A.P.H. POST GRADUATE LIBRARY

B07876

658·5

Business Process Management

D1342529

This book is due for return on or before the last date shown below.

CANCELLED

CANCELLED

About this Book

While the vision of process management is not new, existing theories and systems have not been able to cope with the reality of business processes—until now. By placing business processes on center stage, corporations can gain the capabilities they need to innovate, reenergize performance and deliver the value today's markets demand. This book heralds a breakthrough in process thinking that obliterates the business-IT divide, utterly transforms today's information systems and reduces the lag between management intent and execution.

A process-managed enterprise makes agile course corrections, embeds Six Sigma quality and reduces cumulative costs across the value chain. It pursues strategic initiatives with confidence, including mergers, consolidation, alliances, acquisitions, outsourcing and global expansion. Process management is the only way to achieve these objectives with transparency, management control and accountability. During the reengineering wave of the 1990s, management prophets' books full of stories about other companies were all you had to guide the transformation of your business. Although their underlying theories were based on age-old common sense and general systems theory proposed fifty years earlier, they offered no path to execution. By contrast, the process-managed enterprise grasps control of internal processes and communicates with a universal process language that enables partners to execute on shared vision—to understand each other's operations in detail, jointly design processes and manage the entire lifecycle of their business improvement initiatives.

Process management is not another form of automation, nor a new killer-app nor a fashionable new management theory. Process management discovers what you do, and then manages the lifecycle of improvement and optimization, in a way that translates directly to operation. Whether you wish to adopt industry best practices for efficiency or pursue competitive differentiation, you will need process management. Based on a solid mathematical foundation, the BPM breakthrough is for business people. Designed top down in accordance with a company's strategy, business processes can now be unhindered by the constraints of existing IT systems. Short on stories and long on insight and practical information, this book will help you write your own story of success. It provides the *first* authoritative analysis of how BPM changes everything in business—and what it portends. Welcome to the company of the future, the fully digitized corporation—the process-managed enterprise. Welcome to the next fifty years of business and IT.

What the analysts are saying about BPM

The BPM category may arguably provide the greatest return on investment compared to any other category available on the market today. BPM gives organizations the ability to cut operational costs at a time when the economic downturn makes it increasingly difficult to boost revenues. ... Business Process Management enables government agencies to dismantle obsolete bureaucratic divisions by cutting the labor- and paper-intensive inefficiency from manual, back-end processes. Faster and auditable processes allow employees to do more in less time, reducing paper use as well as administrative overhead and resources. – Aberdeen Group

The BPMI concepts are right on target ...Savvy companies will embrace having a process-centric organization and will adopt Business Process Management software. – AMR Research

Business process integration and automation pick up where BPR left off. Extending process integration and automation solutions beyond the enterprise delivers the efficiency that management has been seeking for decades. – Computerworld

Business processes have been around since the beginning of business. Business Process Management Systems are the next step in making them explicit, executable and adaptable. – Computer Sciences Corporation's Research Services

Few areas of software will receive more attention in the coming months and years than BPM. Yet the greatest challenges to the BPM market are the very forces making it so attractive. – Delphi Group

Firms will need process integration servers that model and carry out broad business processes. ... The adoption of packaged apps and the development of integration standards like Web Services, has primed the market for a new breed of BPM suites. Firms should start BPM projects today to design, execute, and optimize cross-function business processes. – Forrester Research

BPM's potential for business improvements through advanced process auto-mation is the most compelling business reason to implement an "enterprise nervous system" (ENS). Where ENS implementations risk being seen as infrastructure in search of a problem, BPM allows enterprises to raise the level of discussion and make specific business process support the primary reason for application integration efforts. – Gartner

Enterprises should begin to take advantage of explicitly defined processes. By 2005, at least 90 percent of large enterprises will have BPM in their enterprise nervous system (0.9 probability). Enterprises that continue to hard-code all flow control, or insist on manual process steps and do not incorporate BPM's benefits, will lose out to competitors that adopt BPM. – Gartner

For the Fortune 2000 companies, the quest to implement the best business process management (BPM) solution is becoming highly desirable—akin to acquiring the "holy grail" in any given industry. BPM promises to streamline internal and external business processes, eliminate redundancies, and increase automation. – IDC

Business Process Management (BPM) is the identification, comprehension and management of business processes that interact with people and systems both within and across organizations. BPM is quickly becoming one of the hottest top-ics in the IT industry. Many believe the powerful integration story behind the BPM concept has the potential to unlock the e-business market. ... In the current economic climate, business process flexibility is key to organizational survival. But the logic of business process tends to get hard-wired into highly expensive IT sys-tems that are complex and stifle innovation. ... Demand from users for flexibility and functionality is driving the need for systems that can deliver across enterprise processes that are not reliant on a single application, or indeed are not constrained by the boundaries of the organization itself. – Ovum.

Businesses need to constantly adapt their processes, yet they are often held back by static IT systems that aren't designed to exploit future opportunities. Business process management is a new change management and systems implemen-tation methodology that overcomes this problem. – Ovum

Fourth Anniversary Edition

This is the Fourth Anniversary Edition of the seminal book that set forth the vision of Business Process Management (BPM). The limited distribution edition was first published in August, 2002, and the authors have since published numerous follow-on articles that appear at: **www.bpm3.com**

Business Process Management

The Third Wave

Howard Smith
Peter Fingar

Meghan-Kiffer Press
Tampa, Florida, USA, www.mkpress.com
Advanced Business-Technology Books for Competitive Advantage

Publisher's Cataloging-in-Publication Data

Smith, Howard.
  Business Process Management: The Third Wave / Howard Smith and Peter Fingar, - 1st ed.
    p. cm.
  Includes appendices and index.
  ISBN 0-929652-34-7 ISBN 13: 978-0-929652-34-4 (paperback : alk. paper)

  1. Reengineering (Management) 2. Technological innovation. 3. Strategic planning. 4. Management information systems. 5. Information technology. 6. Information resources management. 7. Organizational change. I. Smith, Howard. II. Fingar, Peter. III. Title

HD58.87.S548 2007   2002106051
658.4'063–dc21   CIP

Copyright © 2007 Howard Smith and Peter Fingar. All rights reserved. Except as permitted under the United States Copyright Act of 1976, no part of this publication may be reproduced or distributed in any form or by any means, or stored in a data base or retrieval system, without the prior written permission of the copyright holders.

Limited distribution edition first published August 2002 © 2002.
Book's Web site: http://www.bpm3.com
Web site design by Phillip Heywood.

Published by Meghan-Kiffer Press
310 East Fern Street — Suite G
Tampa, FL 33604 USA

Company and product names mentioned herein are the trademarks or registered trademarks of their respective owners.

Meghan-Kiffer books are available at special quantity discounts for corporate education and training use. For more information write Special Sales, Meghan-Kiffer Press, 310 East Fern Street, Tampa, Florida 33604 or (813) 251-5531

Meghan-Kiffer Press
Tampa, Florida, USA
Publishers of Advanced Business-Technology Books for Competitive Advantage

Printed in the United States of America.   SAN 249-7980
MK Printing 10 9 8 7 6 5 4 3 2 1

This book is dedicated to the business and technology
architects and builders of 21st century corporations.

Build to adapt, not just to last.

Table of Contents

Preface

Like business process management itself, this book was born of necessity and grew in the telling. The third wave of business process management was conceived in response to the chaos companies find around them as they position themselves for 21st century competition.

This is primarily a book for business people, but we do not shy away from technology topics. Anyone will tell you that attempting to address a business and technical audience in the same book is a tough challenge. But because the management of a company's business processes is inseparably about both business and technology, we took on the challenge. Although it has become commonplace to blame the "Business-IT Divide" for the ills of failed projects that depend on complex technology, this book sets out an alternative theory and a pragmatic approach to business innovation and change.

A message that we emphasize throughout is that the last decade's reengineering mantra—"Don't automate, obliterate"—has given way to a deep respect for, and an effective means of, leveraging existing business and technology assets. This opportunity arises only now because it is only recently that methods and technology have become available to fully enable process management in the sense defined here. If the success of data management as the foundation for the vast majority of business software in use today is anything to go by, then, with the third wave of business process management, we are in for the ride of our lives.

Many trends have converged on the third wave of business process management—workflow management, business process modeling, quality management, business reengineering, change management and distributed computing, to name but a few. But there was a vital and missing ingredient. This book explains the nature of that ingredient and what it portends for all companies and the IT industry. We are confident that you and your company will profit from the ideas and information we present. Read it in conjunction with other "management" books, for while they offer business advice, we offer the means to implement both their suggestions and your business instincts.

We gratefully acknowledge many colleagues who influenced, shaped, supported and otherwise contributed to this book, particularly those at Computer Sciences Corporation, the Business Process Management Initiative (BPMI.org) and the Workflow Management Coalition (WfMC):

Adrian Apthorp, Assaf Arkin, Jeanne Baker, Colin Brayton, Ron Brown, David Butler, Lynette Ferrara, Layna Fischer, Ismaël Ghalimi, Nigel Green, John Hamilton, Francis Hayden, Phil Heywood, David Hollingsworth, Scottie Jacob, Bill Koff, Lem Lasher, Stan Lepeak, Bryan Maizlish, Mike Marin, Doug Neal, Bob Olivier, Charles Plesums, Matthew Pryor, Jon Pyke, Robert Reti, Joe Rosenbaum, Malcolm Rudrum, Jerry Scott, Chrysogon Smith, Gillian Taylor, Simon Torrance, Stephen White and Gary Williams.

The BPMI.org and the WfMC develop mission-critical methodology and standards for business process representation and manipulation. Members represent industry leaders in the fields of business process reengineering, workflow and process management, enterprise and application integration, business collaboration and transactions, process discovery and modeling, process analysis and simulation, process outsourcing, programming using processes, business rules management and Web services.

Howard Smith
Peter Fingar
September 2006

While we are confident you will want to read the entire book, we recognize the scarce reading time many of us have and therefore offer a fast track:

Business reader	*Introduction, Chapters One through Nine, Epilog (197 pages), optionally Appendices D & E.*
Technology reader	*Curious about the theoretical foundation? Go straight to Appendix C. Otherwise: Introduction, One through Four, Seven, Epilog, Appendices A - C, optionally Eight.*

INTRODUCTION

Digitization represents a revolution that may be the greatest opportunity for growth that our company has ever seen.
—GE Key Growth Initiatives 2002.

In *The Max Strategy*,[1] Dale Dauten told some interesting stories about Walt Disney, or "Uncle Walt," as he liked to be called. Now *there* was a man fizzing with intelligence. Someone once asked him his "secret" and he said this: "Do something so well that people will pay to see you do it again."

"There's a scene in *Snow White* where Snow is standing beside a well. And she tells a flock of doves that it's a wishing well. She demonstrates, saying something like "I wish my prince would come." Then, we see her from the bottom of the well, right through the water. We watch her face, shimmering in the surface of the water, as drops of water fall into the well and create ripples moving out. Now imagine drawing a shimmering face reflected in water that's rippling out in circles. Imagine how hard that would be, especially since this was long before computer animation."

As workers and as consumers, both online and offline, each of us is enveloped by a myriad of business processes—the intricate, dynamic, ever-changing manifestations of the economic activity of companies. Whether we are disinterested, or actively engaged, in these processes, in large part determines the wealth of those who weave them. Companies are looking for secrets, skills and tools that will enable them to create and mesh together business processes that are so outstanding that customers will "pay to see them" time and time again.

Like Walt Disney, companies are not lacking in imagination, but unlike The Walt Disney Company in 1937 that could afford to employ a thousand animators, companies today cannot afford to be distracted by the labor-intensive animation process. To create the compelling business processes they so desperately seek, companies are now looking for the business-process equivalent of Pixar's computer-assisted animation methods—the ones Disney now uses. This book is the end of their search.

The third wave of business process management (BPM) is a fundamentally new approach to business process innovation and management. For on today's battleground for economic growth, sustainability and innovation, companies like GE, with its Digitization Initiative, are arming themselves with explicitly defined business processes that can be manipulated on a scale previously unimaginable. The strategy they are chasing is not the piecemeal replacement of old processes with new, but a single program, the establishment of a capability for implementing and managing a continuous stream of business process innovations. The goal is twofold: hyper-efficiency and an unprecedented agility. Put simply, companies like GE want to *take change off the critical path of innovation*. GE seeks to empower every business unit and every workgroup to take control of their processes and to make all the assets of the company available to be reused, repurposed and recombined with those of partners. Only by freeing processes from the constraints arising in technology, software and networks, can this be achieved. A similar digitization process happened two decades ago as companies began to use data management systems. The third wave will create a new class of business asset that encompasses data but extends it dramatically so that little is left embedded and ingrained within systems or work practices.

Where last decade's "reengineering" meant "starting all over, starting from scratch," process management builds on and transforms what already exists. The oft-used business engineering terms "as is" and "to be," which in the past referred only to processes, can now be applied to the entire enterprise. Companies can now build change management into the very structures of their organizations, where once it took up valuable resources as a painful "reengineering" item on the corporate agenda. This time it is not just companies that are being reengineered, but reengineering itself.

The problem companies face is how to operate in a state of perpetual change and adaptation. They are no longer wondering how to make a change; they are wondering how to repeat change, over and over again. They also know they need to create and test countless variants of countless processes, but have no idea how to make this happen. It's not for want of trying.

Every day, in every company, someone is challenging the status quo that business processes, and the various automation systems on which they depend, are cast in stone, impossible to understand and modify without wholesale reengineering and replacement. Many companies are trying to break out of that situation by implementing a host of point solutions—piecemeal ways of exposing, integrating, transforming and connecting disjoint processes, information and machines. Their intentions are good, but only rarely do they achieve long term, meaningful results—a system not just built to last, but built to adapt. "Business architects" work to design flexible business systems while "systems architects" work to design flexible software—but the truth is that's still not enough. There are simply not enough analysts and programmers on the planet, let alone working for any one company, to satisfy the pent-up demand for dynamic business processes.

Still, in the course of undertaking these individual process fixes, these companies are gradually creating an overwhelming demand for something new, and when the world wakes up to what the answer is, the demand for it will start a gold rush. At the moment, most companies are completely unaware that anything but piecemeal systems integration solutions exist. Others remain skeptical, as is only natural, and only a handful have yet to join the ranks of the early adopters. Whatever a company believes now, however, the third wave of business process management is inevitable—as sure fire as gravity is gravity.

In *The Agenda*[2], reengineering pioneer Michael Hammer observed that companies know how to do a lot of things that can be understood as processes, such as finding new customers, developing new products and opening new plants. On the other hand, converting a general process description into executable process action is hard for many companies, because it is not something they have a lot of experience doing. Improving processes to better serve current customers; using strong processes to enter new markets; expanding processes to provide additional services; taking a process that you excel at and providing it as a service to other companies; adapting processes that you excel at to the creation and delivery of other goods or services; creating new processes to deliver new goods or services—no one has much practical experience doing these things, the cost and complexity of which were prohibitive in the age of reengineering. Hammer warns that when companies undertake such activities—focusing on processes and customers rather than products—they are operating without a net. And he is right. Here are the things companies need:

- A means not only to conceive of new processes, but to actually put them into action.
- A systematic method of analyzing the impact of business processes and a more reliable way of introducing new process designs.
- Executable process models that are aligned with business strategy, reflecting the complexity of everyday business activity and amenable to complete analysis, transformation and mobilization.
- A managed portfolio of excellent business processes, not only with the customer's current needs built-in, but also with "change built in."
- The ability to respond to the new invisible hands of the market—the abilities to combine and to customize processes.
- The transformation of organizational change from an imprecise art with unpredictable outcomes into an engineering discipline with measurable outcomes.
- A counterpoint to the creativity and innovation of reengineering and the acceleration of all process improvement projects and activities.
- An understanding of a company's trajectory in the process economy—expanding markets and increasing profits, or declining influence, roadblocks, over-capacity or failure to respond to market shifts.
- A pervasive, resilient and predictable means for *the processing of processes*, a permanent business change laboratory, enabling ongoing innovation, transformation and agility.

Such "process processing" should not be confused with automation. Digital process models may have little to do with computers but a lot to do with business. While automation can be readily achieved with a raft of existing technologies, BPM has a wider meaning. Not only does it encompass the discovery, design and deployment of business processes, but also the executive, administrative and supervisory control over them to ensure that they remain compliant with business objectives for the delight of customers. Processes are the main intellectual property and competitive differentiator manifest in all business activity, and companies must treat them with a great degree of skill and care.

Merely perfecting a business process in terms of meeting requirements at a given time is a necessary, but insufficient, response to the challenge of change. Processes cast in stone through point solutions, one-time projects, habitual work practice or the straightjacket of packaged business software are as much liability as asset, no matter how excellent. For if incumbent companies are to compete against market disrupters large or small, they must exploit inherent advantages of the implicit processes embedded within their experience, their assets and their relationships. For this to happen, processes must be explicit. In short, companies must obliterate the business-IT divide, transforming legacy into an asset rather than a liability.

If this analysis seems extreme, consider the fact that every modern management theory ever devised—reengineering, process innovation, total quality management, Six Sigma, activity-based costing, value-chain analysis, cycle-time reduction, supply chain management, excellence, customer-driven strategy and management by objectives—has stressed the significance of the business process and its management. In light of this constant demand, it seems surprising that the IT industry has up to now delivered only "business applications," small fragments of end-to-end processes capable of nothing more than manipulating static business data using prepackaged procedures.

All information systems are imperfect simulations of the businesses they support. Companies understand that the principles of inter-connected and inter-related processes are the reality behind today's IT-façade. This change is structural—a shift in the tectonic plates that underlie the business-technology equation. It will only come about by abandoning the assumption that business information systems design must be based upon the separate notions of data, procedure and communication. Investment in information technology can no longer be justified if business systems remain a weak and incomplete representation of the CEO's strategy. There must be a paradigm shift in the quality and expression of business processes if companies are to apply systematic methods to their development and execution—in strategy, in practice and in information technology. Two decades ago companies implemented data management systems because they recognized the value of business data and the data problems they would face if data continued to be embedded in each and every business application. As companies face up to their process future, similar factors are at work creating the demand for the third wave of business process management. Processes are moving center stage, not just on white-boards, but at the heart of a new business architecture and the systems that support it.

Do not mistake BPM for some new "killer app" or some fashionable new business theory. It is a foundation upon which companies can depend as surely as they depend on database management today. Like the Hubble Telescope peering back into the origins of the universe, the third wave exposes the fundamental basic building blocks that have so far been hidden and by which all business processes are expressed and through which they can be manipulated. Products and services are only the by-product of processes. In every case, the process *is* the product. When World War II broke out, no longer did coal and iron go in one end of Ford's River Rouge plant and automobiles come out the other, tanks rolled off the assembly line. Ford's "product" is its vehicle manufacturing process. In the 1950s, a young Ronald Reagan hosted the top-ranked television program, the General Electric Theater, and made GE's slogan famous: "Progress is our most important product." If that program were to show today, the new slogan would no doubt be, "Process is our most important product." Good processes don't make winners; winners make good processes.

This book sets out a theory and a practical approach to process management that takes what was good about reengineering—the creativity, the insight—but eradicates the pain of discontinuity and new process introduction. If companies want change built in, they must act now to build in an agent of change. Animate your business processes so your customers will pay to see them again and again.

Learn from Uncle Walt.

References

[1] Dauten, Dale, *The Max Strategy: How a businessman got stuck at an airport and learned to make his career take off*, William Morrow and Company, New York, 1996.

[2] Hammer, Michael, *The Agenda*, 2001, Random House Business Books.

One

The Next Fifty Years

The most fundamental phenomenon in the universe is relationship.
—Jonas Salk

Change came slowly in the '20s, when the first Standard and Poor's index of ninety important U.S. companies was formed. In the '20s and '30s the turnover rate in the S&P 90 averaged about 1.5% per year. A new member of the S&P 90 at that time could expect to remain on the list, on average, for more than sixty-five years. In 1998, the turnover rate in the S&P 500 was close to 10%, implying an average lifetime on the list of ten years, not sixty-five! By the end of the 1990s, we were well into what Peter Drucker calls the "Age of Discontinuity."
—Richard Foster and Sarah Kaplan, *Creative Destruction*, 2001.

The Rise and Rise of Business Process Management

Two articles, one published in the *Sloan Management Review* in June of 1990 by Thomas Davenport[1] and another in the *Harvard Business Review* in July of 1990 by Michael Hammer[2] reported on the growing wave of process innovation and radical business process change. Back then established companies were feeling great pain. They were besieged by better, faster and cheaper competitors from emerging markets. Globalization had been set in motion and there was no turning back—change was brewing but few could envision a solution that did not involve abandoning the past. "Don't Automate, Obliterate" became the clarion call of those who set out to reengineer business. The prophets of process kissed the sleeping princess that was Corporate America and awoke her from her "functional" slumber. On the receiving end it felt more like being hit by an atomic bomb. Feelings that had found no previous expression boiled over into a tidal wave of change that saw companies downsize, rightsize, outsource and restructure their work.

American companies had turned to reengineering in response to an unprecedented abundance of customer choice, which had given rise to a shift from producer-controlled markets (supply push) to customer-ruled markets (demand pull). Before the storm broke in that crucial summer of 1990, companies had been less attuned to the significance of business processes and their management. Before the "great awakening," many of them naïvely equated process design with the writing of policy and procedure manuals—painstaking transcriptions of the rigid rules governing the narrow behavior of individual departments—that got tucked away in vaults. Although functional silos still exist in some organizations, the majority of companies have replaced the division of labor with the concept of *process* at the center of their business strategy. Those that have not done so yet will do so soon. Companies no longer trace their roots back to the factory models Adam Smith described in the *Wealth of Nations*, published in 1776. What Hammer defined as the "task-based" organization of work—the fragmentation of human endeavor into its simplest components and their assignment to specialist workers—has finally been extinguished. That which had influenced the design of companies for the last two hundred years has been replaced by the supremacy of the business process.

Companies that survived the turbulent era of reengineering may be tempted to feel that they have already reengineered, reinvented, mapped, analyzed and improved every aspect of their operation. The stark reality is that they know, deep down, they have barely started. The reengineering prophecy—"we've not done reengineering"—is coming true. Now, we are in uncertain times again. Today, companies are experiencing not one broad based economic reality, but a multitude of process problems. Reengineering illuminated only the general outlines and common patterns of necessary change, such as the reduction of hand-offs and the shifting of work to the supplier or customer, and, critically, it offered no explicit method for execution that could be applied to many problems simultaneously. In practice, it tended to create discontinuity between "as is" processes and "to be" forms of the company, and could be completed only by means of expansive and intensive projects of organizational change and new systems implementation. Even if companies were prepared to submit themselves once again to the dislocation and distraction of one-time change, they can no longer afford to fix processes and IT systems one at a time, as the reengineering gospel prescribed. Discontinuous change at the cusp between tradition and novelty is no longer an option for today's companies, and yet change they must. Peter Drucker explains:

> Again and again in business history, an unknown company has come from nowhere and in a few short years has overtaken the established leaders without apparently even breathing hard. The explanation always given is superior strategy, superior technology, superior marketing or lean manufacturing, but in every single case, the newcomer also enjoys a tremendous cost advantage, usually about 30 percent. The reason is always the same:

the new company knows and manages the costs of the entire economic chain rather than its costs alone.[3]

In short, the newcomer, large or small, but not yet burdened with the problem of adapting and retooling business processes, can innovate freely. More importantly, it has the freedom to tailor these innovations precisely to the current conditions of the market. In reality, not just in strategy, it conceives of a new process and aggressively puts it into action across the "white space" of the value chain.

Others had glimpsed the implications of this advantage even before the advent of reengineering. In September 1987, for example, twenty people came together at the Santa Fe Institute to talk about "the economy as an evolving, complex system." One of those was W. Brian Arthur, Citibank Professor at the Institute, who over the next decade refined the notion that a theory of hierarchy alone is not sufficient to explain the organization of economic networks, which involve many kinds of tangled interactions, associations and channels of communication that take place on many levels. Arthur envisioned the global, customer-led economy in which companies now operate as a combative arena, characterized by dispersed interactions, absence of central control, continual adaptation, perpetual novelty and out-of-equilibrium dynamics—what mathematicians call an "adaptive non-linear network."

Discovering innovative ways to improve business processes is now recognized as the path to business agility and competitive advantage. It's something companies are desperately seeking to achieve as they attempt to adapt to the current business and competitive landscape. Business executives cannot look at a trade magazine without seeing that business processes are in vogue—again. Some, however, are asking, "What's new here? Should I pay attention?"

Indeed, business processes are hardly a new idea. Although the term has been in use only for the past decade or so, the concepts of business processes and business process reengineering can be traced back to the early 1920's, under the term "methods and procedures analysis." Companies have always searched for new ways of restructuring work and improving business organizations, but until very recently a practical way to implement and manage the lifecycle of business process design and execution was seriously lacking. This lack led to major setbacks in the delivery of benefits from investments in information technology (IT) and from otherwise excellent theories about the management of process improvement. Some large process and systems reengineering projects failed to deliver any results at all.

In the same way, then, when senior executives hear the term "process management," they explain that they already actively manage their business processes across their companies. When one of the big consultancies hears the term, it also explains that they already work actively with clients to design, implement and optimize business processes. However, very few organizations are actually delivering on the true potential of business process management.

The term "process management" has resonated most strongly in the consciousness of the business world ever since the advent of business process reengineering (BPR). But before that, quality management had introduced a new awareness of the efficiency and effectiveness of business process improvement. Later, enterprise resource planning (ERP) applications gave new visibility to business processes and focused attention on how to control an organization's behavior through automation based on a shared data model. No wonder business people are skeptical of new three letter acronyms.

In fact each development took organizations closer to making business processes visible, understanding how they operate and how they add value to or subtract value from the organization. Each development, however, has also revealed the growing disconnect between business requirements and IT's ability to deliver working systems, let alone to provide a systematic understanding of the value such systems offer businesses. In 2001, corporations worldwide spent over $1 trillion on information technology. Did they get their money's worth?

Industry veteran and luminary Paul Strassman has conducted research that shows only a random correlation between IT spending per employee and return on shareholder equity, and concludes that spending money on information technology guarantees nothing. Those who agree with him often propose moving IT into the hands of people who are competent to make IT decisions that will actually deliver value. When people say this, however, they are usually referring only to placing budget and IT-spend decisions in the hands of the CEO, CFO and COO, leaving the CIO responsible for implementation. They rarely if ever imagine removing application and process development from the IT department (the source of many logjams) altogether!

Business requirements dictate that an organization be flexible—both reactive and proactive. The organization must be able to make informed decisions at many levels, achieve a balance between tactics and strategy, and cope with unforeseen changes. IT delivers logic-based solutions whose quality depends on the foresight of the system designers, who must anticipate different scenarios. The organization requires creative agents who are well informed and empowered to act in changing situations, but what IT provides are drone systems, only able to follow predefined procedures within certain scenarios, with no ability to ad lib in the face of the unexpected. When change occurs, IT is unable to contribute until a new script has been written for the new situation. This disconnect flows from current techniques of capturing business requirements and translating them into system behavior. Each participant in the process, from the business manager and business analyst to the systems analyst and programmer, brings a significantly different terminology and frame of reference to bear on the problem.

Another source of confusion is the effect of time. Once an initial business requirement is introduced, it will go through many iterations as the impact on the business is considered. All too often, the technical specification for the change will be written, or at least started, before the full business specification is documented and signed off. The technical details of changes in a programmer's code may obscure the significance of changes they represent at a business level. The resulting computer program, meant to encapsulate the new process, cannot even be understood by the business manager or business analyst. Once embedded in a computer program, the IT department *owns* the process—forever. This creates a chain of Chinese whispers, where even the definition of "process" is significantly different for each of the participants involved in describing, implementing, optimizing and managing the "business process." Nothing short of a paradigm shift is needed to address these disconnects and to remove companies from the IT impasse they labor under today.

A completely new approach to process design and implementation has indeed emerged to meet this need. We call this new paradigm the *third wave of business process management (BPM)*. The significance of the third wave lies in the ability it provides to create a single definition of a business process from which different views of that process can be rendered and new information systems can be built. This unified process representation means that different people with different skills—business manager, business analyst, employee, programmer—can each view and manipulate the same process via a representation suitable for them and derived from the same source.

For the business manager the process view could consist of a management "dashboard" showing process performance against key performance indicators. For the business analyst the view could consist of a high-level process map. For the employee the interface is a process portal through which they interact with processes. For the programmer the view could be a process language comparable to a programming language. For the process-enabled software system the view consists of executable process code. The capability to derive and render different views from a common source—to build a basis for common understanding among the business community, the IT community and IT systems, based on a shared language—differentiates the third wave of BPM from preceding technological innovations.

Artificial, pre-conceived notions about who is fit to do what with processes, are purely a manifestation of how IT *applications* are built, managed and deployed today. It need not be so. It is not only technicians that can design and deploy new *business* processes. Similarly, do not underestimate the ability of business people to look inside business processes, to examine the fine "technical" details and to identify, and implement, improvements. Technicians and business people alike should be able to do everything necessary to support the full lifecycle of a business process.

The third wave of BPM is not a point solution or a single product that a company can go out and buy. BPM is not merely another three letter technical acronym. Because rapid, endless change is a fundamental driving force in business today, not an exceptional reengineering event, BPM is a mandatory business capability that allows businesses to take control of their current and future process needs. End-to-end process visibility, agility and accountability are now the keys to business innovation. The third wave of BPM isn't for computer programmers and systems developers. It's for *business people*.

Paul Strassman claims that we are done with technology, "From now on it's economics, and the role of the CIO is to make money. Technology has to be good enough to be taken for granted. It must be available when you need it, how you need it, cheaply, reliably and securely." Business people, he says, "will have to worry only about how to use it, not how to manage it." But to use it effectively, they will need business process tools they can use, not data application development. To the CIO we say, stabilize the IT environment so that business people can manage their processes themselves.

The Next Fifty Years

There is something wrong with IT, something dreadfully wrong that goes all the way back to the beginning, to the advent of business computing in the 1950's. For the past fifty years computers have been seen as "data machines," systems of record that reflect the results of business activity after the fact. Companies are stuck in this data-centric vision of the IT role, in which there is an ever growing disconnect between the business and the technology it deploys. Because the data-centric paradigm of IT won't take us past where we are stuck today, we must break it!

Back in the 1950s there was the myth of the great thinking machine. Later, the myth of MIS, the management information system, rose up to replace it. The reality, however, is that to this day, computers are record-keeping machines, not management machines. They can take in, chew up and spit out trillions of bytes of *data*, but where is the management insight, the *actionable information* needed in context, in real time at all levels of automated and human decision-making?

The methods, techniques and mindset of IT today remain fixated on data—on its capture, storage and retrieval. Two influences underlie this arrested development. The first computers were accounting machines, and the management theory that drove them was cost accounting: The lowest cost was equated with competitive advantage in the world of mass production. The second factor reinforcing the data-centric world of IT is that computers don't sense, reason and change course on the fly the way humans do. When early business technologists dreamed of machines that could do these things, they realized that their data-processing systems must separate data from processes, because only data could be structured in a stable, reliable and predictable way, a desirable quality in an accurate cost accounting system. We must now apply a similar technique to the representation of business processes. Business processes and procedures—the dynamic, expanding, contracting, changing activities of the business—are not so stable or predictable. In fact, they are extremely messy.

Because they are so dynamic and such an overwhelming challenge to computerize, business processes have been second-class citizens in the world of IT, limiting that which has been automated and improved. Only the most basic, back-office business processes are incorporated into the majority of today's IT systems. By contrast, and for exactly the same messy reasons, business processes of all shapes and sizes are the focus of management attention today—management wants to overcome the great "business-IT divide" and gain control over business processes.

Numerous strategies and technologies have been proposed over the years for bringing the two worlds together, none successful. The mark of a foolish person is to try repeatedly to solve an insoluble problem. Instead of proffering yet another fix that merely extends the existing IT paradigm, we take a radical approach to closing the divide. We say, "Forget bridging the divide. Don't perfect IT with another layer of complexity, another silver bullet. We've been there and it doesn't work. Instead, place the emphasis where it belongs: Give ownership of business process management back to business people."

Under the data-centric IT paradigm, business people cannot take control. They have no way to obtain the information systems they need in order to compete, not only on cost, but also on quality, speed and service. These competitive variables require, not mere data, but action-able information and knowledge that resides both inside and outside the firm. That actionable information has heretofore not been represented digitally or fully automated.

Furthermore, the business is no longer a self-contained entity. In place of the business owning its value chain, as in the old days of the automotive industry, its value chain "owns" the business, making exter-nal information as critical as internal information. Producer-controlled markets, in which costs were tallied and margins added, have given way to customer-driven value chains in which activity-based costing must consider numerous players to make the total cost of producing value for the customer visible and understood. Companies can no longer only manage their own internal processes; they must venture outside and manage their relationship with the entire value chain. However, no IT vendor and no IT department can provide a "killer app" for this, any more than a company would chose to pay for such an application if it knew a competitor in a competing value chain could take exactly the same step and equip itself with exactly the same tool.

Companies that want to increase their effectiveness in this new way of competing must bite the bullet and take on the challenge of making process, *not* data, *not* the application, the basic unit of computer-based automation and support. They must shift their focus from systems of record to systems of process. In short, "data processing" must give way to "process processing."

This means that employees, customers, suppliers and trading partners must share not just a "data base" but an actionable "process base" that is always on and always up-to-date, reflecting dynamic events in the entire business ecosystem. Businesses need dynamic systems of process, not the after-the-fact "systems of record" of typical back office applications. Systems of process are not only what's *happening now*—they are also what's *happened in the past* and a description of the *path for future action*. We are not speaking about only the past, present and future values of mere data structures. We are talking about the past, present and future of business process structures, for *business processes are the business*.

During the celebrations heralding the arrival of the twenty-first century, many companies were concerned that their industries might get "Amazoned," that a dot-com just might turn their industry upside-down. But with the dot-com clutter cleared away, companies in all industries better be worried about getting "General Electrified." Jack Welch responded to the dot-com era with a destroy-your-company-dot-com initiative. GE's new CEO, Jeff Immelt, has taken the baton and expanded the company's original vision with the Digitization Initiative, which aims to digitize as many business processes as possible, especially those outward-facing processes used to actually conduct business with customers and trading partners.

GE's automated business processes are now required to provide their own analytics so that business leaders can have the personalized digital cockpit instruments they need to navigate their organizations through turbulent times, in real time. GE is intent on making course corrections daily or weekly, rather than monthly or quarterly, saving time and money and better serving its customers. As the prevailing economic winds led brick-and-mortar companies to decimate technology budgets, GE increased IT spending in 2001 by 12 percent, to $3 billion.[4] GE "gets it." It understands the new process-based battlefront of business.

Business Process Management: The Third Wave

Companies like GE and other pioneers are making breakthroughs in the way information systems are conceived, designed and implemented, transforming the very processes they automate and making the reengineering revolution of the past decade look like child's play. The vision of the fully digital corporation has now crystallized, and pioneering companies are already quietly (or secretly) building the agile enterprise. Embracing new game-changing technologies that don't "fix IT," but instead take the software development process off the critical path of business change and innovation, these companies are intent on dominating the decade ahead and achieving never before possible gains in productivity and agility. What GE and other companies are pursuing is a breakthrough that makes end-to-end, dynamic, expanding, contracting and ever changing business processes manageable. What's needed to accomplish this is the third wave of BPM:

- In the first wave of business process management, which began in the 1920s and was dominated by Fredrick Taylor's theory of management, processes were implicit in work practices and not automated.

- In the second wave of business process management of the past decade or so, processes were manually reengineered and, through a one-time activity, cast in concrete in the bowels of today's automated ERP and other packaged, off-the-shelf systems. Even with document-centered workflow added to ERP, such systems only took up discrete roles as participants in processes; rarely did they provide business management control over the processes. Those that did only did so for subprocesses and were generally limited in their capability.

- In the third wave of BPM, the business process is freed from its concrete castings and made the central focus and basic building block of all automation and business systems. They become first-class citizens in the world of automation. *Change* is the primary design goal because in the world of business process management, *the ability to change is far more prized than the ability to create in the first place.* It is through agile business process management that entire value chains can be monitored, continuously improved and optimized. Feedback of results, agility and adaptability are the bywords of the third wave. The question is, however, how can such noble goals be attained?

Business people, unfortunately, remain at the mercy of the technology gods and their data-centric mindsets. What good is a business process innovation if it cannot be implemented in time to make a difference? What good is a new business process vision if the costs to execute that vision exceed the benefits? How can a company participate in end-to-end processes across their value chains when internal business processes are cast in concrete in the software code of individual silo applications scattered throughout the enterprise?

Huge portions of today's IT budgets involve deploying a concrete-busting jackhammer to break out bits of disparate legacy applications systems in order to support and service new or changed business processes. Enterprise application integration (EAI) is what most IT groups do with most of their time and budgets—stitching together existing systems of applications to support new and changing, inward- and outward-facing business processes that deliver value to customers. EAI, and its successor, B2Bi, fill the pages of many trade publications, and there are journals devoted entirely to the topics. Why all the energy, money and words?

It's all about the contortions and unnatural acts needed to support new or changing business processes with today's legacy application packages, their monolithic designs, and their rigid business logic carved in stone. Jeanne Baker of Sterling Commerce and BPMI.org explains it this way: "Imagine a world where people speak a language that brilliantly describes the molecular structure of a large object but can't tell you what the object is—or that it's about to fall on you. You've just glimpsed today's arcane world of application integration." But that's not all. Like the rigid applications they integrate, EAI projects can themselves carve newly developed business processes in stone unless great care is taken.

In the minds of many companies, business processes have become synonymous with integration, but that conception is far from accurate or complete. While systems integration in fact creates "integrated processes," it does not necessarily open those processes to further processing. It does not recognize that processes have a lifecycle all of their own, independent of the IT systems that drive their automation. In addition, integration processes are only one form a business process may take.

Many business processes, such as the movement of goods, the behavior of machines and manual work, are quite independent of any automation support from IT systems. IT may still, however, play a huge role in understanding and improving these "non-IT" processes, through the digital execution and simulation of process models. Conventional thinking about the relationship between IT and business processes must change if companies are to gain the process agility they need to compete in today's uncertain world and super-competitive marketplace.

If end-to-end business processes are the focus of internal and cross-company integration, why not deal directly with the "business process, as application" instead of "data" and "applications"? Because business processes can no longer be cast in concrete the way they are in today's applications, the "business process" must supersede the "application" as a means of packaging software. In addition, companies must leverage existing IT investments as they build new process-aware information systems that understand the enterprise process design right across the value chain. Companies are demanding a breakthrough that shifts the locus of automation from the affairs of IT to the affairs of the business. They want to shift their efforts from further automating integration to make up for the limitations of IT, and move on to managing business processes. That breakthrough is the methodology of BPM and its technology engine—the business process management system (BPMS).

The third wave of business process management of which we speak is not business process reengineering (BPR), enterprise application integration, workflow management or another packaged application—it's the synthesis and extension of all these technologies and techniques into a unified whole. This unified whole becomes a new foundation upon which the enterprise is built, an enterprise more in tune with the true nature of business processes and their management.

The third wave of BPM is not a fantasy, a false promise or hype. For BPM, like other true breakthroughs, is based in the mathematics, specifically Process Calculi, the formal method of computation that underpins dynamic mobile processes, as opposed to static relational data. Pi-calculus, one branch of process calculus, has recently drawn considerable attention in the computer science community and by those building process management systems. The underlying semantics of BPM, the business process modeling language, must be based on an *open* standard available to all participants (people and computer systems) in a value chain. The radical breakthrough is that in the third wave, business processes are directly and immediately executable—no software development needed!

BPM doesn't speed up applications development; it eliminates the need for it. Without its mathematical foundation, businesses would be correct in thinking that BPM is just another buzzword, acronym or marketing ploy. To make BPM a reality, its underlying business process language must be rich enough to describe the process of hosting a dinner party yet also precise enough to describe how computer system "A" talks to computer system "B" while computer system "C" may drop in or out of the conversation, in the same way participants do in real business processes.

The essence of the BPM innovation is that, based on the mathematics, we now understand data, procedure, workflow and distributed communication not as apples, oranges, and cherries, but as one new business "information type" (what technologists call an "abstract data type")—the business process. The recognition of this new fundamental building block is profound, for each element in a complete business process (the inputs, the outputs, the participants, the activities and the calculations) can now be expressed in a form where every facet and feature can be understood in the context of its use, its purpose and its role in decision making. This problem-solving paradigm can therefore provide a single basis not only to express any process, but as the basis for a wide variety of process management systems and process-aware tools and services. Some of these are already available; others will be developed in the future. The implementation of such technology has required a reexamination of some deeply entrenched common wisdom, such as the notion that software is always built from objects and components. Now we can "develop with processes" as well as "manage with processes."

Going forward, this new information type and its associated management systems will be far more important than the relational data model and its associated database management system that underpins the vast majority of today's business applications. The new information services that implement this approach can read, write, query, compose, decompose, transform, measure and analyze end-to-end business processes, internally, with business partners and in the context of external information sources:

- BPM provides enhanced business agility, control and accountability. It will streamline internal and external business processes, eliminate redundancies, and increase automation.
- BPM provides a direct path from process design to a system for implementing the process. It's not so much "rapid application development"; instead, it's *removing* application development from the business cycle.
- BPM supports top-down and bottom-up process modeling, right across the value chain, involving all business-process participants: systems, people, information, and machines.
- BPM is a platform for sharing end-to-end business processes in a manner analogous to the use of a database management system as a platform for sharing business data, both between applications and among business partners. BPM is the platform upon which the next generation of business applications will be constructed.
- BPM supports processes that inherently integrate, collaborate, combine and decompose, no matter where they were created and independent of the different technical infrastructures in which they exist. BPM creates reusable process patterns.
- BPM is defined by the ability to change business processes at a speed governed by the business cycle (day-to-day, week-to-week, quarter-to-quarter), radically reducing the friction arising from today's endemic business-IT divide.
- BPM supports the derivation of key business metrics—for example, activity-based costs—directly from the execution of business processes. BPM processes are accountable, transparent and persistent, and include all the information passed among participants over the process lifetime.
- BPM radically simplifies the deployment of processes that span the value chain, eradicating the point-to-point integration problem that still plagues value-chain execution today.
- BPM supports the fluid movement, management and monitoring of work between companies. It is the operational environment that underpins value-chain integration and business process outsourcing.
- Unlike previous technologies, BPM has the potential to automate the

discovery of business processes arising naturally in the course of business operations, as readily as a database naturally fills with business data during use.

- BPM will enable the industrial-scale collaborative design of business processes among partners, and will provide the tools for the value management analysis of processes supporting virtual organizations.

Management Challenges for the 21st Century

In *Management Challenges for the 21st Century,*[5] Peter Drucker stated two desirable objectives:

> A systematic and organized method for obtaining information about the context of the business in the economy, its markets and its pool of competitors.

> Integration of what was once several procedures—value analysis, process analysis, quality management and costing—into a single analysis.

Third-wave BPM can allow companies to execute on Drucker's vision today. One may speculate that Drucker would have rightfully renamed today's IT as "DT," for *data technology*, from which *information* must still be extracted by users. Climbing on the shoulders of previous advances, BPM is a realizable next step toward elevating the "I" in IT to its proper status. With the advent of the third wave, it is not unreasonable to expect the development of low-cost process tools with capabilities similar to the spreadsheets used for numerical computation.

It was not the development of the personal computer that led to the personal computing revolution; it was the world's first spreadsheet, VisiCalc. In the early 1970s, personal computers were the toys of hobbyists and nerds who loved to tinker with programs written in BASIC. Corporations went to great lengths to keep these toys out of their offices because, if they were to be put to any business use, the business would have to budget for a vast effort from IT to program them for each and every user. Enter VisiCalc. VisiCalc gave business people the ability to manipulate the familiar rows and columns of data directly (a model that business people immediately understood) and the ability to use familiar schoolyard formulae to build what-if analyses aimed at optimizing results. No programming needed—simply design and, presto, calculate! VisiCalc introduced a level of simplicity and convenience that was simply irresistible. It took the IT department off the critical path of personal computing and launched a revolution.

Now, enter BPM. BPM enables business people to manipulate familiar business processes directly and provides the ability to conduct what-if analyses to optimize results. No programming needed—simply design, and, presto, execute! BPM takes software development off the critical path of business process management, and off the critical path of business change and innovation. Do not conclude that BPM is a lightweight solution suitable only for trivial tasks. BPM encompasses a mission-critical infrastructure equal to, or exceeding, that of today's massively scaleable, fault tolerant, data management and transaction processing platforms. Welcome to the next fifty years of business and IT.

It's Inevitable

Most changes in technology have only an incremental effect on the way we do business, but once in a while a new technology creates a fundamental change. The Internet was one, bringing the world e-mail and the World Wide Web. The third wave of BPM is another.

The drivers behind BPM are not technological; they are economic. The two dominant economic trends today are globalization and commoditization. Information about products and prices are available instantly and globally. Trade barriers between nations and regions are being dismantled. Niche markets are disappearing. In this changed world, companies have sought alliances, joint ventures, collaboration and outsourcing as new avenues to achieving competitive vitality.

Today, most, if not all, of a firm's staff may be working on joint projects with other businesses. An alliance strategy is an efficient and effective way of acquiring the skills, assets and processes needed to compete in the new, frictionless world markets. To succeed with such a strategy, however, a business must make itself appealing to potential business partners. Along with the obvious factors in selling yourself—your products, brands, pricing, market access, financial muscle, people and track record—the increasingly important questions to answer are, "What will it be like to work with you? Can you demonstrate that you will be a dependable partner? Is your way of doing business going to be compatible with and comfortable for my customers? Will we be able to easily integrate and collaborate with you? Will your processes add value to ours, or merely duplicate our own capabilities?"

A company's explicit, not implicit, processes are now a key criterion in the competition to attract global partners. The way to provide convincing answers to the hard questions posed by partners will therefore be to make the company's business processes transparent to an extent commensurate with the company's desire for collaboration. This requires a codified universal description language for processes, a method of stating how processes are enacted that is as exact and unambiguous as a computer programming language. Without such a language, companies would have to set up a different, customized shop window for every potential partner it wanted to attract. It would be as though every company spoke only its own language, and each new partnership had to address the translation issue anew. Around the partnering table, the question would be, "How can your company and mine collaborate successfully if you cannot communicate with my supply and customer chains, nor I with yours?" In a world where cooperation and virtual companies are the norm and competition pits value chain against value chain, businesses would have a multi-dimensional problem with answers generated only in one dimension.

As the twin processes of globalization and commoditization gather momentum and the old-fashioned go-it-alone corporation is left for historians to puzzle over, the exploitation of a universal process descriptor language will become an essential passport to the future. Processes are no longer regarded as rigid scripts, intended to replace people or force people to function as cogs in the machine. Participants of all types— systems, people and other processes—work together toward shared goals, sometimes competing, sometimes cooperating. Material flow, information flow, business commitments and computational procedures are equally important to understanding and integrating business processes between partners. Processes are not only the input and output of computer systems. It is not just information that flows, but people, real world objects, results of procedures, even the processes themselves. Processes now model and simulate the real world as readily as they do the internal structure of computing systems.

BPM is now impossible to avoid or evade, for reasons that have been made clear by one of the industry's veteran IT researchers,

David Butler of Computer Sciences Corporation:

> My board must work with your board, your management with mine, your employees with mine and—crucially—your systems with mine. If my systems are to work with yours, then we need a common level of discourse. When my systems describe a customer, an order, a line of account, we must know that we are talking about the same thing. When we talk about the way we handle the goods-inward process, it must be crystal clear. Of course we can sit down and discuss this with my IT team and yours. We'll find a solution. But does it fit with the solutions I've adopted for other firms with whom I already collaborate? Now you call me and tell me that the systems I have agreed with my other partners don't suit yours. Back to the table.

> Then I realize something truly daunting. The companies with whom I am collaborating worldwide have their own suppliers, some of whom are working on components or sub-assemblies that will end up in my product. How can my suppliers' suppliers do their job unless they have access to the latest end product specification in my files? Thus I have to open up my files not only to my suppliers but also to theirs and, even more daunting, they to mine.

Nor is this some theoretical issue conjured out of Butler's imagination: One global firm told him that this is exactly the problem it now faces. The company has hundreds of suppliers linked to its CAD/CAM files, along with hundreds of their suppliers. Tough to manage? Yes, of course, but it's an inevitable consequence of the alliance strategy the company is pursuing. The alliance is not a matter of fashion or made on a whim, it's a bottom-line need mandated by the realities of the industry.

The company is, in effect, becoming a component in flexible, polymorphous, fuzzy-edged extended enterprises that work across corporate borders, trade with competitors, supply suppliers, buy from customers and sleep with the enemy. Butler tells the story of a conference speaker who told a bemused audience that when the short-list of four bidders emerged for a huge multinational defense contract, her company appeared on the list twice with different partners. Her alliance strategy had doubled the chances of winning a contract that would underwrite her company's future for decades to come.

Collaborating through process management, by building the countless process links in a way that can scale up, will be a source of considerable competitive advantage over the next decades. Companies are becoming part of a practically limitless mesh of links. There are so many nodes in the mesh that the number of potential links between the nodes is simply incalculable. It follows that if companies decide to devise an ad hoc method of communication, or a proprietary protocol, for each link in this vast mesh, then they have signed up for an incalculable amount of work. Projects of practically limitless scope are not the easiest to manage—understatement intended.

To this problem there is only one solution, an agreed-upon universal language of process, a language that unambiguously describes "what we do and how we do it" and to which *all* can subscribe. This open standard is precisely that inevitable, universal, language of business process management, the new foundation of competitive advantage in Peter Drucker's Age of Discontinuity.

References

[1] Davenport, T. H. and Short, J. E., "The New Industrial Engineering: Information Technology and Business Process Redesign," *Sloan Management Review*, Summer 1990, Vol. 31, No. 4, pp. 11- 27

[2] Hammer, Michael, "Reengineering Work: Don't Automate, Obliterate," *Harvard Business Review*, July-August 1990, pp. 104-112

[3] Drucker, Peter F., *Management Challenges of the 21st Century*, HarperCollins, 1999, page 114.

[4] Waite, Steve, "Digitization GE Style," *Canadian Hedge Watch Newsletter*, May 7, 2001.

[5] Drucker, Peter F., *Management Challenges of the 21st Century*, HarperBusiness, 1999.

Two

A Walk Over the Hill

What is needed is a relativistic theory, to give up altogether the notion that the world is constituted of basic objects or building blocks. Rather one has to view the world in terms of the universal flux of events and processes.
—David Bohm

In response to hyper-competition and ever-increasing demands from customers for better service, more options and lower prices—compounded by a complex and uncertain economic landscape—business managers are expected to jump through hoops, traverse crevices, tiptoe through minefields and scale vertical walls. The primary tool for alleviating these problems is automation. Why, then, are business managers losing the battle? The root of the problem lies in the very nature of current business software.

For decades, businesses have organized themselves around the very unnatural and unbusinesslike concept of the "software application." Applications automate business functions such as accounts payable, order processing, inventory control, human resources, and so on. Applications consist of a set of data and a set of procedures for operating on the data, as befits their purpose. But today's business applications are often described as *stovepipes* because they are separated by function, time and the data they manage.

Functional stovepipe. Each business application addresses only the specific needs of an individual department or business role, creating a functional silo that is isolated from other areas of the business. Applications are rarely developed with any sense of their context in the end-to-end business processes of which they form a part, with a frequent consequence that employees must devise workarounds to keep the process going. Living in the world of real business processes, employees have to make things work to get their jobs done, so they fix the business-IT disconnect by creating their own process links; manual hand offs, telephone conversations, e-mail and face-to-face meetings. These workaround methods, which skirt the IT domain entirely and which grow over time, become ingrained in the habitual work patterns and practices of employees. In effect, the real business processes move partly, or in some cases completely, "offline" and automated applications become increasingly disconnected from reality. Some fall into disuse, or are used only rarely, which results in incomplete, inaccurate and misleading data getting stored in a company's information systems.

Time stovepipe. Users of today's business applications face another major problem: change. Functional business areas and their associated IT systems are, from an information systems perspective, isolated in time and run on their own clock. Each activity and each application operate at their own pace, quite independently of the dynamics of everyday business life, which naturally require the coordination and synchronization of many different business functions. Business people are again left to their own creative devices to solve these information latency and synchronization problems, usually by organizing themselves using something akin to a "project plan." Designed to ensure that teams work together toward outcomes, and that the right resources are mobilized at the right time, the project plan ensures that each business function waits for dependents to complete interim results before proceeding. Project plans ensure that business processes such as information flow, materials flow and business commitments "make sense." Project plans, formal or informal, precise or just guidelines, coordinate behaviors and create work patterns. Such project plans are, in reality, the central, coordination parts of real business processes. They are rarely supported by the automated computer applications that should in fact understand them and the work going on around them. Companies are asked to understand IT, whereas IT should understand the businesses they support. As it is, project plans have to be executed, monitored and changed manually. This creates further ingrained patterns of sub-optimal work by including too many hand-offs. Changing and optimizing project plans becomes yet another work overlay called "reengineering." Instead of systems adapting to the business, employees are asked to adapt to systems.

Data stovepipe. Today's automated business applications isolate various static data models in "data islands." Each application has its own data, limited to what is required for it to do its job. As a result, data islands spring up all over the business. Once again, business people come up with a workaround. Each workgroup replicates data from other functions, particularly cross-functional data that they need to support their roles and tasks. Workgroups do this in order to see the connections among data, which applications, stranded on their islands, do not illuminate. They set up a host of data hand-offs, reports and additional record keeping, just to keep everyone informed and connected as the real business process requires. Workgroups also supplement IT applications by keeping additional records outside their IT systems, in order to compensate for the fact that as the business changes, so does the structure of the data.

Today's applications are stove-piped by function, by data and in time, creating a source of constant frustration for business users who ask, "Why can't I change this application and all the other things it touches?" Although the reply is often "That's just the way IT *is*," others are challenging this assumption. They are joining up, transforming and connecting different activities that were previously islands, stovepipes and silos. Although integration software is a huge help in integrating software applications, it adds another level of complexity, and doesn't solve the fundamental issue of change. Business people don't want to have to change and then re-deploy applications, no matter whether they or their IT department is responsible, they want *applications themselves* to be able to change.

Business processes evolve, amoeba-like, not only in terms of their programmatic logic, but also through the acquisition or loss of process participants and *their* capabilities. Processes interact with other processes. They divide or combine with one another at a rate that defies the best efforts of applications and application developers to keep up. If you thought you already understood processes think about *Silly Putty;* twist it and pull it and it does not return to its previous shape. That's what real business is like—organic.

Data structures also need to evolve along with business processes, but today's application technology is not up to the task. Data models in traditional applications are relatively static, changing only when there is a "new release," perhaps every few months. Applications also overwrite data, destroying the ability to evaluate the past and project the future. The "present" is tied to static procedures set in stone by today's software packages. In short, today's business technology has no sense of the natural dynamics inherent in business and business management.

What if all business applications were inherently designed to play a role in end-to-end processes? What if all business applications had access to the external data they needed to understand their role in those end-to-end processes? What if all business applications had the means to interact with and coordinate their behavior with respect to one another? What if the data held in applications could evolve naturally with the business as the business evolved and as users found new ways to work with it? What if companies shifted their focus away from "applications" (data and associated procedures) and toward "business processes" as the fundamental building blocks of business systems?

The answer is that business could then focus on real patterns of work, communication and coordination, rather than on working around the limitations of applications that currently do no more than act as disconnected participants within business processes. The perceived role of IT would begin to change as it shifts from providing "systems of record keeping" to providing "systems of process and practice." Today's missing elements—time, connectivity and dynamics—could become a part of the way *all* business applications behave. New applications could adapt to flexible patterns of work, communication and collaboration. The common view of a computer system as "nothing more than a glorified electronic filing cabinet" would no longer be true.

This shift from data-centric to process-centric methods and systems is taking place right now, and will become a major focus of winning companies over the next decade. IT systems will more accurately reflect the way business really is—constantly changing, messy and chaotic. IT systems will then reflect another aspect of reality: that while every employee, department, company, customer and supplier works independently, each is working to achieve common goals. Objectives and work practices will be digitally reflected in business processes, creating a substrate for coordinated teamwork both within and between organizations at all levels. Full visibility of the dependencies and resource constraints will enable process participants, human or computer, to bridge the gap left by the missing elements in today's information systems.

What does it really mean to see and manipulate the whole business process? To find out, let's take a walk over a hill. The footprints along the path represent the evolution of the process, its past, present and future. From a point on the ground we see footprints behind us and ahead of us, but hills and valleys obscure the view of our starting point and our final destination.

Each footprint can be thought of as a change in the business process—new data, new structure or a change of plan. Our route should ideally be guided by business imperatives, but with no way to see where we came from or where we are heading, we sometimes wander without clear direction. Our view and our actions are constrained by our existing computer applications where logic is fixed and predetermined from step to step. We have no way to step off the path set by the designers of our current systems, no way to chart a new course. Previous data values are lost as new structures replace the old, leaving no sense of the past nor of any plan for the future—only a snapshot of the present. And it's not just the value of data that is changing, but its structure as well. Although some IT systems such as the data warehouse and business activity monitoring help us gain some limited business intelligence, they are only partial answers. What we need is a shift in the computing paradigm that makes business processes and their evolution an inherent feature of all business software.

Solving these process related problems on a case by case, application by application, basis does nothing more than create more islands of automation and record keeping. By shifting our perspective to the whole "end-to-end" process—the walk over the hill—and away from data management, we gain a valuable new perspective of the shifting terrain. What business manager would not wish to deal directly with the reality of business today—to gain the ability to leap over clear hurdles, avoid obstacles, implement shortcuts and find the direct path to increased customer satisfaction, increased profits and expanded markets? All these lofty notions rely on putting process, not data, at the center of business and information systems design.

Like actors in a play, today's business applications take on their individual roles, but unlike actors on the stage, they have no access to the complete business script. They are taught to act, but cannot act out of line when circumstances change. The individual footprints of data manipulation are meaningless unless seen in the context of the walk over the hill to reach business objectives. By shifting the focus away from discrete data, discrete time and discrete procedures, companies can create a new business platform for a new breed of "process-aware" information systems that are able to adapt, react and adjust to the reality of business.

Imagine getting in a helicopter and flying above the hills. This elevated bird's-eye view reveals the process level of business design. From this new perspective, companies can clearly see all of the footprints of the business process being enacted. It can take on the role of director and choreographer—improvising, changing course and setting new directions while in flight. Now we can *see* the destination, starting point and current position. Through the wide-angle lens of holistic business processes, the organization can examine, analyze, measure, sense, query and command entire business operations. By casting business processes as the new form of open business information, companies can also transform processes, using countless familiar existing technologies and tools, as well as powerful new collaboration and design tools created specifically to handle processes, not just data.

Such developments herald a new era in business architecture. When corporations make the move to the third wave of business process management described in this book, they equip themselves, not merely to automate, but to exercise executive, administrative and supervisory direction over their ever-changing business processes. Workgroups dependent on supply chain management, customer relationship management and other mission-critical applications will gain direct access to descriptions of the business processes themselves, along with a record of their past performance, their evolution, their current behavior and structure, and alternative scenarios for the future. They will be able to share information about the state of processes as they progress (process data) and how the process design has evolved (process structure). They will be able to see every interaction with every participant in the process right across the extended enterprise. With process designs that offer built-in metrics, workgroups will be able to query the past and present of the process performance and simulate alternate futures, correcting course by making on-the-spot changes to the process design.

Business process management is what makes this possible. It positions process, not data, as the foundation of business design and infrastructure. It is the environment in which all applications are developed and through which all existing applications are reused. It makes possible the discovery, design, deployment, execution, operation, monitoring, optimization, analysis, transformation and creation of processes. It manages the entire lifecycle of enterprise process designs, from creation to disposal. Because process management drives both process improvement and radical change, it provides the missing link between IT investments and the return on those investments. And because it separates business processes from their supporting IT infrastructure, a company can establish a stable environment in which business processes can be fully managed by business units in the dynamic, and often messy, process of doing business.

Think of the most complex thing you do in your business. Think about how to describe this process. Write it all down, in one place. Pick it up and look at it. Can't see everything? Stand back. Too much detail? Zoom in. Something wrong? Reach in and change it. Using tools that are radically different from traditional IT systems, leading companies are building digital models of their business processes that allow them to do all these things. They have begun to realize that their time is best spent, not in writing computer software, but in executing computer-based simulations of their business—finding faults, correcting them there and then, and putting those changes directly into live operation.

You have just glimpsed the world of business process management. The third wave doesn't bridge the business-IT divide—it obliterates it.

Three

Enterprise Business Processes

I cannot think of it this way. It is too big, too complex, with too many working parts lacking visible connections.
—Lewis Thomas, *The Lives of a Cell*

Some business fundamentals really are fundamental—they never go out of style. Today's businesses do what they always have done: They buy, make and sell goods and services. Even after Fredrick Taylor advised robotizing the workforce in the 1920s, even after the reengineering gurus Hammer and Champy advised obliterating work and downsizing in the 1990s, the fundamental mission of business did not change, and will remain the same long after the management guru du jour has come and gone. All management theories center on how to improve the way companies work—how to do what they do "cheaper, better, faster." At the core of most so-called management breakthroughs is an age-old and often misunderstood concept: the business process.

Something Old, Something Very New

Business analysts used to say that a company could compete by being first to market ("faster"), offering products of superior quality ("better") or being the price leader ("cheaper"). Historically, the life cycle of innovative new product offerings went something like this: The initial market leader was the company that was first to market ("faster"); competitors entered the market with similar products of higher quality ("better"); and then came companies offering comparable quality at a lower price ("cheaper").

Traditional business wisdom held that a company could compete in only two of these three areas—until Japanese manufacturers taught other industrialized countries new lessons in the 1970s and 1980s, that is. Sony and Toyota, among others, demonstrated that a single company could successfully pursue all three strategies at once and dominate their markets. This new competitive reality triggered the business reengineering revolution of the 1990s, as companies strove to replicate Japanese successes.

There is more to business success than merely keeping up with the neighbors, however. The three dominant variables of competition now include a fourth: cheaper, better, faster and *with superior service*. For some, service is not a marketing slogan; it's core business. For example, GE has grown from a product-based company into a services company that also makes great products, 70 percent of whose revenue comes from services and, increasingly, from product services. Two decades ago, when Jack Welch took the helm, only 15 percent of GE's revenues came from services. Welch noted in a 2001 shareholder's meeting that product service at GE today is as high-technology as anything the firm does.[1]

This shift from products to product services is a trend whose growth is being propelled by accelerating globalization and commoditization. A hallmark of the industrial age was "supply push"—mass producing goods and pushing them to market, then controlling information about one's products through the mass media with advertising and public relations. This type of competitive behavior worked just fine when markets were geographically bound, but not today. Not that long ago, for example, a customer in search of a new car had a choice among the big three auto makers. Today that same customer can choose from twenty-some-odd fiercely competitive manufacturers from around the world. The growing range of consumer choices makes customers more demanding, and flips the coin to a customer-driven "demand pull" model. People no longer want merely to find and buy a product; they now want full service as they use the product over its entire lifetime. If a given company cannot provide superior support, customers will find someone that can. *Caveat venditor*—let the seller beware.

The pressure to become cheaper, better and faster and provide a whole new level of customer-pleasing service will only intensify as globalization continues at an unrelenting pace. Seven major trends are now evident.

1. King customer is now a dictator

For years, Marketing 101 taught that the customer is king. No more: Today, the customer is a ruthless dictator (and naturally so). A fully-informed consumer is one of the basic tenets of pure competition, and new information media such as the Internet makes it practical to obtain and share information in ways never before possible. Knowledge is power, and a more fully-informed customer has wrested power from producers. In recognition of this fundamental shift, marketing expert Regis McKenna explains, "It's about giving customers what they want, when, where, and how they want it."[2] Customers are asking not only for just-in-time products, but also for *just-in-time processes.*

2. Mass production is giving way to mass customization

As control of markets and economies shifts from the producer to the consumer, companies must establish the ability to customize their offerings. Companies such as the personal computer maker Dell have already demonstrated that the "build-to-order" business model can provide the competitive advantage needed to dominate markets, one customer at a time. Dell customizes each product for each customer. It does not yet customize its processes for each customer, however—nor is it creating processes to meet the needs of special customers, although its corporate programs are modest first steps down that road.

A bicycle company in Japan scans a customer to collect body metrics—weight, build and proportions. Expert systems query the customer about his or her style of riding. A CAD/CAM system works within the parameters of the customer's budget and preferences. Within a few days, a totally customized bicycle is delivered to a market of *one*. Customization is not limited to manufacturing goods, and extends beyond differentiated prices, terms and conditions. Today's competitive financial services are tailored and combined into packages that serve the needs of individual customers. Financial service providers are expected to know their business and markets well enough to provide individual solutions —and in many cases this expectation has a legal basis. Customization is the new invisible hand of the market. Products and services are the result of processes—*in many cases the products themselves are processes.*

3. Customers are demanding total solutions

A plane ticket is not a vacation. Customers in both business and consumer markets want complete solutions. Buying a home, for example, requires many ancillary resources such as a mortgage, appraisals, and title and property insurance. By aggregating and combining many resources of various kinds in a complete value chain around a complete home-buying solution, a company can gain significant competitive advantage. Companies must change their focus from the products and services bundles they now provide to the coherent processes their customers expect to fulfill their complete requirements. Customers want to work with companies in ways that reflect their needs, their culture and their local markets.

Traditional wisdom holds that customers are not concerned about what goes into making a product or service, only that it is fit for purpose and well-provided, a quality often termed "brand trust." Today, however, well-informed consumers of digital cameras may be very concerned about which make of charge-coupled-device (CCD) their camera contains. The same holds true for even more fungible products and services, such as personal financial planning. Brands are in fact the result of processes, or processes themselves—design processes, sourcing processes, customer-service processes and others. The traditional method of bundling and marketing products and services, based on brand trust, will not provide the degree of transparency the market will demand in the near future. Processes provide the means to bundle complete solutions, and processes of excellence are the new form of branding—*processes will replace bundles.*

4. Industry boundaries are blurring

Although today's companies already know how to compete against rivals in their industry—otherwise they would not be in business—it's not so simple any more. New competitors, once thought of as mere enablers—businesses like banks, credit-card companies and even software companies—are marching into other companies' markets with aggregated, on-demand solutions. For example, Microsoft is in the mass media business (MSNBC), and in and out of the credit-card business (MSFDC, renamed TransPoint and later sold to CheckFree). The federal government stopped the company from getting deeper into banking transactions when it halted its acquisition of Intuit, maker of Quicken, the wildly popular personal accounting software. There are no more front lines in the battle for business. It's guerilla warfare now, and competition can come out of nowhere. Yesterday's enabler can turn against you, tiptoe across industry boundaries, and steal your market share. Their burglary tools? *Processes.*

5. Value chains are becoming the unit of competition

Companies must aggregate products and services into total solutions by pioneering complete value chains to deliver those solutions. It's no longer company versus company; it's value chain versus value chain, where the "average" value chain may involve twenty or more discrete participants. It's no longer Sears competing against J. C. Penney; it's Sears' value chain competing against J. C. Penney's value chain. It's Home Depot's value chain competing against Lowe's value chain. If you are, let's say, a realtor, tucked away in your tidy real estate industry, watch out. The "home" in Home Depot, once just a building and improvements supply store, may soon refer to a *total solution*—providing the customer with the finished house and the land it sits on, by establishing new trading partner relationships and developing a totally new value chain. This *process of process acquisition, aggregation and combination* is the new way companies will offer total solutions to their customers, disrupting incumbents and entering new markets.

6. Collaboration and "coopetition" are replacing traditional forms of competition

Wired magazine's Kevin Kelly described the new imperatives of competition:

> The central economic imperative of the Industrial Age was to increase productivity. The central economic imperative of the network economy is to amplify relationships. Since a relationship involves two members investing in it, its value increases twice as fast as one's investment. Outsiders act as employees, employees as outsiders. New relationships blur the role of employees and customers to the point of unity. They reveal the customer and the company as one.[3]

The same goes for relationships with suppliers and trading partners. In the past, companies had to maintain tight connections with a few close trading partners. To aggregate total solutions for their customers in today's marketplace, companies must now establish business relationships and collaborate electronically with suppliers and trading partners that wouldn't even have shown up on their radar screens just a few short years ago.

Some of these new "partners" just might be competitors. Unlike other auto insurance companies, for example, Progressive believes that the consumer should make informed decisions, and so provides rates for three major competitors along with its own quote. Many times Progressive does not have the lowest rate and turns business to a competitor. In such cases, however, Progressive builds increased consumer trust and the reputation of its brand. In addition, it adds considerable information on the insured, including demographic information, to its database: which company had the lowest rate, what the lowest rate was, and contact information for the customer who chooses to purchase insurance elsewhere. Because Progressive constantly monitors the rates of its competitors in order to provide this service, it is able to reestablish contact with the insured when its rate becomes more favorable. Progressive's strategy illustrates the point that *processes encode valuable information for building valuable relationships.*

7. Change has become the only certainty

In the last decade or so, companies responded to the new age of global competition by reengineering how they did their work. They introduced radical changes to organizational structure and supported them using IT as an enabler. A new form of automation called enterprise resource planning (ERP) helped them to tear down functional walls between their departments and to streamline work. But despite achieving some progress, reengineering initiatives and associated ERP systems implementations were one-time affairs and chiefly focused on internal processes.

But that was yesterday. Today what counts is what happens outside the company, and the ability of the company to sense and respond. Y2K, pervasive networks, investment mania, the Euro, deregulation, terrorism, security, bear markets, Japan sinking, China rising, investment in Russia, Indian population hitting one billion, consumer retrenchment, and wildly successful but totally unexpected new products—the fast pace of global business requires dynamic business process. Who could have predicted the major failures of corporate accountability that came to light in 2002? Who knows what new processes employees, stockholders, pension holders, advisors and government regulators will devise or impose to protect investors against further losses? The demand for new processes is apparently endless. *Processes of excellence are able to adapt to change.*

Static relationships defined by long-term contracts will be complemented by dynamic relationships that evolve along with business market conditions, customer needs and the introduction of new technologies. Even if a company is totally efficient in doing what it is doing today, those practices may soon be obsolete, as competition, markets and technology change the business landscape. Companies need "change built in" for both inward- and outward-facing business processes, for in the current Age of Discontinuity, the ability to change is more important than the ability to create.

Inside the World of Business Processes

In his landmark book, *Process Innovation,* Thomas Davenport defined a process as follows:

> Simply a structured, measured set of activities designed to produce a specified output for a particular customer or market. It implies a strong emphasis upon *how* work is done within an enterprise, in contrast to a product focus's emphasis on *what.* A process is thus a specific ordering of work activities across time and place, with a beginning, an end, and clearly identified inputs and outputs: a structure for action.[4]

This definition, although helpful, hardly begins to explain the true nature of collaborative and transactional business processes. At the very least the word coordination is missing.

A business process is the complete and dynamically coordinated set of collaborative and transactional activities that deliver value to customers. Processes are characteristically:

- *Large and complex,* involving the end-to-end flow of materials, information and business commitments.
- *Dynamic,* responding to demands from customers and to changing market conditions.
- *Widely distributed and customized across boundaries* within and between businesses, often spanning multiple applications on disparate technology platforms.
- *Long-running*—a single instance of a process such as "order to cash" or "develop product" may run for months or even years.
- *Automated*—at least in part. Routine or mundane activities are performed by computers wherever possible, for the sake of speed and reliability.
- *Both "business" and "technical" in nature*—IT processes are a subset of business processes and provide support to larger processes involving both people and machines. End-to-end business processes depend on distributed computing systems that are both transactional and

collaborative. Process models may therefore comprise network models, object models, control flows, message flows, business rules, metrics, exceptions, transformations and assignments.

- *Dependent on and supportive of the intelligence and judgment of humans.* People perform tasks that are too unstructured to delegate to a computer or that require personal interaction with customers. People also make sense of the rich information flowing though the value chain, solving problems before they irritate customers and devising strategies to take advantage of new market opportunities.
- *Difficult to make visible.* In many companies business processes have been neither conscious nor explicit. They are undocumented, embedded, ingrained and implicit within the communal history of the organization, or if they are documented, the documentation or definition is maintained independently of the systems that support them.

The three most fundamental characteristics of a business process have little to do with the obvious inputs and outputs of individual work tasks. They are *coordination, coordination* and *coordination!* If activities are collections of individual tasks, it is the synchronization and coordination of those activities and tasks that make them business processes. Coordination is a complex subject—a Center for Coordination Science has even been established at the prestigious Sloan School of Management at MIT to study the subject.

Complexity is something people naturally do their best to avoid: In tough times they often replace deeper thinking with simpler slogans and platitudes. Such was the case when the term "business process reengineering" was thrust on the struggling American business community in the 1990 *Harvard Business Review* article, "Reengineering Work: Don't Automate, Obliterate" by Michael Hammer.

The article that propelled Hammer from professor to management prophet is based mostly on two overly simple examples: Mutual Benefit Life's processing of insurance applications and Ford Motor Company's streamlining of three-way matching for accounts payable. You can forget Mutual—it went out of business and was not included in the wildly successful book that followed the article, *Reengineering the Corporation,* which swept the business world and broke sales records. Hammer and co-author James Champy got rich by selling some very basic concepts to a business community desperate for a remedy, any remedy, for their competitive doldrums. Soon CEOs would be waving the book as they fired people in the name of that now widespread reengineering euphemism, "downsizing." Some downsized to the point of anemia. Employees were supposed to be comforted because they were "downsized" instead of "fired."

Desperation is a powerful force driving acceptance of change, and sometimes any kind of change. Hammer, Champy and other business reengineering advocates took a reductionist view of coordination, restricting the domain of business processes to linear, serial, step-by-step, "input process output" work. Companies began drawing all manner of business process flowcharts, some filling conference rooms and spilling out into the hallways with their reams and reams of tasks, documents and procedures. But work-item driven processes, while easier to nail down and reengineer, are but a small fraction of a company's overall business processes.

Business processes were once thought of as those to be scheduled around people—work that was waiting for a telephone call from a customer, or work that had to be processed at a specific time ("I will expect your call at 10 o'clock"), or work that had to be transferred to a different person because the person who did the first part of the processing got sick or quit before the task was complete. But now, as Charles Plesums of Computer Sciences Corporation (CSC) and the Workflow Management Coalition (WfMC) points out:

> The development and use of workflow technology has moved from simply supporting the routing of work between people to routing work horizontally between resources. Here the resource may be a person, but may also be a system or even a machine. Routing is also vertical (controlling steps that will be performed at each point in the journey) such as when programs will be invoked by the person, or actually invoking the program. And as data is being moved between processes, there is typically integration with the processing systems—which pushes workflow into the enterprise application integration arena.

In addition, the simplest workflow processes offer the least strategic advantages. So what if Ford reengineered its three-way matching problem in the accounts payable department? Coordinating business processes is neither as simple nor as linear as portrayed in the tidy world of traditional task management. Business is constantly changing, messy, unordered and chaotic, and work activities and tasks have to be processed in parallel. Coordination requires the spawning and asynchronous execution of nested tasks and parallel activities in order to capture the richness of complex, real-world business processes. And it is not just tasks that occur in parallel, but decision-making, distributed computation and the movement of information within the company and across the value chain. But many companies have been indoctrinated with the restrictive perspective of the business reengineering movement, in which activities and tasks are to be understood in terms of linear flows, glossing over their true complexity. This way of thinking must be transcended if business processes are to embody the far more complex realities of coordination. Earlier thinking about processes lacked an underlying "science of process" for implementing its insights. Today, process calculus provides the foundation needed to cope with the true nature of business processes and the underlying problems of coordination.

Thus, today's companies should not "throw the baby out with the bath water" by associating the term "business process" with "reengineering," which has become a dirty word. Some companies have unfortunately lost sight of the fact that the business process is the critical path to innovation and performance improvement. Companies have to re-examine their methods for representing and improving business processes with fresh eyes.

As the roaring nineties took off, the *high-tech IPO*, not the value delivered to customers, emerged as the number one goal of many businesses, further diverting attention from business processes and their management. The late nineties were about initial public offerings and "high-finance reengineering," and led to the scandals associated with Enron, WorldCom and who knows how many others. The "cook-the-books" process had superseded the "customer process" because stock markets were—thanks to the dot-com phenomenon—widely perceived to be the only source of new wealth.

As a technique for coordinating work, business processes contain no value judgments. If the object of an end-to-end process is an IPO, experience shows that scandal and the demise of the company are likely results. That's why our definition of a business process includes the objective of *delivering value to customers.* Companies can innovate, improve performance and build new wealth only if they maintain this objective as their number one priority. However, process is also part of the solution in providing more transparent financial processes. *Business processes are the business. The number one job of the business is to create customers.*

The State of Process Management

Business processes today need to be managed and modified for the same reasons they always have been: to adapt to consolidation, mergers and acquisitions, joint ventures, divestitures, regulatory compliance issues, shifts in business models, changing customer expectations, industry standardization and business process outsourcing. Business process management today, however, means manipulating complex processes that were either not viewed as critical in the past or are not now in a form where manipulation is practical. Responding to competition using traditional modes of process reengineering, process improvement and workforce mobilization are insufficient, for the following reasons:

- The new macroeconomic factors affecting a large company cannot be understood without process analysis of its value chain and its relationship to other value chains. Analysis must be performed in the context of market data drawn from inside and outside the firm.
- Just-in-time products are not enough—customers now expect companies to provide just-in-time processes.
- Creating a new process is not enough—companies must be able to efficiently manufacture many process variants.
- Now that many companies provide customers with the means of configuring products and services, they need to customize the processes used to deliver these products and services. Customization will cover everything from how customer requirements are communicated to how products and services are manufactured, delivered and serviced.
- New techniques for process acquisition and process combination are the foundation of a new reengineering discipline in the context of the value chain. Some companies may even demand influence over the way their trading partners improve processes.
- A universal language of process must replace the outworn integration paradigm, because today, a company's partners and competitors are only an idea and a network hop away, if only lines of communication

between processes can be opened.

- The ability to manipulate processes—so-called "process engineering"—is a prerequisite for such business needs as customization for different business channels, expressing best practices and adapting them for re-deployment, and formalizing industry standards for implementation.

How Many Business Processes?

Hammer and Champy once observed that "hardly any company contains more than ten or so principal processes." They quoted examples such as customer communication, strategy development, product development, customer design and support, order fulfillment and manufacturing capability development. Davenport likewise advised that the "fewer and broader the processes, the greater the possibility for innovation ... and the greater the understanding, measuring and changing."

At the time these assertions were made, no technology was available for really managing—within a lifecycle of improvement—even a small number of business processes. At that time, process management really meant re-inventing the business, not reengineering business processes at all. It was therefore logical for reengineering advocates to focus only on high-level strategic "processes." Yet such processes are but the tip of the iceberg in any large business. Principal processes mainly exist in the rarified environment of the corporate strategy office, far away from the "engine and cog" processes that actually run the business.

Under the surface, principal processes require hundreds of tangible supporting processes (see Table 3.1) and thousands of distinct process variants, all of which are needed and all of which need to be managed. These supporting processes include many unique internal processes, industry best practices, and sub-processes to ensure compliance with standards, legal requirements and regulatory guidelines. They encompass not only human work but also multiple stovepipe computer applications that need to be integrated and managed in the context of reusable frameworks. Billions of lines of existing software code contain essential, proven, business rules that cannot easily be recreated. They offer a rich source of reusable components if they can be extracted. In the third wave, both strategic principle processes and all supporting processes are managed together, in one environment.

Table 3.1. An A to Z Subset of Enterprise Processes

Account Management	Organizational Learning
Advance Planning & Scheduling	Payroll Processing
Advertising	Performance Management
Assembly	Performance Monitoring
Asset Management	Performance Review
Benefits Administration	Physical Inventory
Branch Operations	Planning and Resource Allocation
Budget Control	Post-Sales Service
Build to Order	Problem/Resolution Management
Call Center Service	Process Design
Capacity Reservation	Procurement
Capital Expenditures	Product Data Management
Check Request Processing	Product Design, Development
Collateral Fulfillment	Product/Brand Marketing
Collections	Production Scheduling
Commissions Processing	Program Management
Compensation	Promotions
Component Fabrication	Property Tracking/Accounting
Corporate Communications	Proposal Preparation
Credit Request/Authorization	Publicity Management
Customer Acquisition	Real Estate Management
Customer Inquiry	Recruitment
Customer Requirements Identification	Returns & Depot Repairs
Customer Self Service	Returns Management
Customer/Product Profitability	Sales Channel Management
Demand Planning	Sales Commission Planning
Distribution/VAR Management	Sales Cycle Management
Financial Planning	Sales Planning
Financial Close/Consolidation	Service Agreement Management
Hiring/Orientation	Service Fulfillment
Installation Management	Service Provisioning
Integrated Logistics	Shipping
Internal Audit	Site Survey & Solution Design
Inventory Management	Six Sigma
Investor Relations	Sourcing
Invoicing	Strategy Development
IT Service Management	Succession Planning
Knowledge Management	Supply Chain Planning
Manufacturing	Supply Planning
Manufacturing Capability Development	Test
Market Research & Analysis	Time & Expense Processing
Market Test	Timekeeping / Reporting
Materials Procurement	Training
Materials Storage	Treasury/Cash Management
Order Dispatch & Fulfillment	Warehousing
Order Fulfillment	Warranty Management
Order Management	Zero-Based Budgeting

Many processes, especially the ones that deliver direct value to the customer, span multiple organizations and need to be managed as strategic business relationships. These processes and their component tasks must be managed as knowledge assets and integrated with both new systems and with the growing volume of end-to-end, process-related information. Moreover, all of these many processes have many variants—private processes, customized processes for different partners, evolved best practices and new industry standards. The complexity of managing this swarm of process variants is obvious, but complexity is the true nature of business—that's why so much management practice is currently focused on reducing process complexity.

Mergers and acquisitions add another dimension to the challenge of managing numerous business processes. Company A has hundreds of business processes when it merges with company B, who likewise has hundreds of processes. Which are duplicates? Which are variants of the same process? Integrating and rationalizing the legacy systems inherited in a merger or acquisition can be challenging because these are often based on different data models and disparate applications in which implicit business processes are embedded. Rationalizing processes across divisional boundaries, exploiting synergies and removing redundancy is a complex and costly exercise, especially in view of the requirement that the melding of the two companies proceed without disruption to current business operations. Once the merger is complete, these cross-group processes need to be maintained and evolved on an ongoing basis.

One challenge in managing large numbers of business processes is how to identify and evaluate both the general, high-level processes and the detailed, low-level business processes that will yield the greatest benefit if improved or radically redesigned. It should go without saying that the guiding principle for process prioritization must be delivering customer value; if it is not, departments and business units will return to the ruinous pursuit of self-optimization to the detriment of end-to-end optimization focused on the customer. Because no one department is dedicated to looking after the customer, executive management must not confine itself to encouraging process management; it must be directly involved and accountable for it. Process management *is* management.

A business process improvement program often parallels the introduction of new systems from the perspective of performance, quality or resource sharing. Today, no corner of the business is exempt and improvements are required that extend to all processes, business domains and disciplines. This places huge pressure on IT to deliver responsive, general-purpose process-management solutions and tools. Using current methods, IT developers can make a single application more flexible, but this redesign needs to be repeated each and every time the business asks for change in a new area. For this reason, management often focuses exclusively on core processes—those it considers to have strategic importance and great complexity—and either outsources the commodity processes or implements them through shared services.

It comes as little surprise that the high value processes are most complex as they traverse the entire value chain—as they must in order to reach the customer. Nonetheless, companies that want to dominate their industries will take on the challenge and arm themselves with process management methods and tools that are up to the task.

The Need for Process Collaboration

As new technologies emerge, businesses are becoming more ambitious about process collaboration—loosely coupling their business processes with those of trading partners. Research indicates that businesses are now aware of the ability to link processes across organizational boundaries. Although there is still some debate about the best technical architecture for achieving process collaboration, and about the most appropriate standards to use, businesses say they want to be able to:

- Describe the services they need from partners in service level agreements that can be measured and enforced.
- Allow specialist firms to execute certain steps in processes (a credit check, for example).
- Buy in services from partners and service providers as integrated elements of end-to-end business processes.
- Outsource parts of a process to other businesses yet retain control over and monitor the outsourced sub-processes.
- Expose world-class internal capabilities as new services so they can be easily integrated into the processes of potential customers.
- Allow specialists and other third parties to monitor, measure and oversee the improvement of processes.

- Build more sustainable partnerships by asking potential partners to demonstrate that their proposed processes will be feasible and cost effective.
- Compare internal costs and the costs of collaboration with industry peers by providing benchmarking companies with live, *in situ* information about process performance, thereby enabling actionable service level agreements.

Processes are in flux everywhere, right across the value chain. Changes arise as a result of new legal regulations, de facto standards imposed by industry gorillas, competitive pressures or shifting work patterns. Companies seek best practices as a solution, but processes need to change in ways that build on and exceed average performance. Meeting the need to work closely with partners and third parties—either to implement new levels of efficiency or to pursue new business opportunities—can be overwhelming without computer-aided process management.

Custom Business Processes for Competitive Advantage

Companies want to customize their business processes for competitive advantage. Often, they would like to operate several different variants of a particular process, especially where systems interfaces, customers, suppliers and partners have different requirements. In addition, a business unit may be subject to local market conditions, practices, taxes or regulations. The ability to respond flexibly by customizing processes can create considerable competitive advantage—but it also might turn hundreds of processes into thousands of variants that would be impossible to manage without appropriate techniques and tools.

Globalization is also a major driver of the need for process customization. The challenge for any organization responding to globalization is the need to strike the appropriate balance between centralized corporate standards and the autonomy needed to serve local markets. Businesses need control over their business units, but must also provide local divisions with the ability to react to local markets and national regulations. Information systems that support these businesses must therefore be able to customize core processes for local deployment. If these processes are embedded within monolithic applications, such customization and adaptation is either impossible or prohibitively expensive. In addition, if a company does not have an explicit, clearly expressed set of business processes that the local business units can understand and adapt, the locals will invent their own, jeopardizing the overall integrity of the business. Failure to build an appropriate process-management environment to support the dissemination and deployment of corporate-level best-in-class processes results in duplicated effort, unfinished projects, and business units that are forced to work with processes not designed to meet their specific needs. The new focus on process adaptation, reuse, localization and change applies not only to human workflows but also to systems implementation and application integration.

Beyond Best Practice, On to Excellence

A company's processes need to be managed whether they are excellent, best practice or below average in quality. Nevertheless, the implementation of excellence or best practices in business relies upon end-to-end knowledge about, and visibility and orchestration of, these processes. Process management systems must be capable of deploying explicit best practices across the value chain.

Best practices are sometimes discovered within the business. When that happens, the goal becomes to capture them, document them and reuse them across the board. The further challenge is to adapt them for context and localization. A company that wants to propagate a corporate best practice knows it will fail unless the practice can be adapted to local conditions.

Best practices can also be imposed from outside, by government, regulators or industry consortia. Best-practice business processes provide optimal solutions for gaining operational efficiencies within a particular industry, hence the term itself. Examples include:

- Retail: Collaborative, Planning, Forecasting and Replenishment (CPFR)
- Finance: Use of straight-through-processing (STP) in compliance with T+1 SEC regulations
- Telecommunications: Service provisioning and management (TMFORUM)

- Manufacturing: Managing product lifecycles (STEP)
- Hi-Tech: Reducing inventory levels (UCC, RosettaNet, SCOR)
- Insurance and healthcare: HIPAA compliance
- Pharmaceuticals: Computer systems validation (GAMP)
- Banking: Capital risk and accountability (Basel Capital Accord)
- Federal: The Geospatial One-Stop Project, Geographic Information Systems (GIS)

There are literally thousands of government- and industry-mandated best practices. Imposed best practices do not, however, reflect the unique, often proprietary business practices by which companies differentiate themselves and gain strategic advantage. The challenge is to find a way to implement specifications others have produced, and to customize them to the unique practices of a company. No standard industry process can take into account the practical realities of each business. Best practices almost always have to be deployed in a customized way—if not for competitive reasons, then for purely practical reasons. But for lack of an effective process management infrastructure, companies are forced to simplify complex recommendations so that they can be practically implemented without too much additional overhead. Companies then have to refine and maintain them, in compliance with the law or evolving community rules and guidelines.

Today's best practices, whether developed in-house or by an external body, are essentially paper-based specifications. They can be understood in general terms, but provide no plan for implementation. As collaborative business processes proliferate and evolve more rapidly, paper specifications alone will be insufficient. A mechanism is therefore required for deploying best practices onto the IT infrastructure of firms that choose to adopt them—directly, transparently and without distortion. Progress in business process automation will be halted unless descriptions of best-practice processes are formalized to the point where implementation and compliance can be automated. Such specifications must drive process technologies that can implement the best practice directly while maintaining a company's private business processes.

Many companies implement standardized processes as an efficiency solution, but risk becoming a commodity player by doing so. Even standardized processes bring with them the cost and complexity of deploying any large-scale new process. Accommodating a complex standard usually requires large-scale changes to IT systems, as well as associated organizational changes.

An example from the healthcare sector is the Health Insurance Portability and Accountability Act of 1996 (HIPAA), which requires companies to implement and manage specific business processes without adding to the cost of insurance. Similarly, the pharmaceutical industry faces a number of new regulatory issues with respect to the validation and change-control of processes that might impact the safety of new therapeutic products. These arise from government regulations as interpreted by GAMP.org—a forum that reports on the regulation and use of computer and control systems within health care industries. One section deals with electronic records and signatures and could force companies in the healthcare products industries to implement electronic change control systems to replace their largely paper-based procedures, which literally fill whole vaults in many of the programs that bring new therapies to market. It has been estimated that unless supported by automated processes, these regulations can add ten percent to the cost of any ERP implementation in that sector. But the need for process management transcends regulation, for companies in the healthcare sector now have to manage processes extending to the lifetime of a person, involving dozens of healthcare providers that have a common interest in the patient.

In the retail supply chain, processes are used primarily to share such information as stock levels so that suppliers can collaborate with retail outlets to plan for and forecast demand in order to replenish warehouses and supermarket shelves in line with demand and therefore to cut excess inventory. In these supply-chain processes, messages about stock levels flow up and down the chain between participants at every level. These processes are so complex that many companies struggle to implement them fully.

Some industries respond to similar challenges by creating standard data formats and focus less on processes. An example is the Chemical Industry Data Exchange (CIDX.org), which has developed data standards for the industry and is developing standard business-interface processes, but has so far provided no method for expressing these in computer-readable format, let alone in a formalized way that could assist implementation, adoption and drive standardization for efficiency across the industry. Accelerating such value chain integration is one of the major applications of process management.

In the finance sector, workflow automation and transactions across systems and companies is paramount if the industry is to implement SEC regulations and advance incrementally from 5-day to 3-day, to 1-day (T+1) and eventually to "real time" (T+0) trading and settlement. BPM allows financial services companies to collaborate more closely with others electronically, making the Straight Through Processing (STP) paradigm a practical reality.

Best practices can also arise from international conventions. For example, the new Basel Capital Accord was developed by the Basel Committee on Banking Supervision and endorsed by the central bank governors of the Group of Ten (G-10) countries. Its aim is to ensure the safety and soundness of today's dynamic and complex financial system with a combination of bank-level management, market discipline and supervisory review. The Basel Accord places great emphasis upon banks' own internal control and management, the external audit and the supervisory review process. Basel would change capital standards for international banks, in part by allowing them to use internal risk rating systems to help set minimum capital requirements. Industry representatives are said to be less concerned with the transparency requirements of the accord than they are about problems with its size and complexity. When finalized, the accord will run to more than 1,000 pages, and tremendous effort will be needed to comply with it. If new Basel compliance costs end up being high, banks will earn a lower return on capital and grow more slowly. By making operational risk management a requirement, then, the accord creates very strong incentives for financial organizations to come up with a process model of operational risk—one that can be used to drive the behavior of the banks' internal systems, their interaction with the systems of partners and regulators. The new framework should also encourage internal bank management to develop an internal capital needs assessment process. The implementation of these proposals will in many cases require a much more detailed dialogue between internal and external supervisors and banks. Effective disclosure is essential to ensuring that market participants can better understand the risk profiles of banks and the adequacy of their capital positions.

The government sector itself faces process challenges. Requirements for new processes to manage the collection of data from federal, state, local and "tribal" government tiers and other government agencies, as well as from the private sector and the academic community, are ever rising. An example is the Geospatial One-Stop Project, one of President George W. Bush's top 25 e-government initiatives. The initiative aims to create an online geospatial information portal that will be used to support government-to-government operations. Geographic information systems (GIS) analyze spatial information that identifies geographic locations such as latitude and longitude, area code and zip code. These are linked to characteristics of natural, or constructed, features or boundaries on earth, derived from remote sensing, mapping, and survey technologies. GIS is used extensively in areas such as transportation and logistics, public health and safety, environmental, natural resources, utility, forestry, emergency, military and defense. The U.S. federal government spends about $4 billion every year collecting geospatial information, with the state and local governments spending another $8 billion annually.

The One-Stop initiative, an interagency effort led by the Department of the Interior, will accelerate the collaboration, integration of, and access to, existing and planned geospatial data collections. The project has gained further visibility due to Homeland Security priorities that rely on critical information and geospatial standardized data shared across interoperable networks. For example, effective Homeland Security measures require effective cross-governmental and cross-jurisdictional coordination, support and participation. Among other things, GIS data may be used to locate evacuation routes and hazardous materials in response to possible terrorist threats or suspicious activities around nuclear facilities, water plants, bridges and buildings. Such coordination and data sharing processes cannot be established through point-solutions and the integration of existing legacy systems. Nor is the timescale for new systems development commensurate with the urgency to introduce new measures, even if the budget for new systems were approved. Rather, the processes required must be explicitly designed from the top down and deployed across all required participants if they are to meet requirements for accuracy, completeness, accountability and transparency. Whatever approach is chosen, they must be deployed, and subsequently managed, directly onto the existing federal infrastructure, which consists of legacy, hardwired, and proprietary custom-built systems and applications as the starting point. A process, rather than a systems approach, would encourage agencies to work together, to build a holistic view of the end-to-end needs.

The Geospatial One-Stop Project represents only one slice of a solution that is part of a much larger Federal picture, an environment dominated by multiple and redundant applications, interfaces, and operating systems consisting of undocumented ad hoc upgrades and patches, with architectural maps that are analogous to a tangled bowl of spaghetti. The use of process management would therefore significantly alleviate the painstaking effort that would otherwise be required to integrate complex, unaligned and uncoordinated systems. Modeling the whole process in this federated environment, rather than fixing individual elements in isolation, would improve reliability, streamline production planning, and support the collaboration of employees across agencies. Commentators have already highlighted the complexity of such e-government initiatives, and solutions are being sought in the area of data standardization. For example, the Open GIS Consortium has invited expressions of interest from industry to participate in a Model Advisory Team (MAT) regarding a nationwide Transportation Framework Data Content Standard. This task is part of a larger effort to develop data content standards and other capabilities for the Geospatial One-Stop project. The earlier realization of these worthy aims depends, not only on standard data, but also on the deployment of a standard process representation and methodology for process management.

Every company in every industry knows of similar examples, where the changing marketplace is creating a need to evolve existing processes and implement new ones. The cost of IT implementation is often a factor that distorts thinking. It is frequently reported that companies are wary of implementing process collaboration because of its complexity and cost. Many also feel that sharing processes with partners may add risk, create inflexible relationships or compromise their own flexibility and competitive advantage. Without the third wave of business process management, processes baked into systems for all the right reasons might turn around and bite the hand that hatched them, creating rigid maintenance monsters. No wonder some "brick and mortar" companies held back from implementing hard-coded business-to-business (B2B) e-markets.

Today, legacy systems encode core business processes that CEOs regard as their heritage, the source of their competitive advantage and key differentiators. These processes are a form of intellectual property. The challenge for companies is to identify and protect these assets, even going so far as to protect them in law, as Amazon.com did with its 1-Click ordering process. Yet Amazon also uses best-practice business processes to interoperate with wholesalers such as Baker & Taylor and Ingram. Thus, what companies really want are both best-practice processes for operational efficiency and their own unique best-of-breed business processes for competitive advantage. Going forward, business process management systems must address the entire spectrum of business interactions summarized in Table 3.2.

	Simple, Static Processes	Complex, Dynamic Processes
Core and primary activities (Strategic)	Moderate business value. Transaction volume can create value. Standard best practices. Must be supported across different verticals. Focus for collaborative process management.	Tend to be fluid. Difficult to coordinate across numerous partners. Unique to the firm, mission critical. Focus on continual process improvement. Need for increased decision making.
Context and support activities (Processes less strategic to the firm, but oversight needed)	Lower business value. Supported across numerous partners. Focus on automation and standardization to create efficiencies.	Customized processes. Often outsourced.

Table 3.2. The Business Process Spectrum

Every company has its own roster of processes to locate within this matrix. Different companies may locate the same process in different quadrants. Although it offers only the most primitive starting point for analysis, this table makes the challenge clear. Businesses seek an improved way of deploying many custom process designs and are demanding more flexibility so that their unique private processes can collaborate with those of other firms without the need to deploy the lowest-common-denominator, one-size-fits-all public process. Smart companies are now demanding an adaptable process management solution rather than a standard software application. And they must also preserve existing investments, so that any new approach must treat existing systems as full participants in process design.

The CIO needs process management too. The IT function is an integral part of the business and its processes—help desk, service management, applications delivery, incident management, configuration management, release management, service level agreements, capacity management—all are a subset of the business's processes. The extent to which a company can recognize that BPM lies at the precise intersection between business and IT, will be a measure of the company's maturity in applying process management. In IT-intensive businesses the opportunity to define processes that combine both the associated *IT* process with the *business* process they support, will be a powerful technique for creating a more responsive IT-organization. Where the CIO plays a creative role in process design, BPM may actually begin in the IT department before it is widely deployed across the business for non-IT processes. Best practices in IT, such as the IT Infrastructure Library (ITIL), will be fully supported by using process management systems, leading not only to a responsive IT-organization, but an efficient one.

The First Business Process Management Summit

In September 2001, delegates to the world's first Business Process Management Summit confirmed the urgent need for a new generation of technologies to manage business processes. Delegates from business and public-sector organizations heard from researchers, vendors and leading-edge organizations about a new wave of technologies that provide business process management capabilities. This was no ordinary conference, but a groundbreaking executive brainstorm about BPM. The 93 delegates from Global 2000 companies used networked laptops to respond in real time to the presentations and workshops, and to answer specific questions. The objective was to understand, at first hand, how companies felt about processes and process management, based on years of experience with reengineering and other process improvement methodologies. This anonymous form of interactive dialogue generated much data and confirmed that end-to-end business processes are at the top of IT and management agendas. Participants were concerned about their ability to work in the coming process-centric world, and expressed a clear demand for systems to better manage business processes. Yet the delegates also sent a clear message to participating software providers and systems integrators: They are wary of promises. They want to see proof that new business process technologies deliver value.

During the brainstorming sessions, attendees were asked to identify the business processes and process-related issues that were creating the most difficulty in their businesses. Their responses allow us to draw some general conclusions about the state of process management.

Organizations are trying to manage their business processes, but the tools they are using today are inadequate. When asked what processes they were struggling with, most delegates named processes that reach across the value chain: customer service, sales and marketing, and supplier management. Some mentioned processes that share structured and unstructured information with people outside the organization—customers, suppliers and partners—enabling them to perform tasks using the organization's information.

To conference participants, *customer service* meant customer *self-service*: placing orders against existing contracts, assessing technical information such as material management documents, and receiving technical support on-line, either directly through a representative or passively through a list of Frequently Asked Questions.

The *sales and marketing* category encompassed online sales of goods and services. This included direct sales to consumers as well as participation in B2B catalogs, private supplier portals, auctions and exchanges, along with online support for field sales staff.

By definition, *supply chain processes* include suppliers and other partners such as logistics companies. Most of the supply chain projects named by delegates focused on supplier portals, e-procurement or the use of public market sites. An end-to-end view of the supply chain was rarely mentioned. The types of software solution participants were familiar with colored their thinking.

Participants defined *knowledge management* from the inside out. The knowledge management initiatives they cited involved gathering and sharing internal information, although most said they will eventually share knowledge throughout the value chain. The internal projects they identified focused on improving internal help desks or administering human resource programs. Although these are not particularly pressing issues, such internal projects are often seen as a low-risk way to test the application of new business process technologies.

The most surprising finding was that while 28 percent of delegates were aware their businesses faced process-related issues, such as discovery, redesign, analysis and optimization, none of this group could relate these issues to any particular process. Delegates were blinded by the complexity of implementing process change and were seeking solutions that could illuminate their current business operations and offer them a way to make informed choices about necessary improvements. Their response indicated a craving for better, more flexible business process management capabilities in general.

The BPM priorities of participants depended on the competitive environment in their industry and their prior experience with business process programs. Their responses to the question: "What processes would you focus on today?" reflected the very different perspectives of different industries.

In financial services and government, for example, interaction with the customer was cited as the chief concern. For financial services this means developing customer-friendly applications to enable customers to access information, manage their finances and buy financial products on-line. Value chain processes are also very important here because these companies need to access trading partners in order to provide information and offer financial services products.

For government organizations, whose "customers" are their citizens, the chief issue is providing access to information and services on-line. E-government initially promised improved service at much lower cost—but fulfilling this promise will require total transformation of business processes and their enabling applications. Delegates reported that their departments are too heavily focused today on internal operations rather than the customer. Like the financial sector, the e-government sector said it wanted better process management tools.

Delegates from manufacturing companies nominated supply chain and customer-facing processes as their top priorities, focusing on their established supply chain programs and the demand from their customers for more self-service and direct access to information. Manufacturing companies are clearly more focused on specific processes than on their ability to manage processes in general.

Surprisingly, the services sector, which one might have believed should have been focused on customer service and self-service, was focused internally, on back-end processes such as the service supply chain. This focus reflects the nature of their business—solving customer problems rather than providing the customer with the means to solve problems for themselves. They wished to break out of this mold and deploy processes that let customers assist them.

In general, participants saw business process issues both as a product of and a solution to a challenging business climate. They divided the business goals driving their process initiatives into three nearly equal categories: efficiency (39 percent), agility (26 percent) and customer demands (35 percent).

- *Efficiency* is the need to keep cutting costs—both operating costs and the cost of capital. New processes can lower costs by eliminating inefficiencies within the organization, or by cutting cost in the value chain as a whole.
- *Agility* is the ability to cut the time required to develop products and services and to respond to customer and market demands. Delegates expressed this in terms of the need to streamline processes and integrate systems and business units. New processes achieve efficiency and agility by providing better coordination, improved process visibility and reduced cycle times. The need to enable faster deployment of new business processes was reported by all participants.
- *Customer demands* are driven by the need to focus on customer retention and satisfaction. In general, participants believed their customers want better service and self-service. They see the Internet as the primary way of delivering the kinds of interaction their customers demand.

The Surge in Demand for BPM

Business processes are at the heart of several management theories. For example, when Dr. W. Edwards Deming, father of the quality movement, pronounced that the improvement of quality is 90 percent

centered on the system—on the process, in other words—Japan listened
and became an economic superpower, rising from the ashes of World
War II. Other examples of process-related management theories include:

- Value-chain analysis: Porter, M.E. (1980), *Competitive Advantage*
- Excellence: Peters, T.J. & Waterman, R. H. (1982), *In search of excellence*
- Reengineering: Hammer, M. (1990), "Don't automate, obliterate"
- Innovation: Davenport T.H. & Short J.E. (1990), *The new industrial engineering: Information Technology and Business Process Redesign*
- Customer-driven business: Whiteley, R.C. (1991), *The customer-driven company*
- Knowledge management: Drucker, Peter F. (1993), *Post-capitalist society*
- Supply-chain management: Schonberger, R.J. (1996), *World class manufacturing*

Businesses today are under pressure on many fronts. Customers
want improvements in cost, speed, quality, customization, and service
that delights. It is no longer enough to be excellent at just one aspect of
the business—to be cheaper, or faster, or better—because customers
want it all. And these competitive pressures show no signs of letting up.
The technologies on which companies have relied up to now will not
take them past where they are today. Current business applications are
too expensive and too slow to change, and so cannot assist companies
to build *business processes of distinction*—the kind that delight customers and
command markets.

Processes are what partners, customers and regulators impose on,
and demand of, companies. An organization's ability to respond is, in
large measure, determined by three factors. First, if business processes
are implicit, ingrained and embedded, external process influences create
fragility, disruption and the need for expansive changes to both organization and systems. Second, business processes are deeply complex, so
that even if processes are explicit, computer-assisted tools are
required—not only to manipulate processes and create new business
designs—but also create an execution path, a certain way of deploying
and subsequently operating the new processes. Third, deployment out of
business context is nothing more than a cheap trick. Processes must be

deployed upon the existing legacy and heritage infrastructure, leveraging all existing assets, and the functional components manifest in the embedded processes.

To dominate in the years ahead, companies must therefore make their business processes manageable, with formalized, actionable information about how, and how well, they do things. They must manage not only their own business processes, but also their collaboration with the business processes of every participant in end-to-end value chains, all the way to the customer. They need to create extended enterprises in which external value-chain participants work together as one virtual business to provide compelling value to customers.

Companies need these BPM capabilities so they can make course corrections with great agility, embed Six Sigma quality initiatives into their process designs, and reduce the cumulative costs across the value chain all the way to the customer. They need to be able to pursue strategic initiatives with confidence, including mergers, alliances, acquisitions, outsourcing and global expansion. They need the means to respond to changing customer expectations, to cope with unexpected business model shifts and to implement new industry standards. Companies need the means to consolidate their business in times of recession, using cost-effective new tools for business process integration. And they want to be able to achieve these objectives with the required degree of executive management control, visibility and accountability.

Achieving these outcomes requires a universal process language and management platform, one that enables partners to co-design processes and understand one another's operations in detail, and that demonstrates end-to-end corporate accountability to third parties such as regulators, mediators, advisors, lawyers and the federal government. Whether they want to adopt industry best practices in pursuit of efficiency or to develop customized processes in pursuit of competitive advantage, companies want to avoid the high costs once associated with reengineering, organizational change and IT systems implementation. In short, they want a significant breakthrough in the true delivery of business process management, not another management theory or killer application.

Despite the complexity and messiness of the real world of business processes, business process management is no longer optional: It's a mission-critical need. Businesses are under great pressure to *reengineer change management* and get past the platitudes and low-impact linear input-output processes of the reengineering movement, which was long on talk and short on results. Companies that "get it" recognize that they must evolve out of their current "as-is" state into what process engineers call the "to-be" state, becoming a process-managed enterprise. Technology has not been able to provide them with means of doing so—until now.

References

[1] Chairman Jack Welch's remarks at the firm's annual shareowners meeting in Atlanta, GA, April 25, 2001.

[2] McKenna, Regis, *Real Time*. Harvard Business School Press, 1997.

[3] Kelly, Kevin, *New Rules for the New Economy*, Viking Press, 1998.

[4] Davenport, Thomas H., *Process Innovation: Reengineering Work through Information Technology*, Harvard Business School Press, 1993.

Four

Business Process Management

A company is a multidimensional system capable of growth, expansion, and self-regulation. It is, therefore, not a thing but a set of interacting forces. Any theory of organization must be capable of reflecting a company's many facets, its dynamism, and its basic orderliness.
—Albert Low, *Zen and Creative Management*

McARDLE LIBRARY
0151 604 7223

Convergence and synthesis often produce something radically new. Years ago, moving pictures and radio converged, and the result, television, forever changed the world. The third wave of BPM will no doubt also change the world, but there is nothing new about the purposes that BPM was designed to serve. BPM is a synthesis of process representation and collaboration technologies that removes the obstacles blocking the execution of management intentions. BPM is therefore the convergence of management theory—total quality management, Six Sigma, business engineering and general systems thinking—with modern technologies—application development, systems integration, computation, service-oriented architecture, workflow, transaction management, XML and Web services.

For the first time in business history, this synthesis makes it possible for companies to do what they have wanted to do all along—manage their business processes with great agility. A company lacking vision cannot benefit from BPM, but those who have this vision may now use BPM to execute their strategy with speed and precision. The radical breakthrough lies in using process calculus to define the digital representation of business processes, the basis for new corporate information assets. "Process data" based on an open standard for process description allows managers to leverage both old and new technologies for process management. Established companies with great products or start-ups with innovative business models can take equal advantage. The winners in this "radical evolution" are customers, and the companies that master BPM to serve them.

Why So Difficult Before?

Throughout the nineties, companies tried to make their business processes more manageable by reengineering them. Reengineering typically meant designing a simpler new process, then implementing it through a one-time organizational change program. Those efforts had more to do with redesigning processes than with making those processes easy to change and to combine with those of partners. Similar problems remained even after enterprise resource planning (ERP) systems and other packaged solutions emerged in response to the pain of the business process reengineering wave. These packages implemented best-practice processes, but did so by ingraining those processes in software applications. As Doug Neal of Computer Sciences Corporation's Research Services explains, "Historically, ERP solutions had all the flexibility of wet concrete before they were installed and all the flexibility of dry concrete after installation." Today, the management team has no time to wait for IT to evaluate alternative packages, make a selection, customize the package to fit the business, and roll out the new system. Instead, businesses need the capability to manufacture operationally ready processes on demand. Companies must have this now because they are under pressure to perform better and faster, to do more with less, and to provide customers with "super-pleasing" service.

Companies treat processes with care because they constitute vital intellectual property. Processes *are* the business. Operating a process, keeping it updated, operational and effective, is complementary to the lifecycle of its improvement—both must be supported simultaneously and independently. The lifecycle management required might be as simple as keeping track of the versions generated by the design-deploy-redesign loop, or as complex as maintaining project baselines of such long-running processes as those governing tightly regulated product design and manufacturing phases in the aerospace industry.

Based on the experience of ERP, achieving integration inside the enterprise has been perplexing enough. Getting processes to collaborate across the networked value chain is far more so. Business partners may have informal designs for the processes they need to implement, but as they refine these designs, they must also change the technical implementations that support them. This may be possible in simple cases, but in more complex cases such as advanced supply chain design, implementation projects may never be completed. Upgrading applications or adding new suppliers and business units can cause the scale and cost of technical integration projects to escalate out of control. Every process change requires related changes in numerous technical artifacts. This situation is unsustainable. Adding process tools and best practices to existing software integration products helps, but it would be far more practical if process management tools were the foundation for process-centric business information systems.

Several industry analysts have estimated that companies are spending between 20 and 30 percent of their IT budget integrating their internal applications under the banner of enterprise application integration (EAI), but they are, in effect, struggling with a much wider and far more knotty range of process-related issues. One example is preparing for a second phase—business-to-business integration (B2Bi). In the networked enterprise, collaboration is not restricted to any one process domain. Collaboration is 360 degrees, going on at all points on the compass. To integrate business processes, IT departments typically employ a bottom-up technical integration, stitching together application components that were never intended to work together at the business level. This creates a many-to-many integration challenge to which existing tools and techniques are simply not adequate. If completed at all, these projects commonly overrun their budgets and schedules, consuming the anticipated return on investment. Their failure rate stems from the fact they are mere point solutions to a much larger problem; that of enterprise-wide process management.

Why are they going to all this effort and expense? Tying together fragments of internal "stovepipe" applications and interfaces to create end-to-end, multi-company business processes—those activities that bring ultimate value to customers—has produced processes built to last, but not necessarily to adapt. Even those large-scale integration projects deemed initially successful do not necessarily allow companies to readily change processes thereafter. Rarely, if ever, do architects consider the need for subsequent customized process variants or optimization of individual processes for specific customers or partners. And do such point integration architectures offer a holistic approach to process management in larger scale scenarios, such as outsourcing, collaborative commerce, mergers and acquisitions? We think not.

Today's data management infrastructures make it trivial to share data, but despite the rise of middleware and other integration solutions, sharing business processes remains problematic. Many CIOs believe that middleware is the only way to implement processes, although they are rightfully worried about the resulting increase in the complexity of the technology stack. Although CIOs are achieving some success using distributed computing to share functionality inside the enterprise, the complexity of extending collaboration beyond the walls can be daunting.

Meanwhile, CEOs continue to ask them for new and newly improved processes. CIOs are therefore seeking a higher-level, more outcome focused solution to the problem of how to "make this work with that," and want to establish an architectural foundation for tomorrow's process-based business. Sensing these pressing needs, software vendors are stressing the process capabilities of their solutions. Unfortunately, these vendors are sending mixed messages to their markets about the adequacy of different technologies to the problem of process change. Not all process-integration problems are technical, and not all processes are about IT. Integrating computer systems is not the same as integrating the business.

Collaborative commerce requires extending processes beyond the company's walls, and that is not an easy step to take. But if companies are under pressure to be better, faster and cheaper, they will have to do only what they do best and outsource the rest to suppliers and trading partners. If commerce is to be truly collaborative, it's the underlying business processes that must collaborate, not just the IT systems. In fact, collaboration must not depend upon technical integration at all, but the inherent ability of third-wave processes to participate in one another's execution. What is needed?

What businesses need is not a one-time fix for individual processes but an environment that combines business and technical systems to produce processes that flex and recombine as required by changes in the market. Most companies now want more control over their own processes, more interaction between their own processes and those of their partners, and the ability to monitor and control processes performed on their behalf by partners. They also want to package their unique business competencies as processes they can sell, including an ability to sell them over networks, perhaps in the form of Web services. To do all this, firms need a business process management capability, not a new suite of silo enterprise applications.

The current situation is comparable to the period before the advent of centralized database management. Data, and data management, used to be an embedded feature in each and every IT system. The volume of data grew, but it was growing independently in all business applications. Companies found they needed to see connections across the business. From the IT perspective it was soon obvious that data should be managed outside of the application architecture. Now we don't think twice about it. By allowing a company to manage its data apart from the applications that use the data, the database management system supports a variety of shared data models and a variety of shared data management tasks and tools.

Today's business automation packages are largely founded on database management systems. These enterprise applications are primarily concerned with reading from, writing to and manipulating databases. The data-centric view of the world underlying these applications has profound implications. Business logic, data models, time and connectivity all reside within each "stovepipe" application. To date, expensive and overly complex middleware solutions have been used to tie these stovepipes together to create end-to-end business processes. But as the demand for business process innovation accelerates, middleware solutions have reached their limits.

BPM aligns processes more directly with organizational objectives. Business processes literally define the company, representing its critical source of competitive advantage and market differentiation. But business processes are very complex systems. End-to-end business processes are long-lived, unique, and numerous, and are constantly evolving in three dimensions—situation, structure and design. As the drive toward automation, process outsourcing and collaboration continues apace, managing these processes has the potential to overwhelm the firm. Third-wave process management offers vital tools for managing these increasingly complex realities of business.

Today, *standard* business processes delivered in the form of *standard* "off the shelf" applications that are also available to and used by competitors are appearing less and less attractive. Businesses want to shape their processes themselves, performing continuous and incremental process improvement without technological impediments and bottlenecks. But they still want to exploit low cost, best-of-breed application components where appropriate. Third-wave process management systems combine the best of component application engineering and the best of process engineering to give companies the flexibility they now demand. In light of the overwhelming demand for business process management, the era of stovepipe application development will give way to an era of process manufacturing and assembly.

Reengineering Redux

The first step toward business process management is to make processes explicit by abstracting them from existing application software. This approach is hardly a new one. Decades ago, operating systems abstracted memory management, file access and graphical user interfaces from applications. Database management systems removed, from the responsibility of the application, both the management of application data and the management of the schema by which the data was described. Today, the same is true for business rules which are now often held and managed in a separate system. Architects use these management systems to partition the application and make it easier to maintain. Process management is the next logical step, opening the door to a host of new "process" capabilities—analysis, simulation, transformation and inspection—each reliant on access to the new "process data" and therefore amenable to manipulation by all computer systems. Process-centric applications get an end-to-end, bird's-eye view of the business. Companies and their automated tools see the whole process, not just the changes in data as the process executes. The mission-critical business processes such systems support are reliable, transactional and distributed. They enable processes designed independently by different organizations to collaborate. A business process can be represented as a new form of information, and it can be shared and manipulated just as a team of human authors shares and manipulates a document using word-processing software.

Confusion remains, however, about the best way to achieve a process management capability. Virtually every major corporation has an IT group working on an "architecture for BPM." In most such cases, BPM is envisioned as another layer added to a technology stack. Some groups adopt Web services platforms. Some deploy application integration products. Others make extensive use of workflow. A few are piloting departmental process managers. Most use process mapping tools, and many have deployed rules engines. Some use rapid application development tools to speed application delivery. It's a complex picture. Plugging all the pieces together is taxing even the most able IT architects. The current technology landscape seems to offer so many options—and standards—for developing processes: workflow management, application software development, Web services, integration tools, business rules, code generators. Each of these strategies has its strengths, and the variety of existing infrastructures already in place tends to lead different companies in different directions. Such piecemeal approaches to process management simply do not work well enough, however. What started out as a neat top-down design—and the envisioned software system to support it—quickly deteriorates, the process becomes disfigured, and the company's hopes for simplification, improvement and management are dashed. Is there a better way?

There is. Third-wave business process management methods and systems will utterly transform the way companies conceive, build and operate automated systems. And third-wave methods and systems can be used by business people, not just technologists. By placing the representation of processes center stage in business and IT design, companies can develop the capabilities they need to fully manage their processes. The innovation is in the way processes are represented and the way other technologies interact with them. Some companies see this unified framework as providing an opportunity to return to a more centralized model of computing in order to achieve process coherence across the business. A business process can be distributed, end-to-end, long-lived, collaborative, transactional and involve hundreds of participants, yet still reside in one place—the data center. Every assumption is up for reevaluation as corporations refresh their business and technology architectures for the next phase of growth and efficiency using third-wave BPM.

One of the greatest effects of process management will be a shift from reactive to proactive management of change. Managing change must be transformed into and managed as a business process like any other. Given the ability of BPM to simulate change and its effects, companies can build and test multiple projected scenarios, each incorporating information about organizational and process change. With such capabilities, a company like Cisco would have been able to ask those vital "what if" questions such as, "How can we quickly transform our operations if the demand for Internet routers suddenly drops?"—which of course it did when the dot-com bubble burst and Cisco took a $2.5 billion inventory hit.

Process management heralds a renaissance in process thinking and process-centered organizational design. And this renaissance is not being driven by technological innovation alone. Far from it. The principal drivers are economic. Business processes, not applications or databases, are the highest-value assets in business today, but the value of those assets lies not only in their execution but an ability to manage them based upon an explicit representation. Tinkering with existing ways of implementing business change, in the way advocated by the reengineering movement of the 1990s, won't be enough. The payoff of this new wave of collaborative reengineering initiatives will be the ability to *actually deliver on* the decade-old promises of "reengineering."

The Path to Execution

In the third wave of BPM, stovepipe thinking and point-to-point technical integration give way to flexible, business process-based architectures. The complexity and diversity of enterprise systems, the growth of middleware, and the drive for the next level of efficiency and productivity both within and across organizational boundaries—all of these require process thinking. Analysts such as the Gartner Group are now saying that companies that continue to hard-code business logic into software applications or middleware, or insist on manual steps, will lose out to competitors that deploy process management architectures and digitize their business processes.

Unlike yesterday's reengineering designs, today's process-focused designs must be *directly executable* and capable of evolving under their own devices, with minimal impact on current business operations. BPM defines, enables and manages the exchange of business information on the basis of a process view that incorporates employees, customers, partners, applications and databases. The same environment used to create a specific business process can also be used to manage the life-cycle of that business process. Supply chain processes, project planning processes, learning processes and product-data management processes are all represented and managed alike.

BPM recognizes that *change* is as fundamental to business as the law of gravity is to physics, and that agility is therefore a fundamental requirement of enterprise architecture. As Ron Brown of Computer Sciences Corporation explains, "today's CEO is looking to reduce the turning radius of IT, which rivals that of a supertanker in terms of its responsiveness to new business requirements." BPM reorients IT's activities to the trajectory of the business process. IT projects are thus less likely to under perform and to lag behind business thinking, or to over-engineer solutions to problems that no longer exist by the time the solutions are implemented. From the perspective of the business side, BPM streamlines internal and external business processes, eliminates redundancies and increases automation, providing end-to-end process visibility, control and accountability. Corporations adopting third-wave BPM architecture are already claiming that their newfound *agility* is a significant new source of competitive advantage. Brown states, "Companies are only just learning that they need not dumb down process design so that the IT department can deliver, or fall back on acquiring standard applications also available to their competitors." Companies can take charge of their processes themselves. Now there is no excuse, either for IT or the business.

Third-wave BPM can support the automation and continuous improvement of thousands of unique transactional and collaborative business processes simultaneously. BPM spans the enterprise to encompass such basic business functions as marketing, sales, human resources, finance, operations, supply chain, product design, forecasting, logistics and customer relationship management, as well as industry-specific processes. Each process can be customized to meet the individual needs of customers, suppliers, partners, employees, business units and systems interfaces. Processes can accommodate design patterns from industry standards, such as the financial industry's straight-through processing (STP) standard, or the collaborative planning, forecasting and replenishment (CPFR) model used in retail and distribution industries. Process designs can be customized for deployment in geographic business divisions across the globe and managed locally.

BPM is as suitable for the automation of relatively simple support processes, such as human resources, as it is for the automation of complex, dynamic, strategically vital processes, such as product design or contract manufacturing. BPM is most powerful, however, where the processes it manages are complex, fluid and difficult to coordinate, and where continuous process optimization and improved decision-making are the central objectives. Companies are now recognizing that third-wave BPM will allow them to own their business processes and leverage them as a source of competitive advantage.

The third wave of BPM brings business people and software engineers into the same process design environment using intuitive graphical notations. This approach takes IT off the critical path of requirements analysis by allowing the business owner to participate fully in the design, deployment and monitoring of enterprise processes, freeing IT to focus on process operations and integrity, and the management of a scalable, robust, process-driven technology infrastructure. Processes can be tuned and amended under business control without coding changes by programmers. With third-wave BPM, IT can respond to business requirements at a pace governed by the business rather than the complexity of the IT environment. BPM provides lifecycle continuity and minimizes the need for interventions by software developers.

BPM supports the needs of any organization, national or global, that manages a portfolio of business applications. In contrast with an IT strategy based on the selection of a single application image or footprint, BPM can integrate all applications and services. It provides end-to-end visibility and management control of the business processes wherever they reside—in manual work practices, in packaged software or in legacy systems.

BPM manages the challenges of legacy-encumbered environments and the kind of heterogeneous application portfolios that arise from policy decisions, decentralized operations, and mergers and acquisitions. BPM is as adept at supporting a centralized IT strategy as it is at supporting a federated infrastructure. Corporate processes can be easily adapted to local geographic requirements without duplicating the application footprint. Instead of configuring the application and deploying it multiple times—for example for local business units—the process itself is customized, resulting in huge savings.

BPM Over the Years

Process management is nothing new to most large corporations. However, there have been dramatic changes in the way process management is achieved.

The distant past. As the 1980s came to a close, companies were promised dramatic improvements through reengineering, which turned out, however, to involve a lot of manual work and a great deal of pain. Reengineering may have improved performance within the enterprise, but it failed to provide agility or to support ongoing change. Computer systems of the era could not adequately represent the full complexity of processes, let alone provide tools for managing them. Process discovery and design was accomplished in team meetings using little more than a whiteboard. Deployment consisted of nothing more than another team meeting. Execution consisted of little more than new rules and procedures, or perhaps a process map that IT was supposed miraculously to implement. Maintenance was only undertaken in the event of failure, and optimization was a matter of wishful thinking. Follow-on analysis was rarely performed.

The last decade. In the era of ERP and workflow, software packages were marketed at the board level, promising that the CEO would not have to worry about IT again. The idea was that the packages provided "everything required." But ERP systems were inflexible—and installation could literally take months, or even years. Subsequent application flow languages attempted to provide a more complete solution, but they couldn't be configured to meet all business requirements, so business users were forced to add components and customize out of bounds. These additions compromised the base solution, and the distortions they introduced into business processes further reduced overall flexibility. At this time, process discovery was still a manual procedure, bound in books and sitting on shelves. Deployment meant rolling out applications to all participants, with huge implications if they were wrong.

The recent past. Over time, new process mapping tools emerged that could capture and manage enterprise processes in an editable form for more flexible manipulation and subsequent analysis. The primary purpose was to produce documentation about the way the company worked. They were also used as aids to assist the review and refinement of process descriptions. These tools, however, could not carry process models directly to execution, and they used proprietary formats and incompatible notations. They focused mainly on modeling input-output activities and data flows, paying insufficient attention to the collaborative aspects of real world processes and their complexity. In the discovery phase, however, these tools made it possible to integrate multiple views of the business, edit and maintain the process blueprint, and publish reports. Optimization and maintenance initially relied on visual inspection of the process designs, and it was hard to keep the blueprint in step with the live software. This was because the business-IT gap still separated strategic goals from technical implementations. A trend toward process simulation and analysis was evident, but the link from planning to execution was still missing.

From now on. In the era of the third wave, processes can be viewed by human users as information and by machines as executable code at the same time. An open standard is used for describing all processes. Process design proceeds from both the top down—at the level of business strategy and business process design—and from the bottom up, at the level of leveraging existing IT systems.

Discovery activity uses standard electronic formats to create process designs, which populate the process management system and its repository. Process designers use these models to simulate and explore desirable changes in much the same way airplane designers use completely automated, computer-aided design systems and simulators.

Process management separates process design and subsequent process change from integration activities, which are managed in different cycles. Process models developed in different parts of the business, or by partners, can now be related to one another, independent of the technical details, through process level interfaces. High-level models can be further refined. Abstract models can be used as blueprints for subsequent design. Discovery, design, deployment and maintenance occur in parallel, not in ordered series.

The process management system has built-in metrics that provide process-level instrumentation, new forms of management information that can guide process optimization and incremental refinement. Analysis is end-to-end, closing the loop between design and operations. Process improvements achieved in one part of the business can be exported to other divisions and adapted as required.

Process designs are reflected directly in the IT infrastructure and made manifest to employees through enterprise portals. Such an approach leverages existing investments by connecting databases, legacy systems and best-of-breed package solutions into flexible end-to-end business processes, supporting the needs of managers, process engineers, functional departments and employees, as well as IT developers— all in the context of a unified, process-based view of the business.

The reengineering and ERP eras were focused on one-time process change events. Workflow was the innovation that signaled the coming of the third wave. Now BPM has change, integration and collaboration "built in," and not only for input-output processes, but all processes. Processes are represented as a new information type, not a new packaged application. Process designs can be immediately deployed on an IT infrastructure as reliable and scaleable services, with no intervening steps. Process customization is greatly simplified, because processes are *nothing more than data.* Process collaboration is simplified because "integrating" two processes is nothing more than joining two process-data sets. Processes that require the reliable completion of simple business transactions, as well as complex sequences that may continue for weeks, months or years, are well suited to the approach. Even the simplest of numerical calculations can be equally expressed in this form.

Before the third wave, "process" deployment—actually application development—involved translating process designs into an IT deliverable, a complex and unwieldy procedure. In what became known as the "business-IT divide," requirements were "thrown over the wall" for IT to figure out how to implement, often with distorted results. Over the last two decades the IT industry has spent much effort trying to streamline the translation of business requirements to business objects and finally into software code. The third wave complements this approach. In BPM, a rich process representation language can express any process and a dedicated execution environment can immediately put new processes to work. Third-wave process management is a straight-through process—no translation into executable code is required. As a result, process systems can be tuned live. Simulation and analysis are performed on-line in the context of live business operations. Process improvement initiatives can be measured and analyzed, which makes evaluating the return on IT investments far more scientific. Business therefore gets the process model it wants, a model that need not be translated or distorted in any way. All participants can share process designs, and changes can be propagated across systems and business partners.

BPM's top-down design approach does not, however, imply that everything has to be done at once, creating a single enterprise process model—experience shows that would hardly be practical. Rather, the term "top down" implies the ability to model processes simultaneously at all levels in line with business strategy. Business people throughout the enterprise can contribute to the design of processes, even while working independently. This implies an ability to combine process models while retaining their meaning by extending links between processes, based on participants and the exchange of information, and by the use of process design patterns to constrain the behavior of sub-processes.

From Modeling to Management

In a research note dated December 5, 1997, the Gartner Group identified "Nine Reasons Why IS Organizations Do Not Do BPM." At the time, "BPM" referred to business process *modeling* rather than business process *management*. In every instance, business process management can be viewed as the breakthrough that addresses the shortcomings of using process modeling alone as identified by Gartner:

"Business units will not make the effort." Many companies viewed process modeling as an IT-led initiative that would require the participation of business units in facilitating an increasingly complex software engineering process. Needless to say, some business units were indeed quite reluctant to make any effort in that direction. On the other hand, business process management is now conceived as a business-driven initiative that no longer requires the participation of IT organizations for the transformation of business process models into executable processes.

"We tried CASE and did not like it." The shortcomings of Computer-Aided Software Engineering (CASE), which usually led to some form of "analysis paralysis," are now well understood, and business process management incorporates the lessons learned. BPM is not CASE. CASE was an intermediate step that automated the mapping of business requirements and design parameters onto existing software artifacts—objects, components, interfaces and so on. BPM is a new type of software, not based on objects, but on processes—a new first-class information type—and because this new type is oriented to the expression of business, BPM does not require the translation steps of CASE. It provides the fundamental building blocks required for developing complex business logic and computation *without* conventional software development. It has no need of concepts related to the lifecycle of requirements as traditionally defined, such as application design, implementation, testing and deployment. In BPM, testing is largely superseded by simulation.

"We do not have the time." When it was owned by IT organizations, business process modeling was often perceived as an unproductive additional step in the overall software engineering process. It was usually incompatible with increasingly tight delivery schedules, schedules that were squeezed even tighter with the Y2K bug looming on the horizon back in 1997. In contrast, third-wave business process systems can be understood as the fastest rapid application development (RAD) methodology ever made available to business. There is *no* translation of the process model to software—none, zero, zilch. The process model *is* the system. The system is the business. BPM can model not only computer-based processes, but also manual, abstract and real world processes, opening the door for a more complete digital model of businesses. This includes management processes, abstract processes, knowledge management processes, and organizational learning processes. There is no

distinction between these and the traditional view of processes as applications. Models are just models and include all required elements and participants.

"Business units tell us what to build; we do not question them." Business process modeling was often presented as a way to address the divide between business and IT organizations through "a combination of IT push and business pull." This approach ignored the fact that business units typically perceive IT organizations as mere cost centers and have little tolerance for any push coming from IT. Business process management is a similar approach for bridging the gap between business and IT, but is based on a radically different strategy. Instead of trying to reverse the natural chain of command between business units and IT organizations, business process management establishes a *symbiotic relationship*. By delivering a common language for describing processes, third-wave BPM enables business units to pull IT organizations into the business strategy discussion, inviting them to contribute their years of experience with *general systems thinking* to problems of business innovation.

"We cannot keep business and IT models in synch." Originally, business process modeling supported the development of models that merely served as requirements specifications for developing software applications. Requirements specifications are the beginning of a multi-step software development process consisting of analysis, design, coding, testing and implementation. This software development process itself creates a discrepancy between business and IT models which are virtually impossible to keep aligned because the relationships between requirements and the associated technical artifacts of software engineering—components, files, interfaces and so on—are extremely complex and numerous.

Learning from the experience of the software development approach, business process management is based on an architecture that promotes a single model to be shared and preserved over the entire life cycle of any business process. Instead of relying on multiple models and various transformation mechanisms, business process management renders multiple views—for business analysts, for software engineers, for partners and for customers—of a single model.

"Business changes too quickly to model it." Business process modeling's inability to capture business changes in real time was magnified by two

main factors: the need to synchronize business and IT models, on one hand, and the all-encompassing approach usually adopted by most business process modeling projects on the other hand. Because business process management relies on a single model shared by business units and IT organizations, business processes can be more quickly and readily adapted to the rapid evolutions required by the market. Furthermore, business process management, though it advocates a top-down approach to the management of business processes, does not require the modeling of the entire business for this approach to be effective. This pragmatic approach to modeling is one of the key success factors for third-wave business process management initiatives.

"Is applications development modeling not enough?" Business process modeling often conflicted with other modeling techniques designed for software development in IT organizations, such as the unified modeling language (UML). Software development is a process for building and maintaining applications. Business process management is a process for building and perfecting business processes. UML and other model-driven methods will continue to shape application development, but once development is integrated into the business process model, additional application development is no longer necessary for building and maintaining business processes. Integrate applications once, then create, design, deploy and manage business processes anywhere, anytime and as often as you like.

"Is prototyping not enough?" Because business process modeling was sold to IT organizations rather than business units, the very concept of a business process was often confused with technical processes and was commonly represented in terms of technical artifacts such as system procedures and screen flows. This led to the conclusion that business process modeling was just a fancy term for application prototyping. Business process management, on the other hand, does not pay mere lip service to the adjective "business" in the phrase "business process," it considers the business dimension in business processes to be paramount. Though system procedures and screen-user interaction flows can still be captured by business process management as the lowest level of process design, these only represent the interaction side of a higher-level business process that was initially developed by business analysts. Processes exist in their own right, living in the changing world around them, while prototypes are just that, prototypes. Third-wave processes, located

precisely at the intersection of automated and manual work, adjust their own user interface. As processes change, the interface changes—automatically.

"Business process modeling is more trouble than it is worth." For all the reasons listed above, many companies eventually came to the conclusion that business process modeling was indeed more trouble than it was worth. This was to be expected from a technology that was targeted at the wrong audience and therefore created all kinds of tensions and conflicts, both within and between business units and IT organizations. But that view of modeling is changing and with it so are the vendors of modeling technology, who now play a key role in supplying the sophisticated tools that will sit atop process management systems.

Most of today's process-modeling tools started out as application development tools and initially these were sold to IT organizations. Following the business process reengineering wave, IT organizations were faced with the need to implement newly reengineered processes and so told their tool vendors that they now needed a business process modeling capability in addition to a software modeling capability. In response, the vendors started to provide additional tools for enterprise modeling and process modeling, along with a data dictionary for linking these with the existing software modeling tools. The separation of the modeling paradigms, however, quickly led some of these vendors to imagine the next step—a synthesis and convergence of all dimensions of modeling. Process-modeling vendors—who knew from the beginning that process was king—began to shift their target from IT organizations to business units, effectively preparing the ground for the adoption of BPM by business units working alongside IT organizations. Now, the traditional data dictionary within the process-modeling environment has been replaced by the process dictionary, and traditional data by process data. Like the workflow community, process-modeling vendors were also *process-management innovators*, ushering in the third wave.

Taking Control, All the Way to the Customer

Business process management comprises eight broad capabilities: discovery, design, deployment, execution, interaction, control, optimization and analysis of processes. Illustrated in Figure 4.1, these capabilities also form a business process, which itself can be managed using BPM.

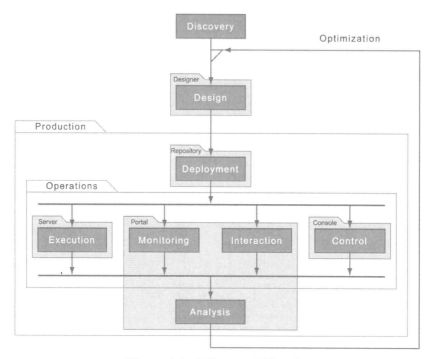

Figure 4.1. A Process Lifecycle

Discovery implies becoming explicitly aware of how things are actually done, as opposed to trying to reconcile the points of view of every individual participant. Business processes—event flow, information flow and control flow—are captured in a machine-readable format from the perspective of all participants, including the computer systems that implement processes and any subprocesses that they use. Discovery involves describing those activities carried out to convert processes that are implicit in work patterns or ingrained in systems and to make them explicit as digital assets.

Discovery may be largely manual (a human labor-intensive effort to map the business) or largely automatic (introspecting the code within legacy systems), or a mixture of both. Third-wave technologies will naturally lead to automated systems that observe the business in action, detecting and mapping patterns of work practice and behavior. Just as today's data management systems readily fill with business data, process management systems fill with process data that reflect the current activities of the business.

Discovery develops a clear picture of how the business processes work, internally and externally. It creates overall process knowledge so that participants can understand the business as a whole, where their responsibilities fit into that whole and how to interact more effectively with others. It synchronizes knowledge about systems and activities across the enterprise and brings customers, suppliers and partners into the process design activity. Discovery tools are increasingly "smart," drawing the process diagrams themselves from process data gathered from the business—for example, from process knowledge elicited from experts.

Design means explicitly modeling, manipulating, and redesigning processes as the organization learns through discovery what is possible. It deals with activities, rules, participants, interactions and relationships. Design includes setting the target metrics for business processes, so that business analysts can restructure processes quickly in response to competitive pressure or business opportunity. Process composition, decomposition, combination, restructuring and transformation are characteristic of the design process. Systems and business interfaces are reengineered internally or with partners. The process repository supports reuse, adaptation and repurposing of process templates, as well as change management and governance. Some organizations will begin to develop repositories of industry best practices and patterns. Simulation is used to explore design alternatives. Unlike previous modeling notations, often designed for software engineers, the notation used by BPM offers an intuitive way of putting process pen to paper, with a clear delineation of the different behavioral aspects of the process, and a brevity that allows even abstract business concepts to be easily captured.

Deployment means rolling out new processes to all the participants, including people, applications and other processes. In the third wave, it's very easy to deploy new processes with little or no manual intervention or additional technical steps. Most, if not all, of the activities are automated. It is possible for IT to develop processes to do just that. Application components can be integrated in advance using a projection of the processes or interfaces to ingrained business logic of existing applications. Participant applications are installed once, independent of the process deployment activity. Similarly, processes can be mapped in advance and bound to standard public interfaces between organizations. At deployment time, it is possible to distribute process work at will to various participants. It is equally possible to distribute the execution of processes across different process management systems. Resources are allocated as a result of these distribution decisions. Fine-grained change management and customization of processes are not only possible, but are absolutely necessary.

Execution means ensuring that the new process is carried out by all participants—people, computer systems, other organizations and other processes. Execution is the responsibility of the process management system—a "dark room" activity. The process management system manages the state of processes as participants interact within them. It implements distributed transactions across new and legacy systems, even within complex nested processes. Existing applications are woven into process execution as fragments of larger processes. The execution state is insulated from disturbances arising from the underlying technologies or the behavior of applications. The business process management system shields the business user from the distributed computing middleware layers, and ensures that processes distributed throughout a mixed technology environment operate properly at all times. Correlating different activities occurring in different systems assures end-to-end process connectivity. The flow of data among participants is controlled, and any required translations are performed. Process data generated by executing processes is permanently stored, so that people or applications can query the state or structure of processes. Processes are persistent, just like databases, and can be trusted, backed up, restored and archived. They can even be transmitted as documents over networks.

Interaction means the use of process desktops and process portals that allow people to interact fully with business processes. This includes management of the interface between manual work (traditionally called workflow) and automation, in which the emphasis falls on work allocation, task management and forms-based data entry. But today's process interaction also includes the ability to observe, monitor and intervene within processes to resolve exceptions. Interaction with processes extends the traditional notions of the windows-based graphical user interface to expressive systems capable of directly representing complex interactions with processes and their participants. This approach can lead to the creation of new *task-oriented* processes, generated at run time from users' recorded actions.

Because third-wave technologies represent processes as data—

or, technically speaking, as an abstract data type—a wide range of tools and techniques will emerge for creating, reading, writing, modifying and extending process descriptions. The situation is analogous to the variety of tools now used to generate HTML pages for the Web, where initially a simple text editor was sufficient. For example, process portals will provide groupware facilities—themselves defined using processes—to help process teams work together. Processes may have knowledge resources encoded within them, allowing them to act as coaches in these interactions and, through simulation, allow users to explore the processes in which they will be required to participate.

Monitoring and control applies to both processes and to the process management system upon which they are executing. Activities focus on the business and technical interventions needed to maintain the health of individual processes, classes of processes and the entire environment. It includes the tasks needed to keep processes running well from a technical perspective, such as resource utilization. Unexpected errors and exceptions must be identified and managed either automatically or manually, with assistance from experts using process collaboration tools. Other monitoring and control tasks include the allocation of processes between partners, upgrading processes on the fly, and adding, removing and changing participants within a process. The activities will be familiar to those responsible for the continuity and upgrades of systems and applications running in a corporate data center, but whereas systems management tasks focus on technical systems, process management tasks are more directly aligned to day-to-day, week-to-week and month-to-month business imperatives.

Optimization means the ongoing activity of process improvement, closing the loop between process design and the analysis of feedback from actual process performance. Optimization can be automated or manual, and expands beyond the organization's four walls. The process management system can automatically detect bottlenecks, deadlocks and other inconsistencies in processes across the whole extended enterprise—that is, in processes used by everyone and everything involved in delivering value to the customer. The automatic optimization of resource utilization, the conversion of serial to parallel steps, and the removal of discovered redundancies are cases in which the process optimizer can perform or suggest adjustments without human intervention. Optimization relies heavily on process analysis.

Analysis means measuring process performance to provide the metrics, analyses and business intelligence needed to drive improvement strategies and discover opportunities for innovation. It provides a wide-angle view of the time and resources consumed by end-to-end business processes, relying on process query languages to provide management-level feedback and operational details about the past and present of business processes. Updates can be applied to individual processes or to sets of processes, to instances of designs or to the designs themselves. Queries can be applied to process data or to the structural evolution of the process, with all its capabilities and participants represented. The process design is nothing more than process data.

For example, the derivation of business metrics from activity-based costing (ABC) or key performance indicators (KPIs) encoded in processes can be automated, streamlining analysis tasks. Current information about the process can be assessed in the context of its history and its projected future uses. The process is measured in terms of business objectives and design attributes. Users can carry out periodic reviews of end-to-end processes to identify problems or shortcomings.

As in process design, simulation plays a key role in analysis and "what-if" validation of processes. Analysis uncovers opportunities to manufacture entirely new processes, services and products, as well as to optimize existing designs. New designs can be immediately tested and put into production operations.

With this new level of control over business processes comes increased responsibility. Previously, businesses were cushioned from the impacts of process change by the long lead times of IT projects. This is no longer the case. If the analogy for BPM automation is power-assisted steering, then simulation must play an increasingly important role in providing a full "BPM" traffic guidance system.

Using the eight core capabilities of business process management, companies can implement an automated lifecycle of process improvement, consistent with any manual approach they already employ. This automated support can be encoded in the form of processes. Change control applies to everything. Change-control processes are no different from other business processes and can therefore be improved in the same manner. The recursive nature of business process management reflects the reality of business operations.

Third Wave BPM at Work

Process management is applicable to a wide range of companies and industries, old and new. BPM is a horizontal, cross-industry approach whose industry-specific uses will evolve over the years ahead.

Start-up businesses need to assemble a complete business infrastructure using a combination of off-the-shelf packages, components and processes. New applications must be acquired and integrated as full business process participants. Such organizations often defer process design decisions to the period before launch and then rapidly evolve processes in line with experience from the first months of operation.

Established businesses using monolithic application packages encounter escalating technical integration costs. Process management can be introduced in parallel with existing systems, tapping their business functionality for new end-to-end processes. Point-to-point integration can be eradicated. Legacy systems can be integrated once and once only, at the level of the business process. Thereafter, business processes drive application behavior and not vice versa.

All companies overwhelmed by the cost of maintaining custom-made applications often move to available commercial off-the-shelf technologies. Process management systems allow for hot-swapping application components into and out of process designs, making such migration activities nondisruptive. Older applications can be retired and the hand-off to new services can be smooth and seamless. Process portals provide consistent interaction with business processes so that users of information systems need not be aware of the infrastructure changes taking place beneath the surface. Process designs remain stable even when the application portfolio shifts from monolithic to component-based applications, or when new standards are adopted.

Customer-focused organizations can design totally customer-driven business processes from the outside in. Processes can incorporate all applications, systems and users across the entire value chain, integrating all the resources needed to delight customers and eliminating manual hand-offs and other inefficiencies that compromise quality of service.

Industry leaders need to respond quickly to new business opportunities or unexpected competitive threats by preempting, creating or responding to market shifts, requiring them to design, produce and launch new products and services. The extreme agility with which third-wave process systems can be reconfigured lets businesses decide between different market strategies, such as "first mover" and "fast follower." Processes can be assembled and deployed in flight to emulate a competitor's offering or to disrupt markets with innovative new products or services. Barriers to the design and implementation of new business processes are removed, since innovation and deployment is no longer dependent on IT.

Operationally efficient companies want to maintain cost levels but cannot afford to stand still. Their need to compete against others who have achieved similar levels of efficiency leads them to supplement replicable best practice (embodied in standard business applications) by extending and evolving their processes in order to differentiate themselves in the market. Process management lowers the total cost of process ownership for such companies, and at the same time increases the range of options for designing and deploying new processes.

By analogy, utility companies employ sophisticated systems for the end-to-end management of their water or electricity networks. Manufacturing plants, oil refineries and computer networks are likewise overseen by systems that manage the processes involved. Process management systems play a similar role and will become the platform upon which the next generation of industrial applications will be constructed.

"The way to cope with rapid change," wrote Michael Hammer in *The Agenda*, "is to create a highly adaptable organization that obliterates time lags. It never looks ahead. It operates entirely in the present, only "now." It spots and reacts to significant change practically in the same breath." This is a grand strategic goal that reengineering never delivered on. BPM can deliver on this promise, by providing and supporting:

- A way of going directly from a visualization of what needs to be done—and that can be understood by all levels of management—to a system for doing it.
- A platform for sharing business processes among systems, people and partners.
- The agility to change processes in use and in design, such as the fluid management and movement of work between organizations, without the usual friction caused by IT considerations.
- Processes that inherently connect, collaborate and integrate; one to another.

- Processes that can evolve and maintain their state, so that both structure and state can be analyzed in order to close the redesign loop.
- Processes whose designs embed business intelligence from as far out as the perimeters of the value chain, giving them the ability to capture such events as an unexpected response to a new product or a sudden change in customer preferences.

The third wave of BPM is a powerful agent of change. When management best practices, legacy systems, best-of-breed software components, workflow, application integration and Web services converge into a unified whole, and focus on a unified model of process, something totally new starts to happen. Using powerful process management systems, process designers are then able to directly manipulate business processes in the way an automobile designer manipulates the design of an innovative new car. Just as the car designer need not go to the IT department with new car specifications in order to make design changes, since direct manipulation of the design is already built into CAD methodology and tools, neither does the process designer need to. Design, deployment and subsequent management are built-in features of the BPM approach.

Process management accelerates the renewal of IT architecture, of project delivery and of integration across business unit boundaries, while lowering the cost of ownership and enabling ongoing process change. The business process becomes the foundation for a new way of competing and of sustaining competitive advantage. The goals of BPM are not at all new: Business remains business. The pace of change has vastly accelerated, however, so that agility assumes primary importance. The third wave of BPM is the holistic business platform for the agile company of the future.

A number of early adopters are at work establishing BPM platforms and deploying process-based systems, tools and methods. They represent a diversity of industries and illustrate a variety of initial uses of BPM in those industries. These companies have begun to apply BPM to their mission-critical business activities in increments. Appendix D presents a summary of lessons we have learned.

Five

Reengineering Reengineering

Reality will not be still.
—Marilyn Ferguson, *The Aquarian Conspiracy*

Reengineering today is in a real state of confusion, with many different opinions of its real value. At one extreme, managers view reengineering as a management fad that never got off the ground. Another view is that reengineering provides a convenient explanation for short-term cost-cutting efforts. At the other extreme, managers point to reengineering as the key force behind the strong performance of U.S. industry during the past seven or eight years. As always, the truth lies somewhere in between. But where?
–Harry Kraemer, from the foreword to *Reengineering Revisited.*[1]

The Promises and Problems of Reengineering

As we mentioned in Chapter 1, Michael Hammer's 1990 *Harvard Business Review*[2] article was the catalyst that launched the reengineering movement with a call to obliterate, not automate work. Three years later Hammer and James Champy published their manifesto for business revolution, *Reengineering the Corporation.*[3] These advocates of radical reengineering—a war on non-value adding work—compared their approach to the continuous process improvement that came before them, as exemplified by the total quality management (TQM) move-ment. In the TQM methodology the primary enabler was statistical control; the incremental improvement of processes based on an analysis of process behavior, defects and exceptions. At that time, few recog-nized that TQM and its modern day derivative, Six Sigma, was itself a process that could be managed.

Those who sought to bring about radical change, however, found it hard to conceive how the big improvements demanded by CEOs could be achieved in this incremental fashion. For them, reengineering was performed when a process was deemed to be broken, or when the opportunity arose to reach a new market and deemed significant enough to justify the costs. The reengineers pointed to the pain, duration and intensity of reengineering. There were two reasons for this. First, the processes that they dealt with were profoundly implicit and inextricably embedded within the work methods and the IT systems of the era. Changing processes meant ripping out and reinstalling entire systems and organizational structures around them. Second, many of the process changes sought during that decade were of a cross-divisional and cross-functional nature, involving the busting up of organizational "silos." To them, this fact implied that such projects must necessarily take the form of a top-down, "management led" initiative. They could not envisage how radical change might bubble up out of a unit at the bottom of the organization, attain critical mass and be adopted throughout the organization.

There was at the time, however, a contrary view to radical reengineering. Japanese industry saw things very differently. They employed the continuous improvement techniques of Kaizen (a word meaning "gradual and orderly, continuous improvement") to boost their competitive edge in all three critical variables of speed, cost and quality, and without the need for step changes in capital investment. Hammer and Champy, on the other hand, were extreme in their opposition to gradual approaches of any kind. They urged their readers to abandon long-established procedures, to toss aside old systems, to go back to the beginning, throw away or dismantle the old, to guard against assumptions, to take nothing for granted, to "reinvent anew," to abandon the familiar and seek the outrageous—their words, not ours. They claimed that radical process redesign was necessary to achieve dramatic improvements in every part of the business, defining reengineering as a search for new models of organizing work in which tradition counted for nothing.

Not surprisingly, Hammer and Champy's agenda for change involved a raft of new job titles, roles and responsibilities: reengineering engineers, leaders, process owners, reengineering teams and steering committees, and even a reengineering czar whose role was to shepherd the reengineering process through "signs, symbols and systems" so that others would not find it "lonesome and frightening." These new "process workers" were positioned as replacing the larger numbers of outmoded corporate controllers, planners and auditors. Hammer urged the new teams to turn the organization inside out and upside down, to persuade people they must accept radical disruption, to make waves and shatter assumptions. Hammer and Champy likened reengineering to a "spiritual journey," a voyage into the unknown. They stated that only people comfortable with ambiguity would succeed in reengineering because only these people were capable of doing and being whatever they liked!

In their 1999 book *Reengineering Revisited*,[4] Bala Balachandran and Ramu Thiagarajan record similar observations about the early days. "The challenges of BPR were many. First, the approach was very radical, as

Michael Hammer's rhetoric demonstrates:

- "In this journey, we'll carry our wounded and shoot the dissenters...." (*Forbes*, September 13, 1993.)
- "Reengineering must be initiated....by someone who has...enough status to break legs...." (*Planning Review*, May/June 1993.)
- "Don't try to forestall reengineering. If senior management is serious about reengineering they'll shoot you." (*Management Review*, September 1993.)

While this had its advantages in bringing "shock value" to what might otherwise have been complacency, it resulted in a rapid loss of what had been built over many years: human capital and employee loyalty. This is because some corporate executives used BPR as an excuse for indiscriminate downsizing." Even the remaining employees felt a sense of uncertainty and displacement, as a result of having their skills and work examined so closely.

The reengineering process itself turned out to be a major undertaking. Hammer and Champy described it as "breathtaking—to throw everything out and start all over." They estimated that a minimum commitment of 75 percent and preferably 100 percent of each team member's time was required to make it work. They pointed out that reengineering was not a ninety-day assignment, but would normally occupy a year, or more—and would require team members to abandon current assignments, sever old ties and say farewell to home departments. This core team, Hammer and Champy said, would have to be supplemented by an outer ring of part-time and occasional contributors, so called outsiders, whose job was to "make waves, ask naïve questions and shatter assumptions." The theory of reengineering and process innovation was more like the theory of the big bang than the theory of evolution. But in the years that followed, and as reengineering was absorbed into management consulting practice, the hysteria was de-emphasized and companies and their advisors started to look for more predictable, less disruptive methods. This was the start of the search for the third wave, a search in part interrupted by the excitement of the Internet and the Y2K problem.

In their original analysis, however, it was not surprising that Hammer and Champy believed that no team could reengineer more than one process at a time, and that only by focusing on one process could improvements be made. In this focus, they also appeared willing to sacrifice existing job designs, organizational structures and management systems—everything associated with the process—in order to design the newly refashioned and shiny processes. They weren't managing processes at all; they were building new businesses from within. In their epilog to *Reengineering the Corporation,* Hammer and Champy proclaimed that reengineering offers no quick, simple and painless fixes. On the contrary they said that it "entails difficult strenuous work."

Thomas Davenport's book, *Process Innovation,* was published the same year. Davenport was less extreme in his analysis of how to achieve process innovation and more theoretical in his methodology and his formula for success. Nevertheless, he agreed with Hammer and Champy that whereas bottom-up participation is a hallmark of continuous quality improvement programs, process innovation is typically much more top down, requiring strong direction and sponsorship from senior management. Davenport's view was that *both* gradual and catastrophic change required *cultural change,* and that many forms of process innovation often involved changes in the locus of power and control in the organization, as well as in skill requirements, reporting relationships and management practices.

Davenport correctly observed that the "wrenching nature of reengineering" made it the most difficult form of organizational change ever devised, concluding that this fact accounted, at least in part, for the long project lifecycles associated with it. He made distinctions between the roles of different employees in process redesign, stating that a clerk in the shipping department was unlikely to conceive of a radical redesign of the entire order-management process. Although ideas from front line workers and lower and middle management should be solicited, he felt, most such ideas would pertain only to incremental improvements. Insofar as workers tend to resist radical change, Davenport did advise the implementers of process innovation to strive to gain commitment and buy-in from all levels. He sought to identify ways to include workers' participation in the design of processes in order to foster commitment from those affected—something we now take for granted and which is supported by third-wave collaborative process design tools.

There are points in Davenport's analysis where he clearly called for some kind of unified theory, a synthesis of both the continuous and the radical process improvement methods. For example, he suggests ways of combining process improvement and process innovation in an ongoing quality program, and we see this today in the application of process management to processes such as Six Sigma and others. Yet even as he acknowledged that continuous improvement is a beneficial practice, he denied it was a prerequisite for innovation. The enabling skills required for innovation, he observed, were radically different in character to those required for continuous improvement. Davenport's idea of a competent expert in reengineering was someone who demonstrates success in a wide range of change disciplines, such as merging large organizations, downsizing, rolling out a major new product or implementing innovations in the process of developing new services.

Davenport's conclusion was that a cycle of continuous improvement could be implemented as a "post-reengineering" follow-up to innovation, "lest it slide back down the slippery slope of process degradation," as he put it. He gave useful advice about how to define clear process improvement objectives, the goal being to reduce confusion and clarify the changes to those who participate in, or are affected by, reengineering. Davenport's emphasis on this point was a response to the findings of case studies showing that companies found it difficult to understand the relationship between incremental improvement and radical change and how to combine these in practical everyday operations. It has taken until now to fully understand how one process can govern change in another and how the introduction of change itself is a process that needs to be managed and supported by a process management infrastructure.

Davenport was more realistic, less dogmatic, than Hammer and Champy. He was willing to say that continuous improvement may be preferable to reengineering in some scenarios—in relatively non-competitive settings, or in cases where basic business practices are not in question, as is the case with regulated industries such as utilities and well-funded government organizations. Radical change was to be reserved for companies responding to extreme competitive pressure.

Davenport also correctly observed that "the breadth of research notwithstanding, process innovation, i.e. reengineering, is more art than science." The use of the term "engineering" to describe process innovation can mislead many to believe that "reengineering" is based on sound scientific principles. Nothing could be further from the truth, as those that experimented with the process of reengineering found out. The literature is filled with studies of the difficult experience of those who had to adjust to and live with reengineering and its results.

In addition, because reengineering provided no fixed methodology for developing new processes or process variants, and no provision for simulating them before taking them live, the new process designs were of uneven quality; they were sometimes unreliable and sometimes unfit for the purpose for which they were conceived. Those companies and advisors that took up the approach, had to develop and refine what "reengineering" actually meant, since the vision alone counted for little. Guess what, these evolutions began to take on the characteristics of a continuous methodology, with more emphasis placed on measurement, feedback and control. Yet these add-ons were external manual "guides," not yet inherent to a single systematic approach.

Despite these extensions to the original reengineering vision, when newly reengineered processes were put into practice they proved to be no more explicit—or manageable—than their predecessors. The new process became just as deeply engrained in and dependent upon work habits and the limits of the IT systems. It was in recognition of this that the innovators of workflow management systems began to conceive of a new IT infrastructure driven by an explicit process model—the work-flow process—not by fixed application logic. They sought to grant control to the business, not IT, for the development, deployment and maintenance of workflow processes. Workflow was, in a very real sense, a response to the inflexibility of software applications of the era. It was a model of computing more aligned to the way a business operated, thought and managed its affairs. Case studies of successful workflow projects proved that the central concepts of explicit process design—a dedicated process execution environment and the integration of process analysis tools—could support reengineering by accelerating the introduction and adoption of new processes.

Early workflow systems provided a component of the path to execution which reengineering lacked. That path has now been completed in the third wave, encompassing even computationally intensive distributed processes. Until workflow management came on the scene, there was no general-purpose collaborative process technology that could support the interdisciplinary teams that were designing and adopting new processes. As a consequence, the results of initial reengineering projects were mixed, with 70 – 80 percent failure rates reported. In some cases reengineering was able to achieve nothing more than to highlight where problems existed. In other cases the chief outcome was organizational confusion. Too often reengineering proved to consume enormous amounts of time and energy, and participants said they never wanted to live through that again—ever. Often results were only achieved by across-the-board layoffs—euphemistically called "rightsizing" or "downsizing"—after which the program was declared a success. Employees were left to struggle, not only with their anger and guilt, but also with a lack of training and technology to support new ways of working.

Some advocates of radical reengineering were not dissuaded by these widespread reports of failure. They addressed the tremendous challenge of persuading people within an organization to embrace change through techniques borrowed from a field called Organizational Change Management. They justified the cost of these "org change" programs as necessary lest the company lose its competitive advantage, undergo a steady erosion of its profit margins or even face outright failure, simply because the body of the company's employees had rejected the newly transplanted process innovation. Today we still hear of such stories, but in the third wave, companies are getting much more savvy at creating a pervasive process environment in which employees conduct their work. As processes change, they hardly notice.

The original change programs usually started with a "case for action" or "vision statement" document. The vision statement was to be a persuasive, high-level description of the compelling argument for change, specifically how the company needed to change in response to the competitive threats and opportunities it was facing. Typically, the case for action contained a diagnosis of why ad-hoc incremental improvement would be insufficient for achieving the company's objectives. It would set out the marketplace demands and the costs of inaction. Examples by Hammer and Champy typically started with,

> The current process is incapable of meeting our growing need for speed and precision. It produces, instead, a stressed and overworked staff, last-minute scrambles, increasing exception processing and creaky systems. Our current process costs the company millions of dollars in overtime and excess expenses, missed deliveries, and less-than-acceptable distributor performance and confidence.

The vision statement, or case for action, served as a kind of banner, or umbrella concept, around which to rally the troops when morale started to sag, and helped structure the reengineering teams and their activities. But beyond this morale-building language and a set of techniques for effective team-based brainstorming work, reengineering offered no clear blueprint for executing the project, let alone for putting the resultant new processes into operation. The reengineering gurus acknowledged some of the failures of reengineering in subsequent articles and books, but often tried to explain them away as failures to take the right reengineering medicine. Revisiting Hammer and Champy's explanations for reengineering[5] failure provides a baseline from which to gain a third-wave BPM perspective (Table 5.1):

Reason given for failure	Third wave perspective
Trying to fix a process instead of re-inventing it.	A smooth and clearly defined path, and managed lifecycle, should lead from incremental improvement toward radical transformation.
Not focusing on processes.	Processes are only one view of the business. Managers should be able to manage processes using systems and metaphors they are comfortable with. Process management systems must be capable of providing the view appropriate to the role and needs of the user.
Bringing in distractions other than process design.	Process management is a part of everybody's job, now that they have the tools needed to manage processes.
Being willing to settle for minor results.	Incremental improvement adds up to significant performance gains; radical, discontinuous changes are rarely desirable, particularly in a downturn.
Skimping on resources required for reengineering.	Process management should not require a layer of additional overhead.

Placing prior constraints on the definition of the problem and the scope of re-design.	Process management should take into account all the constraints senior management wishes to impose, since they understand the fuller context of the marketplace within which they are operating.
Allowing corporate cultures and management attitudes to prevent engineering from getting started.	Process management should be a natural part of business, not create fears, and its results should be measured and predictable.
Trying to make it happen from the bottom up.	Improvement often comes from within and should be amplified by making best practices explicit—wherever they are found—and replicable through process customization for different parts of the business.
Assigning someone who doesn't understanding reengineering to lead the team.	Process management tools and methods should be as intuitively understandable by business people, just as, for example, spreadsheets are today.
Dissipating energy across a great many reengineering projects.	Process management systems should provide an environment in which hundreds of processes can be managed simultaneously.
Attempting to reengineer when the CEO is two years from retirement.	Success in process management should not depend upon key individuals, but on science and systems thinking.
Failing to recognize the unique aspects of reengineering from other business improvement programs.	Process management is not a new management theory you must adopt, it is a practical enabler to help implement your existing strategies.
Concentrating too much on detailed process design.	Detailed process design is useful—process-mapping tools make it easy to generate rich models and these illuminate the need for change.

Pulling back when people resist making process changes.	Collaborative process management provides ways to include everyone both in the process of process design and the process of process deployment.
Dragging the effort out.	Process management is not a project; it's a real-time activity.
Burying reengineering in the middle of the corporate agenda.	Process management should implement the corporate agenda, not become another problematic item on the agenda.
Quitting too early.	Periodic process improvement under lifecycle management should not take so long that the business becomes impatient.
Trying to help reengineering happen without making anybody unhappy.	Change is naturally painful; humans simply don't like change. But BPM is simply a tool that can help people get their process work done more efficiently and with greater ease.

Table 5.1. The New Process Perspective

The third wave of BPM, in other words, recognizes at every point that what reengineering saw as "failures" on the part of businesses are in fact legitimate mission-critical business needs.

A Decade of Lessons Learned

A decade after launching reengineering, Hammer was writing again about how to correct the failures of the movement he started,[6] laying out a new agenda in which the same techniques used by companies to sell products to consumers—marketing communications—were to be used to sell new processes to employees. Change does not have to be *managed*, he said, it needs to be *sold* to the people who will be affected by it. He appears to take this corporate *process education* to extreme levels, even to the point of suggesting *branding* change programs, development of a marketing value proposition and the translation of this into a name, a logo and the rest of the paraphernalia of "spin."

The third wave of BPM has absolutely nothing to say on such

subjective matters, nor does it make judgments about whether such methods are viable or even necessary. The third wave of process management provides a more concrete solution to the problem: a managed, pervasive, resilient and expressive environment within which processes can be more readily adopted, retained and owned by the business, with or without contrived "process heroes" and separate process teams and coaches. This environment is equivalent to a permanent business-change incubator that enables collaborative, ongoing innovation and transformation, where the rollout of change happens no faster and no slower than the business demands or can cope with.

As the IT challenges that arose from reengineering grew, companies turned increasingly to a technological solution to implement best practice processes, with the rise of new enterprise resource planning (ERP) packages. But the software technology of the era was insufficiently flexible to back up the many prescriptions of reengineering advocates. Even if new processes could be successfully deployed, the question remained as to whether they could be changed and improved thereafter. To this day, companies still seek easy answers to difficult process problems by choosing to deploy standard packaged software. They do so at the risk of creating an inflexible, commodity IT system, available to their competitors, and locked into a series of future changes imposed on them by technology suppliers—quite independent of the company's own strategy and its chosen pace of change.

Hammer seemed to recognize this problem in *The Agenda* (2001), where he writes about the reality of constant business change and urges a new approach to implementation, one that is considerably different from the traditional "big bang" in which everything is accomplished in a single step. Hammer now says that implementation must proceed in a series of smaller steps, each of which represent progress toward the ultimate destination. He says that these steps must be accomplished relatively quickly and must deliver some concrete payoff. But how? The third wave of BPM offers a solution.

Unlike total quality management, continuous process improvement and radical reengineering, third-wave BPM is an engineering-based formalism, embodied technologically in the form of a process architecture and management system. The "engineering" in the reengineering movement was just a metaphor illustrating a design philosophy that lacked a concrete plan for execution. BPM is its antithesis.

In *Process Innovation,* Davenport had identified 28 "IT enablers" of process innovation implementation. The list included computer-aided software engineering (CASE), code generation, conferencing, conventional programming, current applications, and umpteen other disparate technologies, each with their own distinct problem-solving paradigms. Only one technology on the list mentioned process modeling. What was available then was a grab-bag of applications, each of which had some potential to take up a role as an automaton in a business process, but never able to manage the process over its lifetime. What companies really needed was a *"native business process technology"* not a bunch of disjoint pieces that could somehow contribute to overall process management—each with its own "understanding" of how business is represented in information technology. We have had to wait years for the development of mature technologies that can directly model, manage and execute business processes—for the realization of a unified, holistic business process-centric approach.

Hammer and Champy were ambivalent about the role technology would play in reengineering. In *Reengineering the Corporation,* they held the view that a company that cannot change the way it thinks about information technology cannot reengineer. They also held that if companies equated technology with the automation of existing processes, then they had not correctly understood the role of technology in process change. According to Hammer and Champy, a company that made this error might achieve a 10 percent improvement in performance instead of the 90 or 100+ percent attained through reengineering. The fundamental error most companies make is when they view technology through the lens of their existing processes, they noted. Teleconferencing, shared databases, electronic data interchange (EDI), expert systems, telecommunications networks, modeling software, wireless networks, portable computers, purchasing software, interactive videodisk, automatic identification and tracking devices and high-speed computing: all of these Hammer and Champy viewed as disruptive technologies that opened up new reengineering possibilities. One example they gave was:

Old rule: Managers make all the decisions
Disruptive technology: Decision support tools
New rule: Decision-making is part of everyone's job

This analysis of technology's role was limited, however. It focused strictly upon technology's role as a participant in a business process, such as a shared database supporting a distributed team of caseworkers. Hammer and Champy missed the point that the business process itself needs its own technology, its own organizing principles and its own paradigm. Hacking at the holistic BPM paradigm by throwing a grab-bag of preexisting technologies at it is just that—hacking. Over time, as reengineering practice and IT practice became ever more inextricably linked, because customers demanded it be so, the discrepancy between the management thinking (around process) and the IT thinking (around data and procedure) grew ever more dissonant.

Davenport was clearer about the way in which technology can directly support business processes. He identified nine effects of technology on business processes:

- *Automational:* Eliminating human labor from a process
- *Informational:* Capturing process information for purposes of understanding
- *Sequential:* Changing process sequence, or enabling parallelism
- *Tracking:* Closely monitoring process status and participants
- *Analytical:* Improving analysis of information and decision making
- *Geographical:* Coordinating processes across distances
- *Integrative:* Coordination between tasks and processes
- *Intellectual:* Capturing and distributing intellectual assets
- *Disintermediating:* Eliminating intermediaries from a process

The list, published in 1993, provides the early blueprint for the third wave, a technology attuned to the management and execution of business processes. The third wave incorporates preexisting technologies—but it goes much further than that. In BPM, preexisting systems are full participants in the process, with the freedom to interact with and exchange information with all other participants—human or machine. Indeed, these interactions are themselves modeled as processes in the BPM paradigm. In addition, the processes ingrained in existing IT systems, such as those defined by packaged business applications, can be exposed through process projection and component interfaces, opening them to further design improvement, customization and reuse.

Yet even these remarkable features cannot fully capture the essence of the third wave. BPM is not just a participant enabler; it fully supports the *management* of the business process as well. The CIO should have to be no more concerned about what processes are running on the IT infrastructure than he or she is about the content of every email message flowing across the corporate email network. Such "process neutrality" —the ability to execute any business process in the IT infrastructure— places the control of processes with the business, not IT technicians.

Before the third wave, each business application was a kind of "hard-wired" process management system for those discrete parts of the process it supported. This may be why advocates of reengineering were dismissive of IT efforts to automate the business, missing the opportunity to see the potential of the third wave. As a result, many of the radical new process designs developed during the 1990s outstripped the ability of IT to deliver new applications to support them. Processes dreamed up in the "process team action room" required superior support from IT systems, but in practice employees wound up being asked to take on radical new ways of working with systems that were poorly designed, under funded and under supported. The gap between business and IT actually widened as a result of reengineering. The hope that standard ERP systems would save the day was only partly fulfilled; mainly because such systems could handle only a limited menu of "best practice" processes, not the unique processes of the firm. Companies were asked to adapt to ERP, because ERP could not *easily* adapt to them.

Hammer and Champy thought it was useless to ask a business person how to use technology to enhance, streamline or improve what they were already doing, preferring to pose what they thought was the more radical question, "how can we use this technology to allow us to do things that we are not already doing?" Their example: A market research firm asks a regular traveler what would make her life easier; she replies, "A faster way to reach the airport," or perhaps "A private plane." As Hammer and Champy pointed out, nobody would ask for a teleportation machine, because nobody could imagine such a device outside of science fiction.

The technologies of the third wave may seem like science fiction to many people. For example, in the past, reengineering teams had to make decisions about sequencing and timing in order to specify new process designs. With BPM, these aspects of process design are largely automated. BPM focuses on interactions and relationships, not sequences, because sequencing is mainly to do with process execution, not process design, except where it adds value to the latter. For example, some processes require controls that provide more transparency and accountability.

Companies learned a lot about reengineering over the last decade, most of it the hard way. It's only with the advent of the third wave—a development that the reengineering prophets could not have been expected to foresee—that the lessons of that period can be seen clearly. We can now put the assumptions of reengineering behind us, and move onto a fresh way of thinking about processes and their management.

Beyond Reengineering, On to Process Management

In *The Social Life of Information,* John Seely Brown points out that reengineering focused most heavily on the flow of work, the inputs and outputs of individual process stages.[7] He says that reengineering was relatively indifferent to the internal workings of these stages—to the specific practices that comprised the process and their meaning from the perspective of process participants. Brown urges organizations to attend not only to processes, but also to *practices.* He agreed that reengineering presented "a clear antidote to organizational inconsistency, inertia and gradualism," but, in his view, it was a paradigm in which people were merely inserted into processes as needed—or as not needed. Though lip service was paid to improvisation in process design, local knowledge about work practices played a minor role.

By *practice* of course, Brown was not referring to the sort of rote exercises people associate with phrases like piano practice. Rather he meant the activity involved in actually getting work done—the sort of activity that lies at the heart of medical practice or legal practice, for claims processors are practitioners of their own craft just as doctors and lawyers are practitioners of theirs. It has been observed that many of the problems faced by "process workers," for example in claims processing, can be traced to clashes over meaning and sense making—such things as what the *input* to a process signifies, why similar *inputs* need different responses, and who or what should be responsible for resolving ambiguity and providing the agreed *output.*

If one accepts this thesis, reengineering will always be associated with the second wave of process thinking, with rigid forms of input-output work automation. But as Michael Hammer pointed out in response, a high-performing process requires both a high-performance process design and a high-performance process execution. Without the latter, the potential of the former will never be realized.[8]

The third wave of process management is an environment that enables high-performance execution of both process *and* practices, for it can combine data and information in the context of its use. Prior to the third wave, automation was applied to a fairly narrow spectrum of "back-office" operations—procurement, shipping, receiving, warehousing, fulfillment, billing, and so on. The third wave is equally at home with the creative processes of the "front office"—demand creation (marketing), order acquisition (sales), and product development (innovation), for example. Herein lies the real learning challenge, for BPM pushes process innovation and management into realms where few companies have yet ventured: the application of *whole systems thinking* to all aspects of the enterprise.

BPM is a method, a system and a standard that amplifies the execution of any given management theory and that facilitates the formalization and adoption of new theories into business more readily. If a company's approach to change and improvement is Six Sigma, or a similar method of total quality management, process management will help the company achieve its goals at a lower cost and with less pain. If the company seeks change based on radical reengineering, process management will clear the IT bottleneck and avoid discontinuities. If management prefers a networked control structure, process management will help it implement customized processes both locally and globally. If the market demands new efficiencies and increased automation, process management will adapt to the specific structure of the organization, not the limits of legacy applications. If the company uses a balanced scorecard to measure performance, process management can generate the needed data, and perform the analysis. The third wave of BPM is entirely indifferent to each of these management methods and theories. It's devoted solely to managing the processes needed to apply whatever business practices a company chooses to use.

For this reason, process management is not just another form of computer automation that provides more efficient ways of doing the wrong kinds of things. Process management provides the means to discover and describe exactly how a company operates, and the process-tools for controlling and analyzing the business. It enables companies to control the lifecycle of business processes and enables them to put new processes into practice without writing software or procuring new applications.

In a downturn, companies must focus on delivery and cannot afford to implement the latest fashionable management theories, new organizational structures or esoteric new applications, especially not on the basis of dubious or tentative "return on investment" cases. Business processes must manage themselves as much as possible. Companies can use process execution to reduce human involvement if required, but they should recognize that its role is far more significant than mere automation. Processes can amplify the productivity of employees and improve the quality of their work. By contrast, in an upturn, process management is just what companies need to accelerate innovation ahead of competitors.

The third wave of process management takes process-based methodologies out of the hands of specialists and technicians and provides business people with the tools they need to create, improve and deploy processes. Reengineering will be greatly simplified when those that actually have to be part of a process can change that process and ensure that everyone else affected is included. Business process management rejects or overturns many of the assumptions inherent within traditional reengineering as shown in Table 5.2, which is adapted from Davenport's *Process Innovation.*

Factors Compared	Process Improvement	Process Innovation	Third Wave BPM
Level of change	Incremental	Radical	Total lifecycle
Interpretation of "As is" and "To be"	Current process, Improved new version	Old process, Brand new process— Discontinuity	No BPM capability, BPM capability
Starting point	Existing processes	Clean slate	New or existing processes
Frequency of change	One-time or continuous	Periodic one-time change	One-time, periodic, continuous or evolutionary
Time required	Short	Long	Real time
Participation	Bottom-up	Top-down	Top-down and bottom-up
Number of processes	Simultaneous, across several processes	One at a time	Simultaneous, across many processes
Typical scope	Narrow, within functions	Broad, cross functional	Enterprise-wide process management
Horizon	Past and present	Future	Past, present and future
Risk	Moderate	High	Low
Primary enabler	Statistical control	Information technology	Process technology
Tools	Offline	None	Online
Involvement	Industry specialists	Business generalists	Process engineers and all employees
Work	Practice	Process	Process and practice
Path to execution	Cultural	Cultural, structural	Mathematical foundation and process tech. standards

Table 5.2. Davenport's Process Improvement and Innovation
Comparison Extended With Business Process Management

In 1995, the reengineering wave was beginning to crash, ERP implementations were underway and the rise of the Internet was attracting attention. In that same year, Davenport revisited the subject of reengineering, observing, "The most profound lesson of reengineering was never the reengineering, but business processes. Any company that ignores them or fails to improve them risks its future. That said, companies can use many different approaches to process improvement without ever embarking on a high-risk reengineering project."[9] The third wave fits this description perfectly: an alternative path that accommodates many different approaches.

In 2002, John Hagel and John Seely Brown wrote in a similar vein that reengineering is only one of a number of possible approaches to what they call "process renewal."[10] They argued that few businesses would want to repeat reengineering more often than every five to ten years, and proposed a more loosely-coupled architecture as an alternative. Our view goes one step further: Whether loosely coupled or tightly linked, whether incrementally improved or radically transformed, processes must still be explicitly described in a standard language and managed in a lifecycle of process improvement using business process management. Reconfiguring loosely-coupled services as the mean of achieving business agility, as suggested by advocates of Web services technology, is an incomplete approach, although it plays an important role. Web services are about simplifying the process of application integration to enable the formation of composite applications.

Advocates of Web services point to the power of combining little things to make bigger things with surprising qualities. BPM, however, is about integrating Web services on the level of business processes, enabling companies to choreograph, orchestrate, tailor and otherwise manage their business at the level of the enterprise. Loose coupling is only a part of a more comprehensive approach. Long-running business contracts and mature joint ventures or powerful alliances typically require just the opposite, tight coupling, to achieve operational efficiency and scalability. The different approaches focus on different entities, in BPM the process, in loose-coupling the service or component.

In the years following the initial wave of reengineering, workflow management systems and computer-assisted process mapping became popular. Metrics began to be incorporated into process design. These developments were the first glimmers of the third wave as they integrated concepts from activity-based costing, value analysis and quality management. They added empirical data to business processes linked to the objectives of the organization for the first time.

The aim of activity-based costing, for example, is to calculate the resources required to complete a process, such as producing a particular product or providing service to a particular customer. In value analysis, accessing the costs and benefits associated with processes involve studying process participants and the way information flows among them. In quality management, cultural procedures are developed to provide a robust "system"—actually another process—by means of which processes to be improved are analyzed and adjusted in a series of incremental steps. Over time, these methods, and related developments in the field of information engineering, led to the tantalizing vision of a top-down approach that translates strategic business objectives—time, cost or resource requirements, for example—into business process designs.

Top-down process design allows businesses to describe their operation in general terms from the point of view of upper-level management, retaining a single model as an executable, transactional process, with no translation steps. This allows others to add more detail to refine the model over time without creating discontinuity. These expansions of the model are not details added to provide missing "technical aspects" so that the process can be an executable software program, for in BPM, even high-level models, without detail, are already executable. BPM enables businesses to support process design throughout the value chain, allowing higher-level process models and lower-level (more detailed) process models, developed quite independently, to be integrated to form executable end-to-end processes, both horizontally and vertically.

The term "top-down design" also implies an ability to create process variants, custom processes that adhere to defined higher-level process patterns. In addition, top down processes will normally encode metrics so that running processes can measure organizational and participant performance and monitor progress against targets. This is much like goal-seeking analyses that can be performed automatically by current spreadsheet software. In this sense process management has attained characteristics similar to that achieved by industrial engineering—an efficient process of product design and design-variant evaluation based on collaboration, analysis and the evaluation of relationships of the product to its environment and modes of use.

The Industrial Engineering of Third Wave Processes

The advent of computer aided design and computer assisted manufacturing (CAD/CAM) brought radical new efficiency to industrial engineering, starting with the aerospace and automotive industries and later spreading to all industries based on product design. At the outset, reductions in the time from concept to production were of the order of 25 to 50 percent. As the new approach matured, ten-fold and even hundred-fold reductions were achieved. Collaboration was vastly simplified as suppliers and specialists in a given industry adopted new tools based on standards such as STEP (the Standard for the Exchange of Product Model Data). But even before standards were adopted, computer aided design processes had reduced the number of design hand-offs. In the long term, design quality improved and production costs were lowered, resulting in high quality products at a better price. These processes are now standard practice in the industrial sector.

As business process management and its associated technologies matures it will be adopted as standard practice, much as occurred with data management. Processes will be created, discovered and designed much more readily. Hundreds of variants will be generated and tested now that the cost efficiencies of BPM give designers the luxury of creating processes the majority of which they will simply throw away. Processes will be deployed more readily, closing the ends of the loops that link design, optimization and analysis. As this approach gains wide acceptance in an industry, or as industry gorillas turn collaborative process design systems into de facto industry standards, the kind of business-to-business reengineering that Champy defines under the brand "X-Engineering"[11] will become possible.

Because they will be opened to computer assisted refinement as a result of the new focus on explicit process models—just like 3-dimensional CAD/CAM product models are today—processes will improve in quality. BPM will eventually emerge as an integrated process design system for the business as a whole, including product design processes. The next generation of product engineering applications, built on a database foundation today, will be rebuilt on a process foundation. Already companies are using process management systems in conjunction with product data management (PDM) applications. Companies will start to think of business process engineering as routine standard practice. In effect, BPM will assume the role in a business analyst's day that product data management plays in a product engineer's. Boundaries across all discrete application-centered activity are going to blur.

Champy himself recognizes a significant business opportunity in this scenario. In a May 2002 article, he said, "If we could improve the efficiency of these cross-organizational administrative processes by 50 percent, that would result in annual savings of $400 billion."[12] He sites the example of logistics—the processes by which goods move from company to company or from company to consumers—as a comparable case. Globally, companies spend about $2 trillion a year on logistics-related services, 40 percent of which is administrative costs, according to Champy's estimate. Similar issues plague other industries, with health-care a notable example. To scale down costs and prices, customers, suppliers and partners will need to collaborate on new process designs. This can only be accomplished using BPM. The technology of the 1990s was simply too expensive and complex to support open process collaboration in dynamic value chains. Proprietary Electronic Data Interchange (EDI) systems were complicated, expensive and rigid: oriented only to simple trade processes which fell far short of the richness and nuance inherent in truly collaborative inter-company, value-chain, relationships. They too will be re-invented in the third wave.

Boeing is a world-class example of this type of collaboration. The company designed its 777 airliner "in cyberspace" by electronically sharing its CAD/CAM design tools and processes with engineers, customers, maintenance personnel, project managers and component suppliers across the globe. No physical model. No paper blueprints. The nature of this process is captured in the slogan, "The 777 is a bunch of parts flying together in close formation." As a result, Boeing's customers no longer have to wait three years for a new airplane. Through process collaboration Boeing aims to deliver a plane in eight to 12 months, and the company expects to have the capacity to build 620 airplanes annually, up from 228 in 1992. Companies that can imagine the same capability applied to their business processes will have taken their plunge in the third wave of BPM. It need not be on the scale of Boeing computer-aided methods, but the principle is the same. CEO's that recognize the potential of BPM will create value chains where companies, their suppliers and trading partners "fly together in close formation," dominating their markets and delighting their customers.

New Rules for the Process-Managed Enterprise

Process management will create new rules for the company of the future. Reengineering sought to rip out and replace outdated processes. Process management provides a way to capture existing processes, test multiple variants, manage any mode of innovation or improvement the company sees fit to adopt, and readily deploy the result.

How exactly is BPM different from BPR? Using the style employed by Hammer and Champy in their original book—Old rule, Disruption, New rule—let's count the ways:

1. Old rule: Process-based clerical work and practice-based skilled work are different. *Disruption:* Process desktop. *New rule:* All forms of work can be described and managed using a single system.

2. Old rule: Processes are rigid scripts, focused mainly on the inputs and outputs of discrete steps. *Disruption:* Process calculus. *New rule:* Processes are fluid, dynamic, amoebic and adaptable.

3. Old rule: Executing a process means locating it in one place and under centralized control. *Disruption:* Distributed process execution and end-to-end processes. *New rule:* Processes can be as easily managed in a federated environment as in a centralized one.

4. Old rule: Collaboration requires standard processes. *Disruption:* Business process modeling languages. *New rule:* Firms are free to innovate because collaboration rests on a standard representation for processes, not a standard process.

5. Old rule: Companies have to start over. *Disruption:* Process discovery, introspection and projection combined with application componentization. *New rule:* Companies build on and transform what exists.

6. Old rule: Process must be kept simple in order to be manageable. *Disruption:* Process participants. *New rule:* Processes can be as complex as they need to be, yet still be manageable.

7. Old rule: Processes have to be changed in order to reduce the manual checking required of accountants, auditors and supervisors. *Disruption:* Process metrics and process lifecycle. *New rule:* Processes can monitor themselves.

8. Old rule: A choice must be made between incremental process improvement, and radical reengineering. *Disruption:* Lifetime process lifecycle management. *New rule:* There are no discontinuities.

9. Old rule: Incremental process improvements produce minor gain. *Disruption:* Process analysis and transformation. *New rule:* Processes evolve in fits and starts, sometimes incrementally and sometimes radically, but always non-disruptively.

10. Old rule: Radical change is painful and disruptive. *Disruption:* Computer-Aided Process Engineering. *New rule:* Replacement of organizational change with technological implementation.

11. Old rule: Companies need a large, dedicated, long-standing, reengineering team. *Disruption:* Process portal. *New rule:* Process management vanishes, becoming a part of everybody's job.

12. Old rule: Process innovation is an art form, with uncertainties and ambiguities. *Disruption:* Process calculus. *New rule:* Process management is a precise science.

13. Old rule: Radical change takes a long time to implement. *Disruption:* Process deployment and execution. *New rule:* Not all radical changes require radical changes to IT systems or organization.

14. Old rule: No team can reengineer more than one process at once. *Disruption:* Process management system. *New rule:* Continuous process improvement across many processes.

15. Old rule: Radical change is top-down and continuous change is bottom-up. *Disruption:* Integrated process model. *New rule:* There is no distinction—circumstances govern the approach you take. Process models developed quite independently can be easily combined.

16. Old rule: Reengineering never happens from the bottom up. *Disruption:* Process intranet. *New rule:* Insights for process streamlining and process re-design arise naturally in the business, and are readily accepted by those affected.

17. Old rule: Managers make all process design changes. *Disruption:* Collaborative process design and closed-loop process optimization. *New rule:* Change-making is part of everyone's job.

18. Old rule: There must be a single process owner. *Disruption:* Collaborative process analysis. *New rule:* Everyone that needs to be involved in process improvement can be involved.

19. Old rule: Processes can be designed only by the process team. *Disruption:* Shared process repository. *New rule:* As many designers as required can be involved, deep within the business.

20. Old rule: It takes work to have to find out where you are in a given process. *Disruption:* Process metrics. *New rule:* Processes measure themselves and tell you where they are.

21. Old rule: Every process team needs a human coach. *Disruption:* Process training built into process designs. *New rule:* Processes as coaches.

22. Old rule: Plans get revised only periodically. *Disruption:* Process modeling language. *New rule:* Plans are processes, guiding the enterprise in real time.

23. Old rule: The only feasible processes are those supported by the existing IT systems. *Disruption:* Process virtual machine. *New rule:* Any process can be modeled and executed; it may have nothing to do with IT.

24. Old rule: As few people as possible should be involved in the execution of a process. *Disruption:* End-to-end processes, process data correlation, distributed process execution. *New rule:* Everyone and every system needed can be involved without degradation of automation or efficiency through manual hand-offs.

25. Old rule: Don't bury reengineering in the middle of the corporate agenda. *Disruption:* Process modeling methodology. *New rule:* Value analysis, process analysis, quality management and costing are combined into one analysis.

26. Old rule: Tradition counts for nothing. *Disruption:* Process discovery. *New rule:* Tradition is everything, and must be built upon. Those who fail to learn from the past are condemned to repeat it.

27. Old rule: Design processes so that only a small number of variants are needed. *Disruption:* Process customization and process patterns. *New rule:* Any process can be reused to construct or constrain the design of hundreds, even thousands, of variants.

28. Old rule: A company has no more than ten to twenty processes of interest to process engineers. *Disruption:* Process discovery. *New rule:* Organizations are more complex than they think.

29. Old rule: The processes to be improved must be carefully selected and prioritized. *Disruption:* Process optimization, analysis and transformation. *New rule:* Process improvement is built into the methodology; pain points emerge naturally.

30. Old rule: Processes must be designed to eliminate excessive information exchange and data redundancy. *Disruption:* Process data. *New rule:* Strong processes are those that include all required participants who can freely and efficiently exchange and re-process all required information.

31. Old rule: Work must be structured so that suppliers and customers can plan and schedule their respective activities in dependently. *Disruption:* Collaborative processes. *New rule:* Coordination of independent activities is built in.

32. Old rule: Divide overly complex processes into a smaller number of simpler processes. *Disruption:* Enterprise process model. *New rule:* Manage processes as intellectual property and derive what is required for execution automatically.

33. Old rule: Technology only participates in the process (as cogs in the engine). *Disruption:* Third wave. *New rule:* Technology implements the process (drives the pistons, orchestrates the cogs).

34. Old rule: Processes change only when people change them. *Disruption:* Capability passing, external process participants, business rules. *New rule:* Processes can change themselves within limits set by process design.

35. Old rule: Processes take a long time to design. *Disruption:* Real-time process manufacturing. *New rule:* Just-in-time, single-purpose, throw-away processes are both possible and useful and reflect the way business is really done—experimentally *and* systematically.

36. Old rule: Changing processes across organizational boundaries is virtually impossible. *Disruption:* Process interface definition language and end-to-end processes. *New rule:* Process management knows no organizational boundaries.

Putting it All Together

Companies have always sought to achieve and maintain competitive advantage. That's just business. For example, when American industrialists were besieged by Japanese manufacturers in the 1980s, they saw, in no uncertain terms, that their competitive advantage had slipped away. So great was the pain that the extreme remedies prescribed by the reengineering school made sense. Unfortunately, the IT infrastructure was not capable of fulfilling this prescription, so the advocates of radical change fell back on a talking-cure in lieu of the scientifically developed antidepressants that the economy needed.

Lacking any empirical foundation, "reengineering" lost credibility in the world of business. To an extent this was justified, as its most honest advocates have admitted, though they can hardly be faulted for lacking the proper medicine to cure a disease that they otherwise treated to the best of their ability. As we have seen, however, the third wave of business process management can be thought of as a way to *reengineer reengineering*, capitalize on the lessons learned, and profit from process.

Old rule: Business-IT divide
Disruption: Third wave BPM
New Rule: Process owners design and deploy their own processes, obliterating, not bridging, the business-IT divide

---

References

[1] Balachandran, Bala and Thiagarajan, Ramu, *Reengineering Revisited,* Financial Executives Research Foundation, Inc., 1999.

[2] Hammer, Michael, "Reengineering Work: Don't Automate, Obliterate," *Harvard Business Review,* 1990.

[3] Hammer, M. and Champy J., *Reengineering the Corporation,* Harper Business, 1993.

[4] Balachandran, Bala and Thiagarajan, Ramu, *Reengineering Revisited,* Financial Executives Research Foundation, Inc., 1999.

[5] Chapter 14 – Succeeding at Reengineering, *Reengineering the Corporation,* Harper Business, 1993.

[6] Hammer, Michael, "How to Sell Change," *Optimize* magazine, December 2001, optimizemag.com/issue/002/pr_marketing.htm

[7] Seely Brown, J. and Duguid, P., *The Social Life of Information,* Harvard Business School Press, 2000.

[8] Hammer, M., "Process Makes Practice Better," *CIO Magazine*, March 1, 2000, www.cio.com/archive/030100/reply_content.html

[9] Davenport, Thomas H., "The Fad That People Forgot," *Fast Company* Magazine, November, 1995, fastcompany.com/online/01/reengin.html

[10] Hagel, John III and Seely Brown, John, "Cut Loose From Old Business Processes," *Optimize* magazine, December, 2001.

[11] Champy, James A., *X-Engineering the Corporation,* Hodder and Stoughton, 2002.

[12] Champy, James A., "X-treme Business Reengineering," *Optimize* magazine, March, 2002.

Six

Business Process Outsourcing

All ethics so far evolved rest upon a single premise: that the individual is a member of a community of interdependent parts. His instincts prompt him to compete for his place in that community, but his ethics prompt him also to cooperate (perhaps in order that there may be a place to compete for).
—Aldo Leopold, *The Land Ethic*

Change occurs at many levels within an organization. Some change takes place on a grand scale, some on a small scale. Some change is gradual, some radical. Employees come and go, teams morph and take on new roles, existing processes evolve, new processes are introduced and the company responds to the market by honing its products and services to expand its market share. Change is everywhere.

What about the process of entering brand-new markets, or shifting business models 180 degrees, adding new lines of business, or other forms of truly radical *business model* change? The costs and difficulties involved in such strategic change, if it is to be accomplished with reengineering, are well known. Companies have to deal with new channels almost as new businesses, transferring core competencies with superior process design so that the company can attract, motivate and retain the right people. The unfavorable cost/benefit curve of traditional reengineering precludes a good number of the desirable strategic options to achieve this. And reengineering focused on improving processes one by one, mostly inside a single company. There is another way.

What if a company could reinvent itself without painful reengineering? Instead of reengineering its existing processes and building new processes from scratch, what if it could simply *acquire* the best practice and best-in-class business processes it needed to transform its business to the extent of radically redefining what the company is and does? What if a company could use plug-and-play business processes to aggregate completely new lines of business—to establish new market channels, to cross-sell new goods and services that complement their current line, to expand their product line without additional capital investment—what some have called "competition by outguessing links in the supply chain"? Business process management makes a whole new world of business process outsourcing (BPO) not only possible, but also practical, manageable and cost effective.

Under the reengineering model, a company could rebuild selected processes; with BPO it can restructure its *entire* business. BPO becomes a new form of "mergers and acquisitions." What BPM adds to BPO is the capability it gives to partners to retain control of business processes even if they reside partly or wholly with others. With this ability, companies can both produce and consume numerous business services. They can acquire new "virtual" processes, as represented by assets such as people, skills, machines and intellectual property, which makes it a

totally different proposition from *reengineering* existing in-house processes. Instead of process design, the emphasis is on process combination
and the construction of a *managed virtual enterprise*.

Building and managing process-based relationships shifts boundaries and introduces new capabilities without diverting capital, time and
organizational energy. A classical example is contract manufacturing.
Cisco doesn't *make* routers, Levis doesn't *make* jeans, Boeing doesn't
make airplanes. Their contract manufacturers do. The key tools for
importing business resources are process management, outsourcing discipline and value-chain integration. Procurement expert Stan Lepeak
paints a concise picture of how businesses are changing through
outsourcing.[1]

> The G2000 organizational model continues to evolve from
> insular and self-sufficient to open and specialized. Gone are the
> highly vertically integrated business and organizational models
> of the early to mid 20th century. No longer does coal and iron
> go in one end of Ford's River Rouge plant and automobiles
> come out the other. Newspapers no longer own forests to sup-
> ply newsprint. More recently, organizations have been getting
> out of the business of managing their facilities, logistics and
> back-office operations. Organizations today are focusing on a
> narrowing set of core competencies. Already many supply chain
> functions are being outsourced, including inventory manage-
> ment, transportation services, and even manufacturing.

> What's driving this trend is the fact that competitive differ-
> entiation is increasingly a function of horizontal business proc-
> ess expertise and not vertical integration. Organizations strive to
> excel at one or two core processes (e.g., customer care, or
> research and development) and to direct as many resources to
> those processes as possible. Furthermore, operating in today's
> global, high-tech and complexly regulated economy has become
> so complex that no organization can host internally all the skills
> and processes it needs to compete.

> Influenced by this trend, spending on outsourced services
> has become a huge part of the economy. Today, on average,
> over 50 percent of the spending of Global 2000 companies goes
> to outside services, an amount that exceeds $2 billion in a typical

Global 500 enterprise. This amount will continue to grow at 20 percent CAGR or more through 2005 (CAPS). These services take many forms, ranging from individual contractors and temporary staff to retainer services, project-based services and business process outsourcing.

Once a process is digitized, an organization can then "unplug" it and outsource it to a third party for management. Increasingly, it is these third party experts who—as a result of focus, skills and resources—have become the most proficient at carrying out these processes. Processes that were once considered too crucial or too sacrosanct for outsourcing are now considered viable candidates. Chipmakers no longer manufacture their own chips; pharmaceuticals outsource new drug research; the government outsources prison management; and apparel firms outsource their manufacturing. In the near future, few if any processes and tasks will be viewed as off-limits when it comes to their potential to be outsourced.

Once an organization buys into the outsourcing concept, it needs a process to determine which of its functions and processes are viable candidates for outsourcing. There are two reasons for outsourcing a business process, whether it is procurement-related or not. The first is that the organization cannot perform the process well enough to compete. The second is that the process does not contribute to an organization's competitive differentiation and should either be outsourced or eliminated in order to free up resources.

As Lepeak suggests, however, outsourcing "is not a one size fits all proposition."

Organizations must assess outsourcing viability for each business category, such as strategic procurement, commodity procurement and services procurement and management. Strategic outsourcing can provide an organization a competitive differentiation if performed to excellence. Commodity business process excellence can save organizations money, but rarely can it provide competitive differentiation, at least for any length of time. Rather, commodity process outsourcing can provide a negative differentiation when it's performed poorly. It is a process that only gains visibility when there is a problem.

The traditional distinctions between outsourcing, value-chain integration and process management are blurring. Where once companies outsourced well-defined, bounded, functional business domains (and the associated stovepipe IT applications) process management lets companies slice and dice *end-to-end* processes they choose to outsource in different ways and with finer granularity. Outsourcing is becoming more collaborative, and value-chain integration is growing more dependent on business process management. Collaboration is defined through processes, and companies can be both consumers and providers of outsourced business processes. Many outsourcers wish to emulate value-chain integrators, while many companies who have already integrated their value chains have unbundled services for distribution to others. Process management will make possible further progress along these lines. Shared process management, and a standards-based language for process representation, not a standard process, will allow processes in different companies to collaborate, and a wide range of outsourcing and service models will emerge.

Even the smallest of companies can digitize a business process of excellence and offer it as a business service. Some companies will become world-class BPO specialists in the way that Computer Sciences Corporation and EDS became world-class IT outsourcing companies. BPM will enable such BPO specialists to master all facets of business process management. These tools are really no different from the systems and data management tools used in data center outsourcing, without which IT outsourcers could not exist.

Some companies may not set out with the intention of becoming an outsourcer. A classic example is American Airlines. American created a subsidiary, the SABRE Technology Group, to concentrate the highly specialized expertise needed to develop and operate its airline reservation system. SABRE became so good at what it did that it sold its business services to other airlines and thousands of travel agencies. It was so successful that at one point, Robert Crandall, former CEO of the parent company, AMR, said if he were forced to sell one or the other, he'd opt to sell the airline.

Some companies fall into the outsourcing business simply by

excelling at what they do. GE's Trading Process Network was established to streamline procurement for the parent company's independent lines of business. GE became so good at this process that it eventually established GSX, a massive online procurement marketplace, although it later decided to sell off 90 percent of GSX when the market for online procurement waned. This leads us to another key business fundamental: No business is static. A company's long-term success depends on its ability to bundle, unbundle and rebundle what it does—or even what business it's in—as it adapts to changing markets.

Outsourcing can range from a tiny procedure such as plugging FedEx or UPS into the shipping function to a complete new line of business. Borders Books took its entire online bookstore and outsourced it to the best-in-class "enemy," its competitor, Amazon.com. This "coopetition" put Amazon in the outsourcing business. Amazon started its virtual bookstore by outsourcing its warehousing and fulfillment to the book wholesaler Ingram. Now Amazon is both an outsourcer and an outsourcing client, a state that will be typical of the company of the future.

Outsourcing of business services is already commonplace. In addition to payroll and IT services, one thinks immediately of human resources, retirement services, expense management, credit processing, insurance claims management, sourcing, learning services, logistics, call center operations and literally hundreds of other specialized business services. Take finance, for example. The inventory of related services that can now be outsourced includes accounting, planning, budgeting, reporting, general ledger, accounts payable, receivables, treasury functions, cash management, foreign exchange, fixed assets, revenue accounting, joint-venture cost accounting and tax management. Just about anything can now be provided as a service, and integrating service processes over both private and public networks is getting easier and easier.

The strategy of some vertically integrated organizations is to retain core competencies and outsource everything else. Others have set out to retain excellent processes and outsource processes they execute less well, lest they drain the company of its energy and its ability to respond to customer expectations. Companies may retain excellent processes even if they are not core, and find new markets for them. Some may even set out to *acquire* excellent but non-core processes if these processes are synergistic with their core business and the combination might allow them to move into profitable new areas. Firms will no doubt seek to develop new market channels for processes they have acquired through outsourcing, often in conjunction with capabilities only they can provide.

There are, however, huge differences between the procurement of standard services, such as payroll processing, and the blending of best-of-breed processes from different providers into highly differentiated processes that create competitive advantage. Commodity "sourcing," with hundreds or thousands of specialized services to choose from, is largely a matter of portfolio management—evaluating, selecting and adopting external business services. Sourcing may require only a relatively simple hand-off to third parties, which in effect decouples the process provider from the process consumer. As Champy explains in his book, *X-Engineering the Corporation,* "Companies began to outsource everything from information technology to building maintenance services—arms-length transactions that involved little or no cross-company integration and certainly no harmonization." Building new end-to-end value chains, however, is not an arms-length process; it requires the collaborative management of business processes such as the delivery of financial services, healthcare, order-to-cash and "molecule to manufacture." Using BPM, the smart value chain integrator adopts and integrates new processes—and process service providers—into the whole, combining and customizing as required.

Access to "processes on demand" changes the economics of acquiring new capabilities. It reduces capital expenditure, minimizes risk and enables companies to scale process capacity and volumes both up and down, and quickly and efficiently. Some process relationships will be based on a variable, pay-as-you go model, others on subscription-based pricing or the risk/reward model typical of participants in a value chain. In any of these models, however, past methods of bundling products and services don't provide the transparency the market will demand in the future. In the third wave, process management provides the foundation for outsourcing and value chain integration. Outsourcing requires coping with frequent change within and among value chain partners. Processes grow more intricate and complex as they traverse organizational boundaries. They are deeply enmeshed in the organizations involved, so that managing them requires far more than mere automation. The outsourcing capability must include analysis, simulation and optimization of processes, as well as the ability to manipulate, combine and recombine process designs.

A capability for flexibly dividing and allocating responsibilities for process activities within an end-to-end relationship is paramount, as is the ability to change the contractual basis for those responsibilities as the outsourcing relationship deepens or grows obsolescent. The phrase "process management" signifies that it is processes as a whole, and not merely IT assets or human resources, which have been brought under the strategic control of the business. Process management also provides business intelligence derived from measuring the performance and resource consumption of end-to-end processes.

During the reengineering era, IT was seen as only one participant in a larger process, and IT outsourcing focused on operating specified IT systems and making sure they kept pace with the evolution of the business. For example, outsourced billing services rely upon a billing system, but the billing system itself has no real understanding of its role beyond providing the billing service. It's merely a shared component. In the third wave, process outsourcing provides visibility, accountability and control of the entire process. Partners demand insight into the processes of the firms they work with, particularly those whose performance can impact their bottom line. Partners seek to measure the performance of processes they entrust to others, and in some cases need to exercise a significant degree of control over them. A one-size-fits-all business process is clearly not adequate, since in the era of personalization and mass customization, delivering services and products means providing variants tailored to the needs of each customer.

The roles of different partners may vary for different processes. One partner, for example, may be responsible for discovery of new processes; another may be responsible for integrating them; and yet another may be responsible for executing them. Similarly, optimizing and benchmarking a process may be the responsibility of one company, while the responsibility for monitoring and managing performance may be shared. Specialists may be employed to analyze process performance and suggest strategies for improvement. In complex industries, such as industrial supply chains, smaller firms specializing in process integration at end-customer sites may be involved. Process intermediaries, such as marketplaces and trading hubs, may emerge in the value chain.

The New Look and Feel of Outsourcing

Whether delivered in the role of outsourcer, alliance partner or a value-chain participant, companies that provide business services to others will be skilled at recognizing, evaluating and acquiring processes and managing a large process portfolio. Process management will be the tool they use to manipulate processes as easily as companies handle their data needs today. They will deliver processes through multiple channels and customize them to meet every requirement. New enterprise applications, based on process management, will enable the efficient management of these collaborative sourcing and service-chain strategies.

Many firms that have not yet digitized, or even documented, all of their processes will use process-modeling tools for efficient, sometimes automated, process discovery. With third-wave business process management systems, it will be possible to move these captured processes directly from design into production, execution and operation.

Processes will be the outsourcer's intellectual property. Knowledge management will complement process management to help the outsourcer's customers and trading partners make smarter and faster decisions. The best companies will build a repository of best-practice and best-of-breed processes and will use this repository to further analyze, optimize and improve processes, with the aim of increasing customer satisfaction and their own profitability. They will be skilled at helping themselves, and others, manage the transition to new processes, a skill that will require the ability to modify subprocesses independently of supervisory processes and with a fine degree of evolutionary control.

Some outsourcers will provide process management capabilities as a service. Mature process suppliers will be skilled in all of the process management disciplines without reference to any specific process domain, such as human resources, finance or logistics. As they build competence in process management across different domains, these suppliers will seek out opportunities to operate as process management service providers, much as American Airlines did with its online reservation system, SABRE. For a time, process management itself will be a valuable competency, but it will end up as a utility business as process expertise becomes more widespread. Over the next decade, process-powered networks will become as commonplace as hypertext networks are on today's Internet. In supply chains, value-chain integrators will extend process management to small to medium sized companies that otherwise could not afford to participate. They will extend process interaction facilities and workflow to niche suppliers, or even to individual workers, so that they can fulfill roles in end-to-end processes without incurring debilitating overheads.

Companies using processes that belong to others will exert influence over the design and delivery of new processes. Companies will seek to monitor the performance of even non-core processes, along with how they are managed and billed by the service provider. They will demand complete management of the process lifecycle. Changes must be controlled in order to reflect the changing contractual basis of relationships, which will be defined, not by service level agreements, but by the integration of metrics into the process designs themselves. Process designs will be included in the legal contracts governing such relationships. Service levels, not details about the idiosyncrasies of individual processes, will be used to define the performance of process management services.

At the desktop level, the workforce must be provided with a rich environment that enables them to interact with processes and that facilitates self-help. Changes in processes must be visible to users. "What-if" scenario planning and analysis using metrics will help everyone, not just managers, understand how processes are performing and how they could be improved.

It has been widely reported that relationships between companies are increasingly becoming true partnerships, involving collaborative work of individuals and teams across the partnership. Other than checking payroll, it will be hard to know who works for whom, the end-user organization or the process service provider. These closer relationships will need to be organized around the process of change itself. Successful companies will rely on process collaboration tools to manage task lists, resolve exceptions and coach people in the execution of processes. Teams responsible for delivering processes will therefore be able to work efficiently with process users, avoiding complex hand-offs while ensuring that everyone is kept informed.

With sound process management, the introduction of a new process or a new system can be nondisruptive and less dependent on training. Cross-company teams will work through a process portal—a system interface designed for interaction with a business process—that allows work to continue as processes change. Employees will be kept fully involved and amenable to changes in work patterns, by providing them with insight into their role in the process and its associated tasks. Collaborative processes, including voting, reaching agreements, together with the identification, escalation and resolution of issues that cannot be attributed to a single individual. The process model must support the implicit network of commitments made by employees, companies and their customers.

Radical Change Through Business Process Outsourcing

In a world of end-to-end, customer-focused processes, what matters in the marketplace is the cost of entire processes, regardless of who owns which part of the chain. Tracking this cost requires end-to-end visibility and value management. Cost advantages are the way newcomers enter and dominate mature markets. Almost always, these newcomers succeed by bundling superior processes and associated technologies to form a new "killer value chain." As Peter Drucker noted in *Management Challenges of the 21st Century:*[2]

> Executives need to organize and manage, not only the cost chain, but also everything else—including strategy and product planning—as one economic whole, regardless of the legal boundaries of individual companies. This is the shift from cost-led pricing to price-led costing.

The very same point can be applied to outsourcing, alliances and joint ventures.

The flipside to the outsourcing and value-chain integration advantages is that the associated business models rest on complex commercial and financial arrangements. Such financial engineering will also have to be fully transparent and accountable. Fortunately, end-to-end process control will help. As Drucker pointed out, achieving this outcome once depended on establishing uniform systems of accounting management, along with their associated IT systems, and required participants to share competitively sensitive information. This is no longer the case. Now, companies can create and deploy the processes required to share, harmonize and manage the *controlled flow* of accounting information across the value chain, made secure by the use of business process level firewalls. A standard process language replaces a standard process or a standard system.

Companies with a BPM capability will be able to serve their customers better and faster. They will be able offer higher quality at a lower cost with greater economies of scale, increasing their profitability. They will be able to respond to new marketplace opportunities more readily by bundling or unbundling business relationships in both demand and supply channels. In its various forms, business process outsourcing, enabled by process management, changes the rules of engagement on the battleground of business competition.

References

[1] Lepeak, Stan, "Procurement's Future: Outsourcing?" *Line56.com*, August 20, 2002.

[2] Drucker, Peter F., *Management Challenges of the 21ˢᵗ Century,* HarperBusiness, 1999.

Seven

Management Theory, Return on Investment and Beyond

My friend, all theory is gray, and the Golden tree of life is green.
—Goethe

While each scientific theory selects out and abstracts from the world's complexity a peculiar set of relations, philosophy cannot favor any particular region of human enterprise. Through conceptual experimentation it must construct a consistency that can accommodate all dimensions of experience, whether they belong to physics, physiology, psychology, biology or ethics.
—Alfred North Whitehead

The third wave is not a new management theory. Rather, it supports, accelerates and amplifies existing approaches to management. To illustrate this we consider the application of BPM to the processes of Six Sigma and Change Management. Then we visit the measure by which process management itself is measured, Return on Process Investment, and go on to envision how management theory will evolve.

The Process of Six Sigma

Six Sigma is a management technique that aims at developing and delivering near-perfect products and services. It has been claimed that Six Sigma is only useful for problems that are "hard to find, but easy to fix"—as contrasted with the radical reengineering approach, whose advocates focus on problems that are "easy to find, but hard to fix."

The term "Six Sigma" refers to statistical constructs that measure how far a given process deviates from perfection. Six Sigma is of course a process, a discipline in its own right that measures how many defects exist in a business process and then systematically determines how to remove them. Its focus on process quality evolved out of the quality movement that began in the 1980s. It is, however, now used for a much wider range of process improvement activities. It could in fact be applied to many different types of processes, since the measured attributes can be very varied. Companies such as GE have completely internalized Six Sigma as a way of doing business (see Figure 7.1).

The principles of quality applied in implementing Six Sigma are almost always defined in terms of the company vision and its strategy. Processes are designed from the perspective of the customer and involve an infusion of process thinking across the firm. Metrics such as performance, reliability, price, on-time delivery, service and accuracy provide the targets. The customer focus creates market knowledge that can illuminate the need for process change in areas where the company can add value or implement improvements that customers themselves value most. Advocates of Six Sigma believe that customers are interested in comparing, not the average performance of companies, but the relative merits of each and every process touch-point used to deliver goods or services to them.

GE's Evolution Towards Quality

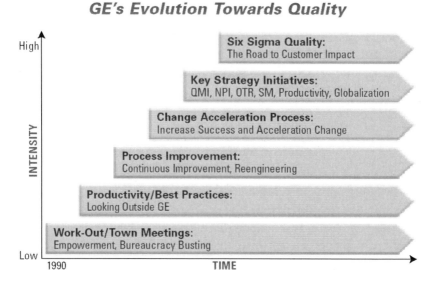

Figure 7.1. GE's Roadmap to Customer Impact (Source: GE)

Rigorous Six Sigma requires that a process produce no more than 3.4 defects per million occurrences of the process, but its main goal is continuous improvement. Its principles apply not only to manufacturing but also to the delivery of services. Six Sigma can be used by the travel industry just as easily as it can be by the automobile industry. In GE's conception, Six Sigma revolves around just a few core concepts:[1]

- Critical to quality: Attributes the customer values most.
- Defect: Failure to deliver what the customer expects.
- Process capability: What a process can deliver.
- Variation: What the customer sees and feels.
- Stable operations: Ensuring consistent, predictable processes to improve what the customer sees and feels.

- Design for Six Sigma: Designing to meet customer needs and process capability.

Because Six Sigma is itself a process, it can be defined and deployed by a business process management system to provide several advantages:

- For many companies, introducing Six Sigma is itself a process of reengineering, and each Six Sigma activity is a project in its own right. Powered by BPM, a Six Sigma process would be visible to everyone in the extended enterprise, which would accelerate its adoption across business units and business partners. All of the advantages of change, integration and collaboration that BPM can provide to a business process can be provided to the Six Sigma process. Just as BPM can speed implementation of reengineering, it can do the same for a Six Sigma program. To the BPM system, Six Sigma is just another process.
- Six Sigma is a process that focuses upon improving other processes. Meta-processes like Six Sigma govern the lifecycle of change in other processes. But the changes still have to be implemented and put into production. BPM's ability to link process design directly to process execution accelerates implementation and reduces the costs associated with manual Six Sigma initiatives. In other words, BPM enables "straight-through" Six Sigma.
- BPM can provide the tools for conducting Six Sigma activities. It can provide a central repository of process designs, as well as a consistent process modeling language and representation methodology that obviates the need for ad-hoc Six Sigma process design tools. Although many companies perform Six Sigma with nothing more than paper, pen and a spreadsheet, BPM permits a process-centric enterprise to take a more managed approach to the discipline. Because BPM extends to all process-related activities, BPM sits at the cross hairs between Business and IT, and a bottom-up (organic) and top-down (enterprise) view of process innovation.
- BPM can be used to define and execute the data retrieval processes needed for Six Sigma activities, including the automated delivery of data from IT, reducing the time and training that would be needed if people were to handle these tasks. Six Sigma team members need vast amounts of data to perform their work. BPM is a heavy-duty

forklift for Six Sigma data collection. It can also play a large role in assisting with process discovery activities.

- Six Sigma inevitably requires the detailed mapping of processes for analysis. BPM's process-modeling language provides the most complete and most consistent approach known to the formalized description of business processes—IT and non-IT. The BPM paradigm makes all processes more transparent to an analysis of their strengths, weaknesses, cycle times and defects—for example by separating the modeling of control flow and data flow.

Within Six Sigma, various schemes—in effect processes—are used to conduct the key phases of the total lifecycle—definition, measurement, analysis and improvement. Many of these standard approaches claim to be systematic, scientific and fact-based. This may be true, but none until third-wave BPM has been able to directly deploy new process designs once they have been changed, or to continue to measure them automatically thereafter.

One such Six Sigma process is called DMAIC (Define, Measure, Analyze, Improve and Control). Applied to a variety of Six Sigma projects in many different industries, from product design to supply chain improvement, DMAIC defines a series of activities—a process, in other words—for ensuring the best possible results from continued process improvement. Here is another example from GE Capital:

- *Define* the customer, what their Critical to Quality (CTQ) issues are, and the Core Business Process involved. Define who customers are, what their requirements are for products and services, and what their expectations are. Define project boundaries—the stop and start of the process. Define the process to be improved by mapping the process flow.
- *Measure* the performance of the Core Business Process involved. Develop a data collection plan for the process. Collect adequate data from many sources to determine types of defects and metrics. Compare with customer survey results to determine shortfall.
- *Analyze* the data collected and the process map to determine the root causes of defects and identify opportunities for improvement. Identify gaps between current performance and goal performance. Prioritize opportunities to improve. Identify sources of variation.

- *Improve* the target process by designing creative solutions for fixing and preventing defects. Create innovative solutions using technology and discipline. Develop and deploy an implementation plan.
- *Control* the improvements to keep the process on its new course. Prevent reverting back to the "old way." Require the development, documentation and implementation of an ongoing monitoring plan. Institutionalize the improvements through the modification of systems and structures (staffing, training and incentives).

BPM can facilitate the DMAIC process in at least the following ways:

- *Define activity.* BPM helps express the process under study. The process can be described in as much or as little detail as required—from the finest details of implementation to the highest-level abstract expression of a business model design.
- *Measure activity.* A BPM process can express the DMAIC data collection plan precisely, whether it involves analysis of a single element or of many elements from across multiple systems. It can also immediately start to collect the data from the operational systems and work patterns under study in a fully automated manner and on a regular basis. Metrics data will be more complete and more accurate as a result of being collected automatically.
- *Analyze activity.* BPM can encode metrics within any process design so that the comparison of variations in current performance against stated goals can be readily derived. The data contained in the BPMS about the end-to-end state, structure and design of the processes under study, can be queried by existing tools.
- *Improve activity.* BPM tools can assist Six Sigma practitioners in their work. For example, the generation and exploration of process design variations, in conjunction with simulation.
- *Control activity.* BPM prevents the process reverting to the "old way" by directly implementing the automated parts and by generating the required workflow interfaces that adapt to process change. Process portals and a process desktop can expedite knowledge transfer related to new processes by keeping employees totally involved in and interacting with the evolving digital process.

Because a third-wave BPM process can express and execute both the DMAIC process itself and the collection of data for DMAIC analysis, it can provide the foundation for improving an entire class of processes under study. Because a BPM process is able to perform arbitrary calculations, procedures, algorithms and business logic, it can encode the calculation of Six Sigma in terms meaningful to a particular industry— defects in products, uptime on a power grid, reported telecommunications faults, ability to supply, and so on. In short, BPM provides a rigorous platform for Six Sigma projects.

The application of BPM to Six Sigma is but one example of the way third-wave methods and technologies can assist a company in implementing its process improvement strategies, whether they are incremental or radical in nature. BPM can be applied to any number of methods, including Activity-Based Costing, Balanced Scorecard, EVA, Excellence Models, and Supply Chain Management—even Business Games Theory. BPM can integrate these methods as required to create "Our Company Strategy"—a process that encodes metrics and measures that drives toward outcomes, and that can be used as a *design pattern* and applied to any process a company subsequently develops.

Of course, Six Sigma with absolutely no support from BPM methods still generates bottom line savings, enhances customer satisfaction and improves quality. With BPM, these benefits are amplified and become "built-in" to all enterprise processes and architecture. The loop between process analysis and execution is closed. Many companies have applied Six Sigma with nothing more than a spreadsheet! Imagine what can be achieved, or achieved faster and more pervasively, when the third wave of BPM is applied. The objective of including process management systems in a Six Sigma initiative is to help organizations deepen their focus on processes, include automated systems, and take change off the critical path altogether. With BPM, even companies that have never applied Six Sigma may do so easily. We believe process management should merge into the corporate background—no more thought about than the use of email today. Some are predicting the possibility for BPM not only to build in change, but to build in process and quality improvement as well.

Change Management is a Process, Too

One of the most challenging and costly problems faced by companies today is change management, a process closely related to process lifecycle management, since each change request can be viewed as a process instance in its own right. BPM provides the capability to manage the entire lifecycle of the change management process from design to deployment to execution to continuous improvement. The change-management-process design can incorporate all the participants in the change, including employees, value-chain partners, systems and other processes. It can also model both the automated and manual interactions in a single environment.

Aside from processing costs, time-to-market is the key factor that makes the change management process so critical. Most manufacturing companies complain about the time that it takes to process a change request—a change order, a notice, or the like. It can take weeks to turn one around when they actually need it in days or hours. According to one estimate, the average cost of processing a paper-based change request is $2,500. Companies that fail to adapt their products and services quickly to changing market demand incur considerable opportunity costs that can spell the difference between success and failure. Change management is central to that adaptability. What's more, changes that occur early in the product design cycle are far less costly than those implemented later on, when product changes have broader implications for the entire supply chain. Using BPM to implement an electronic change management process across the supply chain allows problems to be addressed early on and reduces cycle times significantly.

An effective change management process spans multiple business functions, including engineering, finance, support, marketing and manufacturing, and extends outside the firewall to suppliers, subcontract manufacturers and distribution partners. A variety of information systems must be integrated and coordinated in order to extend the change process to all these participants. Managers responsible for change management need to be able to view and track the progress of any change at any time and determine where current responsibilities reside. They also need a complete audit trail of activities pursuant to change requests and of all the members of the supply chain involved in the process. Such audit trails are particularly important in industries such as pharmaceuticals, aerospace and financial services, where change management must ensure compliance with regulatory guidelines and requirements.

Today, the vast majority of companies utilize manual change management processes. Even where electronic document management is used, it is rarely linked to all of the participating systems and procedures that are subject to change management. A manual change-order process usually begins something like this:

- A change request is handwritten
- Supporting documentation is attached
- The request is submitted to document control
- Document control makes sure that the form is complete and accurate

Then, a specific person or workgroup is assigned responsibility for the change request. In a manufacturing environment, those charged with the responsibility will want to see such detailed information as:

- The parts affected
- Where the part is used
- Inventory count of the old parts
- Disposition of the old parts
- Cost impact analysis

Parties who need access to this information must log on to multiple systems to gather data stored in multiple applications. Typically, the bill of materials will either be in the enterprise resource planning (ERP) or in the product data management (PDM) system. Cost data used in the impact analysis and for materials disposition might be in the ERP financial system, while the level of on-hand inventory of affected parts is distributed in systems across the value chain.

When the change request form has been completed and all of the appropriate information made available, it is usually routed through a convoluted approval process. When it comes back approved, activities are launched and the product changes must be incorporated in all affected systems. The PDM and ERP systems need the revised bill of materials. The financial system needs the new cost data. The product catalogs, quote configurators, customer-care applications and sales-force automation systems must all be updated to reflect the change, and the change needs to be made available to supply and demand chain partners as well. Today, this largely manual process is error-prone, slow and expensive, and yet is commonly practiced by many organizations.

Using BPM, systems such as document management, ERP, manufacturing execution system (MES), product data management (PDM), CAD/CAM, and others can be integrated. Once integrated, they can contribute to many subsequent change management processes. BPM can streamline and automate the entire change management lifecycle, reducing cycle time across the process or implementing additional levels of audit and control. A process design can capture and orchestrate the activities of all the participants involved, including employees, partners and information systems. BPM combines aspects of workflow, process automation and transaction management to provide global visibility and control.

A BPM process can power a completely "paperless" change control system, both inside a company and across its firewall. Participants in the process may, for example, log a change request on-line, outlining the details of the request. The request will be automatically routed to heads of departments, change owners, change controllers and evaluators, as applicable. Tasks will be allocated to roles at design time and assigned at run time to users, who will have access to all the information they need to perform their tasks. The owner of the change management process can also customize the process to enable task delegation, escalation and alerts, taking the guesswork out of how a change request should be processed. Customization is critical in change management if change managers are to take into account working practices that naturally arise in the course of process execution.

A BPM system can provide a full audit trail for the change request that encompasses the activities of all participants in the supply chain. The audit trail can track the change request from initiation to completion across the extended enterprise and make the results visible to management in real time. In addition, the BPM system is able to assure reliable execution of long-lived change management processes that require hours, days, or even months, to complete. In the aerospace sector, change management processes that last a year or years are not uncommon. In a distributed environment the BPM system can ensure that all systems are automatically updated, and that the change is consistently applied, rolled back or compensated for in the event of failure. Because the electronic change-control process is not hard coded in back-end systems, the processes handling the change request can expand, contract, back-track or otherwise adapt, as required by changing circumstances over the lifecycle of the change request. In short, change requests can be processed more efficiently, with greater speed, fewer errors and far less paperwork. Users know at all times where their request is, what its status is, and who is handling it, since all information about the change request is constantly updated in the BPM system.

BPM can therefore eliminate or greatly reduce the need for costly supporting activities such as change control meetings, faxes, shipping paperwork, additional couriers, travel and e-mail. The use of a process portal can reduce training requirements and enable employees across the value chain to initiate change requests. When thousands of change orders are processed this way, the costs savings alone can be substantial. More importantly, product excellence can be improved while customer service is enhanced at the same time.

Return on Process Investment

The third wave of BPM makes multiple, parallel process improvement initiatives possible. One process may be in the discovery phase as another is designed and deployed and a third is undergoing analysis. In fact, when hundreds of processes at various stages of readiness can be managed simultaneously, the process of process improvement starts to feel more like document management than the waterfall model of Six Sigma or the discontinuous approach of reengineering. Putting a new process into operation is as simple as the save file function at the end of an edit. Because the system manages the intricate dependencies between processes, process engineers need worry less about such matters. This efficiency brings a faster return on investment to more processes. The traditional process beginning with the production of a long-winded "business case" for each software engineering project—a process which analysts tell us results in 80 percent of projects never being given the go-ahead—gives way to continuous development.

Companies always want to know the expected return on any investment, and return on process investment is no exception. With the advent of the third wave of BPM, return is a twofold proposition. First, what is the projected return on investment for third-wave BPM methods and technologies compared to current methods—or lack thereof? This is measured in terms of the "total cost of process ownership," not the result of those processes on the business's bottom line. Second, what is the projected return on investment of the proposed new or improved business processes themselves—the result of the process management activity? The two criteria are related, since if the cost to implement a new process exceeds its benefit, there is no business case. On the other hand, if the cost to implement new processes is driven down, a new world of possibilities is opened.

Measurements can be made by asking questions—which point to associated metrics—whose answers demonstrate a measurable impact on the business. A balanced scorecard approach is useful in formulating the right questions because it's important not only to measure things right, but also to measure the right things. For example: What if this process could be deployed within this time frame? What if this process could be deployed within this budget? What will it cost to design and implement this new business process using our current change management methods as compared with third-wave methods? What if this process could be fully automated? What if this process could be tailored to each customer's needs? What if this process could be completed in one day instead of three? What if this process could be updated on a daily basis? What if this process could be executed with ten times fewer errors? What if this process could involve these business partners? The total cost/benefit picture is an aggregate of the following factors:

- *Process design to production time and cost.* An aggregate measure of the time and resources required to design—or redesign—and then deploy a new business process. A significant element is the extent to which digital process design can naturally capture and express all the resources required in the real business process.
- *Process design automation coverage.* The degree to which a process is capable of modeling and including all needed process participants—humans, systems, and machines.
- *Process customization level.* The degree to which the process management environment makes the creation and maintenance of large numbers of process variants easy and manageable.

- *Process lifecycle continuity.* The extent to which the modification of processes to meet new requirements does not require any departure from managing within the "pure" process paradigm, such as writing additional software, implementing technical interfaces or configuring packages.
- *Process transaction capability level.* The extent to which processes can include managed business-level, multi-participant, cross-functional transactions and compensating activities, and the extent to which these operate independently of the participating applications' "technical" transactions.
- *Process value-chain coverage.* The extent to which the process can be extended to reach all participants in the value chain.

The aggregate of these measurements reveals the total cost of process ownership and the cost benefits of nondisruptive change management. An analysis of these measures compares the total cost of process ownership against the hidden cost of unmanaged and usually unmeasured process methods already in place. These measurements also apply to the return on the business process itself as a contributor to the bottom line. This dual analysis of process ownership, including both the cost/benefit of process ownership and the bottom-line return on new business processes, provides the new balanced scorecard needed for effective business decisions.

Management Theory Yet to Come

Management theory emerges in response to major changes in the wider world in which companies operate. For example, Fredrick Taylor's theories arose in response to the early days of the Industrial Revolution. The Chaordic Commons, a network of researchers and practitioners that study the application of chaos and complexity theory to organizational design, take inspiration from Dee Hock, founder and CEO emeritus of Visa International. Some claim that it was he who first conceived of a global system for the electronic exchange of value. The group attributes the success of Visa—that now links in excess of 20,000 financial institutions, 14 million merchants, and 600 million consumers in 220 countries—with a Chaordic form of organizational design.

Hock contends that success in business depends less on rote and more on reason; less on the authority of the few and more on the judgment of many; less on compulsion and more on motivation; less on external control of people and more on internal discipline. He advocates that computer simulation will be needed to allow people to quickly see how clarity of purpose and Chaordic principles allow institutions to self-organize, evolve over decades, and link in new patterns for an enduring constructive society. Judging by the success of Visa he might just be right. The chaord lies precisely at the discontinuity between order (rigid, predictable process) and disorder (random, unpredictable behavior). Advocates claim that flexibility, innovation, adaptability, and inclusiveness are the hallmarks of organizations that adopt the principles of the Chaord.

Such complex systems are attracting management attention. Megan Santosus writing in CIO Magazine[2] stated that a growing number of consultants and academics are looking at complexity theory, once the domain of biological and physical sciences, to help managers improve the way they lead organizations. They state that businesses are adaptive complex systems and have three ways of functioning. There is the stable zone, in which the company is in a state of inertia, not responding to opportunities nor adapting to changes. The stable zone is undesirable because it leads to an unresponsive system. Then there is the chaotic zone, in which the organization is bouncing off walls, haphazard, led by events rather than choices and overreacting. Then there is a zone between these two, the creative zone, the place to be. Researchers claim that creativity, versatility and adaptability emerge from tolerating the ambiguity between the two extremes.

Companies are now seeking out successful business models and, through process modeling, coming to understand the basis of their success more fully. They are creating the third wave of "process knowledge" and putting it to work in their companies. This endeavor will intensify over the coming years: IT systems are simulations of the businesses they support, whose degree of alignment with reality depends on the ability of IT tools to reflect the real world. An example is the field of logistics, where, as Nigel Green of LINE.net points out, "Messages flowing between computers represent physical packages being carried by trucks and aircraft. They are, quite literally, one and the same."

In Brian Arthur's work at the Santa Fe Institute[3] he points to the problem of examining the resulting trajectories of individual participants and emphasizes the discovery of structure, and the processes through which structure emerges, across different levels of the organization. The study of such distributed multi-participant processes, grid-like systems, emergence, chaos and self-organization are going to set the stage for the theoretical work that will underpin the scientific application of third-wave process management over the coming decade. For business people don't want to have to change and then re-deploy "applications," no matter who, business or IT, does the associated work. Ultimately end users of technology just want business processes to be able to change. In the third wave, the business process is the self-organizing app! What would Fredrick Taylor—arguably the world's first management consultant and practitioner of time-and-motion studies—make of all this? What new "killer management theories" can be envisioned? How do we calculate their ROI?

Of course, in the short term, process management systems will be deployed for more prosaic reasons: agility, control, efficiency, visibility and accountability. For this to happen, businesses must understand their value today, and compute the return they can expect from an investment in business process management.

Note: For those who want to understand more of the theory behind process management, Appendix C will help.

References

[1] http://www.ge.com/sixsigma

[2] "Simple, Yet Complex," *CIO Enterprise Magazine,* April 1998.

[3] Arthur, W. Brian, "Complexity and the Economy," *Science*, 2 April 1999, 284, 107-109

Eight

Implementing Business Process Management

The Tao that is told is not the Tao.
—Tao Te Ching

What if, at the conclusion of a meeting between the senior executives of two companies, the new alliance they had just formed could be implemented within days after each side returned to their respective offices? What if the world's most common excuse—"The IT department says it will take 18 months to implement"—was no longer to be heard? Agility has been on the agenda of companies for quite some time, but inflexible technology and the lack of an ability to manage business processes has hampered efforts to achieve it. Now, however, it's time to remember the venerable proverb: "Be careful what you wish for, because you just might get it." Until the third wave of BPM, the business-IT divide was a comfortable excuse for not implementing change. Until the third wave of BPM, companies could not manage their business processes. Because the third wave of BPM places technology and business processes firmly in the control of the organization, the naked organization itself is all that lies between business change and innovation.

Two Out of Three Ain't Bad

Process, organization and technology combine to form the inseparable triad of business change. Alter the balance, and chaos and waste are sure to follow. For example, companies recently pumped indecent amounts of money into technology, trying to renew and reinvigorate their businesses by technological means alone. Forrester Research calculates the technology overspend in the years 1998 to 2000 at $65 billion in the U.S. alone, as large companies engaged in a historic tech orgy. Forrester's CEO, George Colony described the result: "Bewildered CEOs and CFOs who felt burned by the dollars lost (and who are now slowing capital spending to a trickle), lost credibility for IT, lost stature for vendors, hardware for sale on eBay at 10 cents on the dollar, and pressure on operating margins. Oh, and by the way, you also get one toxic technology recession."[1]

But now, the third wave of BPM allows companies to master technology and process management, leaving the organizational factor as the primary determinant of successful change and competitive advantage. With two of the three factors driving business change taken off the critical path, the options that organizations have for structuring work to conduct business has become the overriding management issue. As Colony explained,

Whether it's the stirrup, the PC, or electricity, technology has always required change in the way humans work. You don't farm the same way with a hoe as you did with a plow. General Motors didn't organize its robotically driven Saturn production line the way Rolls-Royce structured its hand-built assembly process.

Learning new ways of doing work poses an immense challenge, however, involving not just the individual company but what organization theorists call the "organizational ecology"—the entire industry value chain through which the effects of change cascade. The concept of organizational ecology traces its origins to a 1977 paper coauthored by sociologists Michael Hannan and John Freeman.[2] While we defer to the experts on this organizational theory, we will summarize works in this field as these relate to the assimilation of business process management. In addition to organizational ecology, critical factors for success involve systems thinking, building learning organizations and developing practical guidelines for assimilating BPM.

The key word is *assimilation,* for, over time, BPM will pervade the entire extended enterprise. BPM is not a single "big bang" event. It's a framework for corporate evolution. Its guiding principle is "do no harm" as it implements the new and phases out the old. What it calls for is a sustained approach—exemplified by GE's Digitization Initiative—that minimizes the impact of change on current operations, while incrementally moving aside the old in deference to the new.

Business processes are best managed as a portfolio, and high-value processes will no doubt yield greater returns on investments. Winning companies will prioritize and manage their process portfolios using an analysis of return on equity. Early projects and initiatives will require only a subset of all the possible features of a business process management system. The BPM infrastructure should then grow in step with the growing number and sophistication of processes brought into the process management framework. Companies should research a little, implement a little and watch their process portfolio grow, for BPM is an *incremental revolution.* The impact and enhancement of capabilities is huge, but the path to execution is incremental and nondisruptive.

Process improvement and process management now apply to all of a company's processes. Point solutions to process components, rather than whole processes, can and should be avoided. In previous reengineering and improvement activities, individual processes were typically treated symptomatically—that is, individually and piecemeal. Each improvement effort was usually accompanied by its own change program and its own IT systems implementation project. This approach added to the total cost of ownership of each process and left many potential improvement initiatives on the shelf, lacking sponsorship. Critical analysis of such approaches will demonstrate the enormous advantages of a holistic approach to the management of all processes that comprise the business, for processes are what a business does: They are the business.

Once brought into the BPM infrastructure, no one process deserves more attention than any other: Process management becomes everyone's business. Each process can be discovered, continuously monitored, optimized and analyzed. The third wave of process management allows the company to treat all processes equally, in terms of their representation in computer systems and their subsequent management. This new foundation allows businesses to implement the process systems needed to manage all business processes on a continuous basis. Implementing BPM allows companies to avoid implementation of point solutions that solve only immediate points of pain in individual processes or sub-processes. Process management provides a unified foundation for the entire organization, covering its information systems, its people and its business processes—as well as those of its trading partners.

In a less competitive economic climate, a business could simply watch and wait for early adopters to experiment with the third wave of process management. They could then develop their action plans and business cases by extrapolating from the results achieved by those who tried it first. This strategy had much to recommend it when change involved a major initiative such as ERP deployment, but today's economy requires a more proactive approach. Fortunately BPM fosters incremental change and leverages past investments in technology. Existing applications are preserved. Existing processes are preserved. In short, all existing assets can be reused and adapted.

When BPM is implemented, a more immediate and proactive approach can be taken to the business issues facing the company. Some unscrupulous consultants will no doubt seek to cash in on the fear, uncertainty and doubt (FUD) that surround any advanced breakthrough, and yet there is really nothing new about BPM—though it will no doubt change the world. BPM is merely a synthesis of business best practice and process collaboration technologies that removes many of the obstacles blocking execution of management intent. Thus, transitioning to a process-managed enterprise requires that a company trust what it already knows and avoid being mesmerized by IT industry hype. BPM simply makes it possible for companies to do what they have wanted to do all along—manage their business processes with great agility. With two out of the three variables of the change triad firmly grasped in the hands of BPM, companies can now become laser focused on the organizational dimension of business innovation.

Systems Thinking:
The "Core" Core Competency

As W. Edwards Deming, the father of the quality movement, pointed out, it is "the system," that is the problem. End-to-end business processes are dynamic systems, but today's business professionals are generally not trained in general systems thinking. Too often constrained to a perspective limited by ingrained business practices, rigid scripts and structured input-output work, few professionals have a wide-angle view of, or experience dealing with, end-to-end business processes.

The worlds of business and technology are growing more complex, however, and managing that complexity is the goal of systems thinking. It focuses on the whole, not the parts, of a complex system. It concentrates on the interfaces and boundaries of components, on their connections and arrangement, on the potential for holistic systems to achieve results that are greater than the sum of their parts. Mastering systems thinking means overcoming the major obstacles to building the process-managed enterprise—for every business process is a whole system.

Systems thinking provides a new perspective on business process analysis and redesign. Imagine holding your hand at arms length in front of your face and blocking your view of the earth, the entire earth? Astronauts can do that. The world below them looks drastically different from their perspective: They see the whole earth. Workers, however, only see bits and pieces of their company and their industry in the course of their earthbound daily work. Within individual specialties, workers lose sight of the overall business. They are deprived of knowing the results of their individual actions. They do not get to see outcomes in cause and effect relationships, and therefore stop learning. Feedback, specifically knowledge of *effects*, is absolutely required if workers are to learn from daily experience. Today's workers need an astronaut's perspective of end-to-end business processes. Systems thinking is a formal discipline of management science that deals with whole systems and in terms of the interconnections and interactions of their parts. But because today's business rests on automation, practitioners of building lasting, growing, profitable businesses are going to need tools to help them take the holistic systems thinking perspective. As we have explained in this book, BPM provides those tools.

The hard part of process engineering is understanding the interconnections and the interactions of business processes and subprocesses, the variables affecting processes, and the overall effects of decisions made by process designers. Systems thinking provides a basis for understanding the environment under study, and long-term effects are revealed by running simulations of the models. Such business simulations have been termed *management flight simulators* and *management practice fields*. Mistakes and erroneous design assumptions can be discovered in the laboratory rather than in live operations. If reengineered business processes are tested in the real world, the very real results can be disastrous. What avionics engineer would introduce a new airplane without testing it in a real or digital wind tunnel? Simulation is one of the foundations of the business process management system. Hands-on process simulation also provides a learning tool for reinforcing systems thinking. Process designers can make assumptions about improved business processes and test those assumptions. Feedback closes the loop and facilitates learning.

Learning to Become a Process-Managed Enterprise

Peter Senge, a senior professor of behavioral policy science at MIT and author of *The Fifth Discipline*, is a leading exponent of the concept of the *learning organization*. Senge describes four other core disciplines, in addition to systems thinking, required to build such an organization: *personal mastery, working with mental models, building shared vision* and *team learning*.[3] These disciplines have yet to be written into the personnel manuals of today's corporation.

Teams and organizations can learn, just as individuals can, but the learning process is more complex. Personal mastery is a prerequisite for team learning, just as team learning is a prerequisite for organizational learning, but learning disabilities abound in all three domains: individual, team and organizational.

The process of individual adult learning is a compound challenge because learning new ways of doing work requires "unlearning" existing, ingrained thinking and work patterns. Learning is often a painful experience as it disturbs existing, deeply held, assumptions, beliefs and generalizations (*mental models*) people use to get through the day, at home and at work. The pain level can be so significant that adults practice defensive procedures in learning situations that threaten their existing mental models.

Successful corporations of the 21st century will systematically manage their mental models. The discipline of working with mental models is a vital enabler of change, the kind of change needed for corporate transformations. Individuals are not simply updating or adding to their current knowledge. Instead they are fundamentally altering the way they think about problems, and altering the way they view their world. Companies will no doubt need to take specific steps to help individuals think "outside the box" of existing mental models. A first step is to embrace the field of creative thinking. A classic book on creative thinking is Roger von Oech's book, *A Whack on the Side of the Head*. This classic takes a refreshing look at the 10 mental locks that keep us from being creative.

Team learning, in contrast to individual learning, must be given special attention. Teams often have built-in learning dysfunctions as a result of the individual behavior of team members. Senge asks, "How can a team of committed managers with individual IQs above 120 have a collective IQ of 63?" On the other hand, successful teams know how to do team learning, and the collective intelligence of the team exceeds the mean of the individual IQs.

Sports teams exemplify team learning where total team performance is greater than the sum of the performances of the individual players. That is why teams "jell" during the season to create something extraordinary. But when the all-star teams are formed at the end of the season, the collections of individual stars from different teams produce less than optimal teams. All-star teams are often clumsy. They have had too little time for team learning. Companies should keep in mind the concept of team learning for they will be putting together multi-company all-star teams as they build winning end-to-end business processes.

Finally, in the world according to Senge, a vision of the future is needed, a sense of where the company is going and what it is trying to build. But few concepts are more elusive than that of corporate "vision." A *shared vision* is not a handful of pearls of wisdom handed down from an enlightened CEO. Shared vision boils up out of individual insights. How are individual insights to be captured, except in a collaborative learning environment? Isn't the discovery of shared vision a part of the learning process, just as process discovery is part of process management? Isn't it, in fact, the end result and purpose of learning at all levels of the organization? A shared vision provides common direction and focus, and motivates personal, team, and organizational learning. A genuine shared vision, as opposed to vague corporate "vision" statements, enables all workers to keep their eyes on the prize, and all participants in a value chain to work toward common goals.

Here is a surprising fact about what has been said up to this point in this discussion of learning—most of it was written during the 1990s, as companies were grappling with internal reengineering projects in which command and control issues were confined to an individual company.[4] Companies then were merely trying to manage the "white space" in their organizational charts. Today's companies must manage the white space in entire value chains. Value-chain leadership requires cultivation of a shared vision in all participants. Because multiple value-chain participants must collaborate to deliver value, they must all participate in process analysis and design—and achieve team learning. Only with the visibility provided by process management can end-to-end processes be understood, anomalies spotted, redundancy eradicated and inefficiencies eliminated. Process management integrates everyone and everything once; thereafter, process design, transformation and experience take place freely and continuously, not as a series of infrequent, long-winded, piecemeal and distracting "integration projects" for each new process design. In this way, participants truly learn about the process and the side effects of change on the business.

When corporations react to threats from global competition by forming partnerships and alliances and set out to transform processes accordingly, failure can be expected unless the five disciplines, characteristic of a learning organization, are understood and mastered. The often-quoted 70- to 80-percent failure rate of early reengineering efforts indicates that process innovation and improvement are not trivial undertakings. If deep cultural and learning transformations cannot be accomplished, process reengineering will likely prove a waste of time. Corporations that do not, moreover, treat the learning as seriously as they do the technology of process management, stand to lose the competitive edge to those who do.

Mastering Business Process Management

Although implementing business process management can deliver immediate value, BPM technology alone is not enough. Implementing BPM technology will not make a business "process competent" any more than the act of buying a car means a person knows how to drive. Experience with prior technology acquisitions, such as ERP, shows that businesses that adopted the same technologies—and even used the same implementation consultants—achieved very different business results as a consequence of how they actually learned to exploit the strengths, and avoid the weaknesses, of the technology. Thus, to use BPM effectively companies must develop and acquire process management competencies.

Building a BPM competency requires three components: a sound understanding by senior managers of BPM's strategic importance to the business; the setting of clear targets by strategists, defining precisely how BPM is going to be used; and the possession of appropriate skills by implementers so that they can do their work effectively and efficiently. Because these three competencies reinforce one another, they must be developed together.

Companies need to create a virtuous circle in which understanding, targets and skills reinforce one other to earn support for the BPM initiative by demonstrating its real value to the business. They need to make sure that the business and its customers, suppliers and trading partners fully understand and exploit the power of process management. They must consciously nurture the competencies that they gain from using and evaluating the methods and technologies.

When an organization adopts a new tool, a common assumption is that training is a binary proposition, i.e., that people are either trained, or they are not. Experience indicates that this assumption is flawed. Meilir Page-Jones, industry luminary and president of Wayland Systems, developed a seven-stage model of expertise that describes what people actually go through as they learn and develop skills associated with a new paradigm.[5] Developing an environment and a process for moving people through these seven stages should be high on the CEO's and CIO's priority lists. The following discussion outlines how Page-Jones' stages may be applied to a BPM implementation.

Stage 1: Innocent—Never heard of BPM. Some have never heard of BPM. Others have already seen references to business process management in trade publications. They may be vaguely aware of the existence of BPM, but may not see the possible relevance to their situations. Someone may be considered innocent if that person has not learned enough about BPM to be aware of some of the tradeoffs associated with it, some of its costs, some of its benefits, or where and when it might be appropriately applied.

Business processes have become insidiously more and more complex, yet there was no sharp transition. The earth was not hit by a complexity asteroid that suddenly made business processes three orders of magnitude more complex and cast our reptilian process techniques into extinction. Page-Jones calls the way in which process complexity actually increased the "Frog in the Pan." This is because although a frog will jump out of a pan of hot water, a frog that is placed in a pan of cold water and slowly heated will fail to leap forth and will actually boil to death. The temperature gradient is so gradual that there will never be a point at which the frog declares, "Boy, it's suddenly gotten hot in here! I think I should hop out." Many Innocents are experiencing "Frog in the Pan" and are trying to tackle problems of the 21st century with approaches of the past without realizing that the problems they're facing are the very ones that the third wave of BPM was created to alleviate.

Moving someone from the innocent stage to the next stage is a process of providing gentle introductions to the technology through articles, presentations, seminars and participation in related associations. The goal is to inform and educate. Management-level introductory presentations can place the more global issues of BPM into perspective.

Stage 2: Aware—Has read something about BPM. Stage 2 people have noticed that the water is getting decidedly warm, if not downright hot. So, they are actively seeking BPM methods and techniques that will get them out of the pan or at least reduce the heat. Their interest level is high but their knowledge level is low, being limited to a few terms and definitions and not based on any practical BPM experience.

At stage two, the person has become aware of the benefits and costs of the technology, as well as when and where it might be successfully applied. The Aware can generally describe what is involved with BPM, and at a high level can compare and contrast BPM with older approaches. The person has a talking knowledge of the subject. The Aware technicians may seek to examine the relationship of BPM to existing EAI, workflow, portal and B2B implementation strategies. The Aware business architect will seek to understand how BPM may lead them to change the way they conduct process modeling and process improvement.

A person at this stage has not yet achieved the paradigm shift. The Aware's intellectual framework for BPM is still based upon drawing analogies to the old ways of doing things, and the person probably still draws upon erroneous assumptions when thinking or making decisions about third-wave BPM. Moving a person from this stage to the next involves establishing and executing an initial training program of readings, seminars and workshops in the working fundamentals of BPM.

Stage 3: Apprentice—Has studied BPM. At this stage, the person is well aware of the high level concepts of BPM; however the Apprentice may or may not have experienced the paradigm shift. This person cannot effectively apply the technology on his or her own, but can begin to contribute to the use of the methods and techniques. If a Stage 3 person absorbs everything from a seminar, then the Apprentice is minimally equipped to tackle a true, full-sized project in the corporate jungle. Usually, however, an Apprentice does not grasp everything or has difficulty scaling the techniques up from a case study to a real project. It could be said that most Stage 3 people know just enough to be dangerous!

Moving the person from this stage to the next involves establishing and executing a training program that focuses on the details of BPM. It is now appropriate to introduce selective BPM tools training. At this stage and its transition to the next, hands-on training becomes very important. To this end, an apprentice should be teamed with a *mentor*, someone who uses the technology naturally and automatically and can explain the internal process involved with BPM technology.

For the Apprentice, it is sink or swim at this stage. It is time to throw the Apprentice into a project using the new methods and technologies. The mentor expects that the Apprentice will swallow a little water and, at times, gasp for breath. Fortunately, the mentor serves as a lifeguard. The mentor has to closely monitor the Apprentice to ascertain progress, capitalize on the lessons that are learned from mistakes, and adjust the detailed goals of the development process.

Stage 4: Practitioner—Ready to use BPM. The rite of passage to Stage 4 is the use of BPM methods and techniques on at least one significant project. Achieving "Stage 4-hood" is for many people the most difficult transition of the six transitions between stages. The fledgling Stage 4 is asked to take newly learned techniques and apply them to a corporate project with the usual demonic cocktail of politics, deadlines, changing requirements and distractions. At the same time, the Practitioner is attempting to recall what he or she learned in class and scale up the examples 10- or 100-fold.

At this stage, the Practitioner is ready to make process-engineering decisions on his or her own. Mistakes are a significant contributor to the learning process at this level, and the Practitioner should be allowed to make them. That's okay, because in the third wave backing out of a process change is as simple as flipping a switch and larger changes can be simulated before use. This stage is generally a self-managed process but still needs the presence of a mentor to make assignments and observe results. The Practitioner is given full responsibility for assignments and is an active participant in project review activities. The Practitioner will have begun to consider a host of related issues, including:

- The organizational implications of BPM.
- Requirements for deep integration of BPM in existing methodologies such as Six Sigma.
- The need for training and tool support.
- Implications for industry data and collaboration standardization efforts.
- Examination of the benefits to value-chain integration and adaptation.

Movement to the next stage is a function of time, practice, an increasing knowledge base and specific mentoring.

Stage 5: Journeyman—Uses BPM naturally and automatically. At this stage, participants are able to apply the technology in normal situations and do not require the presence of a mentor to accomplish quality work. This stage also requires a self-managed learning program to increase understanding. The Journeyman still calls upon the mentor when new or especially complex problems appear. However, the Journeyman is self-sufficient and more often the source, rather than the recipient, of BPM advice. Like those who can develop sophisticated financial planning spreadsheets today, the Journeyman commands respect because he or she has both the skills and the knowledge to build new models. The Journeyman continuously seeks opportunities to apply BPM within his or her business.

Movement to the next stage is a function of experience, increasing depth of knowledge, and the evolution of the generic, problem-solving framework. This problem-solving framework is developed through interacting with a Master-level person on new or complex situations. In this stage, the solution process is more important than the solution details.

Stage 6: Master—Has internalized BPM and knows when to break the rules. The Master is not only adept with BPM techniques and technologies, but also possesses a profound methodological foundation. Beyond the "whats" and "hows," the Stage 6 knows the "whys" of BPM. This depth allows the Master to sometimes break a surface rule, while adhering to a more fundamental methodological principle.

The Master will carefully consider the intersection of business strategy and BPM—how a company competes in a world where business processes can be captured, demonstrated, shared, instrumented, analyzed and deployed within and between companies. The Master may ask questions about BPM regarding complex issues such as intellectual property, the ability to formalize and potentially protect process designs through copyright, patents, contracts, trademarks or other devices.

The Master is a good instructor because his or her theoretical and practical knowledge provides the wherewithal to tackle difficult questions from others climbing the competency ladder. For the Master, continued learning is a matter of keeping up with progress being made with BPM methods and technologies. Every organization needs access to

Masters, either on staff or on retainer. The Master can handle new or complex applications of BPM, review Journeyman level work, show alternative or creative solutions to problems, point out subtleties in process engineering decisions, and help keep the organization up to date.

Movement to the next stage is strictly up to the individual. It is based on the individual's thought processes and experiences. Moving up to the Expert stage generally requires the individual to be actively engaged in a broad range of applications of BPM in new or unusual situations.

Stage 7: Expert—Writes about BPM modeling and methodology, publishes learned articles, gives lectures and develops ways to push the envelop and extend BPM methods and technologies. The Expert is at the pinnacle of BPM methods and technologies. The Expert is generally recognized for his or her contributions to the industry, and is often asked to lecture or give presentations at national meetings for peers. In short, *knowledge transfer* is the key to success in implementing business process management throughout the enterprise. As we mentioned before, BPM is not a big-bang conversion. The seed must be planted, initial BPM infrastructure put in place, and pilot projects undertaken to establish BPM competency. Having established such a greenhouse for nurturing competencies based on the seven-stage process of BPM mastery, a company can grow into a mighty process-managed enterprise.

Corporations won't be the only "greenhouse" for developing BPM mastery. The business world needs properly trained university graduates who can hit the ground running and contribute to building the company of the future. *Internet World* magazine's August 2002 Digital Tapestry column, "The New M.B.A. Curriculum," explains and is reprinted in Appendix E.

At some time during the journey from *innocent* to *master* an epiphany will occur. It will be something like, "This is as it should always have been." However, no methodology and no technology is a silver bullet—including BPM. BPM is as powerful as it is precise because the designers chose trade offs based on the first principles of business and technology architecture. Even though BPM can be considered to stand at the leading edge of enterprise computing today, the underlying concept of a design-driven—in this case business-process driven—architecture is hardly new. BPM is not a panacea for software development. While the abstraction of process data and a process virtual machine—based on process calculus—does not limit the ability to develop any process, any procedure or any algorithm, initial process management systems will not be used for all application development tasks. While theoretically unlimited (because of process calculus) in its application to the construction of enterprise processes and applications, companies will find the most appropriate, unique and creative uses for BPM as they build mastery. As companies learn more and gain experience, they will then demand more from BPM systems and tools. The spreadsheet and relational data management systems were initially more limited in their capability than they are today. Likewise, BPM will advance in step with the growing communal knowledge of those who master it.

Getting Started

After 20 years of experience with computer-based processes and process management, there is little new to be said about how to introduce new theories and new systems into a company. What is new is that, as a result of the third wave of BPM, the technical issues are receding and new tools are now available that can facilitate all business process work. Whether companies start at the top and work down, or from the bottom and work up, they will use BPM to rapidly build their process capability.

Like data management tools that spurred the growth in data-aware applications, process management systems are now available to spur the growth in process-aware information systems. Companies will adopt BPM much like they adopted relational data management—organically. Companies will identify a business domain where managing the process has become problematic and will apply the new tools naturally and readily. The shift from hierarchical, to relational, data management, was triggered by a realization of the significance of data embedded in the previous generation of applications. As the volume of data grew, and the relationships across different data sets became apparent, companies rushed to deploy a standards-based DBMS that could share data across several applications. By taking this step they put in place a consistent, reliable and manageable capability to manage all business data. Companies will do the same with process management systems. With a commitment to processes as a way of enabling business change, and armed with BPM capabilities, companies are free to concentrate on the harder cultural and organizational issues of developing the process-managed enterprise.

A company's first BPM implementation should kick-start the virtuous cycle by delighting business managers, inspiring them to think of new opportunities and equipping implementers with a set of useful new tools and skills. The ideal inaugural project will be highly visible, address an issue of real importance to the business, hit exactly the right level of risk for the business culture, and provide a convincing demonstration that BPM can achieve what other technologies could not.

The two key parameters in developing such a project are the phase of process management to be undertaken and the scope of the process to be managed. Companies have to decide whether to attack the discovery and design of a process before moving on to manage it, or whether to integrate systems in order to implement, execute and refine a process. A company can opt to focus on an internal process that is well within its zone of control, or it can deliberately go select a cross-business process that will be key to the future of the enterprise. There is no right answer—the choice depends entirely on the business context and the availability of resources.

Vision alone is not likely to win support, or funding, for the implementation of BPM. Although the amount of funding required is modest compared with the size and scale of the largest reengineering projects of the past, BPM advocates must still deal with skepticism on the part of executives who have invested in past programs ranging from ERP to e-business, many of which failed to deliver the promised business results.

Companies should build support on a process-by-process basis, and each "project," as demonstrated in chapter seven, must show a meaningful *return on process investment*. The second process will then be easier to justify than the first, and companies will be able to accumulate evidence of success. They will build out BPM starting with one department, division or workgroup. This bottom-up approach to business case design recognizes that executives are unlikely to accept a justification based on the practices of other firms or on industry benchmarks. Too many reengineering investment decisions were made on the basis of anecdotal benefits that are no longer credible, especially in light of exposés of questionable accounting practices uncovered at the very companies that provided many of the benchmarking numbers for e-business and ERP.

Given that companies tend to remain loyal to the unique styles of strategic planning that have already made them successful, the following guidelines serve as points of consideration for the initial assimilation of BPM methods and technologies into the organization (each company can provide its own elaboration of the guidelines to place them in its specific context):

- Build a learning organization around process management: inform, educate and train.
- Start with process discovery and design proof-of-concept pilot projects.
- Seed the BPM platform and integrate tools into existing projects.
- Implement BPM program management to spread BPM competencies.
- Design new business processes from the outside in, starting with the customer and the customer's customer.
- Take on initial BPM projects in *parallel* with current projects in order to manage risk and to discover opportunities for accelerating current "laggard projects" using BPM.
- Look for small mission-critical projects that will yield a large mission-critical payback. Alternatively, try to solve a big problem, such as total value-chain management, that other approaches have so far failed to address and whose "return on investment" is unclear if it went ahead based on a more traditional implementation approach.
- Take on projects containing elements of application integration, workflow, service-oriented-architecture, application component orchestration, Web services and value-chain integration to gain a broad base of experience.
- Seek opportunities to test the promised benefits of BPM. For example, focus on process designs oriented toward achieving any one of the key goals such as process customization, end-to-end process design, reduced cost of process ownership, full leverage of existing systems, self-aware and self-metering processes, business level transactions, continuous process change, unified enterprise process modeling and collaborative process design.
- Experiment to find out what distinguishes BPM from existing preconceptions of quality management or traditional reengineering.

- Use BPM to amplify what the company is already doing. Don't stovepipe BPM as the latest new initiative or killer-app. When people say, "Why should I replace my XYZ program with BPM?" reply, "Keep right on with XYZ. BPM can help."
- Outsource commodity processes and measure the provider's performance, or identify a business service you have wanted to sell to others but lacked a practical means for doing so.
- Establish enterprise-wide standards for process management and a centralized process repository.
- Use cross-industry standards to collaborate at the business process level, powering implementation with a private process management system.

Once BPM is proven in practice, companies should consider how to gradually phase out work on existing "process point projects." They should start in one business unit and establish a center of excellence, using BPM to draw together existing process-related activities to create synergy and add systematic support. Partners will also acquire BPM capability, and a network of BPM systems will develop at key nodes in the value chain.

Companies can expect many people in the organization to be interested in BPM and to want to take on their own initiatives. That's okay, because the beauty of BPM is that processes can easily be connected, whether designed separately in different divisions, by different people, from different perspectives, top-down or bottom-up. The process description language allows multiple processes to combine and collaborate. One process can exchange data with another. One process can become a subprocess of another. One process can govern the lifecycle of another set of processes. One process can inherit a new capability from another. One process can monitor another. These capabilities are not reliant on technical integration of systems, but inherent attributes of process data.

When the "lights turn on," companies won't turn back. They will build new applications with processes and build new processes with processes. The process data generated by processes will become a valuable asset upon which companies will build new process-aware information systems. As companies discover the possibilities, they will open their thinking to new and innovative ways of introducing process management into their organizations in order to drive agility, collaboration, connectivity, visibility, accountability and control. By establishing a stable and scalable BPM environment, a raft of process improvement initiatives can be undertaken at the speed of business thought, rather than the snail's pace of traditional integration and software development.

By taking on a wide range of initial projects, companies can establish a broad BPM knowledge base that will serve as a foundation upon which to build the process-managed enterprise. The goal is to achieve double leverage: gain immediate benefits from BPM, and build the foundation for process management growth, continuous change and innovation.

The Process Portfolio

Along the road to BPM implementation, companies should never lose sight of one overriding principle: that the primary objective of process management is to deliver compelling value as perceived and measured by customers. Cost reduction is a necessary but not a sufficient condition of success. If a company is not also achieving simplicity, convenience, quality, and customer satisfaction—or some other outcome that provides value to customers—it may be unwittingly committing to a strategy of competing solely on low price rather than on value. Process improvement is not simply a cost-cutting exercise. A process-managed company eliminates low-value work and automates tasks to carve out time so that its people can work with business partners to find new ways to create value for customers. As Peter Drucker observes, "Because its purpose is to create a customer, the business enterprise has two—and only two—basic functions: marketing and innovation. Marketing and innovation produce results: all the rest are costs."

The strategy firm McKinsey & Company similarly maintains that competitive advantage consists of the progress a company makes as its competitors, paralyzed by confusion, complexity and uncertainty, sit on the sidelines.[6] According to McKinsey, the key is to be ready to act as soon as it becomes possible to estimate, with reasonable accuracy, the risks and rewards of an investment in process. In process management, the advantage lies not with the first mover alone, but with the first mover that can scale up process improvement and process innovation once process analysis has shown the way forward, making it possible to forecast substantial benefits from larger investments.

CEOs who approach corporate strategy as a portfolio of initiatives, each aimed at achieving favorable outcomes for the entire enterprise, can extend this approach to the high-level management of a portfolio of processes—the challenge being to convert raw processes into new profits. To achieve the desired outcomes, a company must manage its process portfolio with the same rigor that a venture capital firm uses to manage its portfolio of investments. They must organize a disciplined search for the best processes, inside and outside the firm; nurture and enhance promising processes; and consider the option of acquiring process from third parties through collaboration, purchase or alliance. Process portfolio management is a business process like any other and we recommend placing it too under "process management."

The Critical Factor for Success

Learning how to deliver ever more compelling value to customers is the ultimate goal of process management. Over a decade ago, in the *Harvard Business Review*, Arie DeGeus of Royal Dutch/Shell described the critical factor for reaching that goal: "We understand that the only competitive advantage the company of the future will have is its ability to learn faster than its competitors."[7] Let the learning begin.

References

[1] Colony, George F., "Naked Technology,"
http://www.forrester.com/Info/0,1503,287,FF.html

[2] Cherian George, "Change, Easier Said than Done," *HBS Working Knowledge*,
August 2002.

[3] Senge, Peter M., *The Fifth Discipline: The art and practice of the learning organization.*
Doubleday/Currency. 1990.

[4] Fingar, Peter, *The Blueprint for Business Objects,* Prentice Hall, 1995.

[5] http://www.waysys.com/

[6] The McKinsey Quarterly, 2002 Number 2, *Just-in-Time Strategy for a Turbulent World*

[7] DeGeus, Arie, "Planning as Learning," *Harvard Business Review*, p. 74, March-April
1988.

Nine

Tomorrow's Interview in BPM3.0 Magazine

A system must have an aim. Without an aim, there is no system. ... A system must be managed. ... The secret is cooperation between components toward the aim of the organization.
—W. Edwards Deming, *The New Economics*

This book has covered a lot of material that we'd like to consolidate into an everyday conversation. To help understand how business process management can help companies, we reflect back from the future with a fictitious interview in the equally fictitious BPM3.0 magazine. In this interview Acme Express suffered, as many companies have, from the business-IT divide. But they did something about it and tell their story to Editor-in-Chief, Paul Hollander.

ACME Express wins industry award for innovation

Yesterday, the Logistics Industry Council presented ACME Express their annual award for innovation and best practice. *BPM3.0* was granted an exclusive interview with ACME Express executives Hilary Rosen, President and CEO, and Barry Jay, CIO, explaining their different perspectives on how business process management systems have enabled them to move beyond the tyranny of legacy systems and regain control of their future business direction.

BPM 3.0: Thank you for taking some time out from your busy schedule to meet with us today. Our readers watch the Logistics Industry Council's innovation awards closely for they provide great insight into what companies should be thinking and doing as they prepare their own futures. Hilary, can you tell us a little bit about what set your company on the path that led to this prestigious award?

Rosen: ACME Express was first established in 1970. Our parcel delivery business had grown rapidly through the first decade, expanding to all parts of the globe. It looked like the bubble would never burst and although business slowed toward the end of the 90s, things still looked rosy despite an ongoing debate over how to best manage our considerable investment in IT. Much time and effort had been put into understanding how IT might enhance our business and we understood that the future of the business was irrevocably tied to technology. The question we posed was how to manage technology to gain a greater competitive advantage.

We were always being presented with a plethora of new "innovations" many of which seemed promising at first, but ended up costing much more than we estimated and delivered much less than was promised. We were frustrated with the lack of delivery, finger pointing when things went sour, and ever increasing IT costs. Our board would revert to organizational realignment of the IT function. We went through cycles of decentralization and re-centralization, outsourcing and in-sourcing for over a decade. With every restructure a new CIO was put in place. And with every new CIO, a different approach to the provision of business applications—in-house development, consulting led development, purchased packages, purchased on-line service. But every approach came with a sting attached. By the end of the nineties, the complexities of managing a global service, with ever more demanding customers, in an increasingly competitive market were putting unsustainable pressures on our business.

It felt like the company was about to implode. It didn't matter which way we turned, which IT innovation we implemented, which management technique we employed or business model we adopted, we just couldn't see an end to the madness. Everyone was hurting: customers complained at the lack of response to their needs, function heads continuously complained about and fought over control of IT, countries protested over lack of localization capabilities, suppliers failed to deliver on promises and shareholders expressed concerns over the dwindling earnings per share. It was time to regain control and we began our journey to do just that.

BPM 3.0: You obviously faced many challenges our readers likewise face. How did you get started in the face of such tremendous challenges?

Rosen: We initiated the ACME 2020 Vision program, a strategic program that would examine all aspects of the business with, first and foremost, a focus on customer needs. With that in mind we then turned our attention to our information assets, opportunities to leverage technology and an inward analysis of competencies that are truly core to our business. As this exercise developed, a number of organizational inefficiencies and spurious or even insidious behaviors surfaced. There was a glaring disconnect between our strategic vision and the services delivered by IT. Many ineffective and inefficient processes had become ingrained in our IT systems. IT systems were dictating business processes and had become an easy target to blame for any or all mishaps in the company.

Past reorganizations of the IT department didn't solve these problems. In fact, the turnover of IT staff and the ensuing different approaches further deepened the confusion. An increasing amount of mission-critical data was embedded in desktop applications and "shadow" business processes emerged, developed by user departments in a reaction to a perceived lack of response to their needs. The process of communicating our global business requirements was error prone and time consuming. It was so cumbersome that the process often rendered applications out-of-date before they were implemented.

BPM 3.0: What other problems did you uncover from your company-wide introspection?

Rosen: A number of key facts became clear. IT permeated every aspect of the business and this was brought home by the risk assessment of the Y2K Bug. IT innovations rarely delivered break-through business results and typically just added more complexity. Globalization required a flexible balance between global standardization and local autonomy. Customers were no longer satisfied with a generic service; they wanted customized solutions. Growth through acquisition fuelled our growing business process complexity and associated IT diversity. The company was losing the very foundation blocks of its early success: agility, operational excellence and service quality. Integrating customers and suppliers electronically was much more difficult than we had imagined and the solutions developed were rarely reusable. Contracts and service level agreements with our service providers were often badly conceived and ill managed, leading to rancor and confusion. Our supply chain integration initiatives had partly failed due to a lack of trust between partners and a concern over visibility of one and other's business processes. Core intellectual assets of the business were often hard to identify and impossible to untangle from the contextual activities and systems we were using.

BPM 3.0: That pretty much sets the stage for a situation any CEO would be happy to walk away from, especially if they didn't come up through the technology ranks. How were you able to help find a cure to this technology conundrum?

Rosen: I consider myself to be somewhat technology literate, but I don't mind admitting that this is the first time I have actually felt in control of the information technology that runs my business. What really surprises me is that the success of our 2020 Vision program can be attributed to a genuine breakthrough that grew out of the IT industry!

In our business IT had always been a "black art." I knew it was vital to our future, but it proved impossible to manage effectively. Now, however, we're able to use IT as the infrastructure for our business process ecosystem and it is this that provides me with a completely fresh view of every aspect of our business. My CIO provided me with a dashboard, fed from our new company-wide BPM systems. The dashboard gives me up-to-the-minute information against our key performance indicators. Better still, our business experts are able to accurately simulate changes in our business processes and if necessary, demonstrate their value to the board before implementing them the next day.

Our business process approach, however, extends way beyond technology. It's now a way of life. It permeates the entire business. Our process repository has become the most shared and reused asset in the company. Our sales force uses it to negotiate deals. Our operations personnel use it to derive new efficiencies. Our marketing department uses it in simulations and what-if analysis. Our IT department uses it to negotiate contracts with service providers and our legal and administration team use it to protect our intellectual property and for ISO standards qualification. In fact, the whole organization has become infused with a new form of business intelligence that has empowered everyone and stimulates new ways to tackle planning, design and operational challenges.

BPM 3.0: What's so different about the BPM approach compared to traditional solutions in business applications, knowledge management and workflow?

Rosen: The answer lies, in part, in your question. Previous attempts to align IT applications with business behavior are, by their very nature, separate and independent solutions to a particular problem. The very names of the applications tell the story: enterprise resource planning, customer relationship management, supply chain management, enterprise marketing management, product delivery management, trade settlement management, demand management, warehouse and logistics management, procurement management and so on. Each solution has its own strengths but tends to set up a center of gravity that extends beyond its original purpose. In doing so it subsumes the essential nature of our business processes into its own value system and behavioral model—what I call the Holy-Grail effect. The great strength of the BPM approach is that it doesn't attempt to replace these applications, it orchestrates them and binds them to the way we want to conduct our business. A business process methodology can therefore be viewed as a horizontal layer of business level infrastructure, or glue, that enables us to manage the business rules, behaviors and events regardless of the underlying IT application. It has also allowed us to change the way we develop applications themselves. In fact, we hardly think about applications today, we design and deploy business processes.

BPM 3.0: A number of CEOs will be skeptical; they're still recovering from the last "Killer App." Isn't this just ERP on steroids?

Rosen: No, that's the point. ERP has its strengths, but because of its closed architecture, it failed to address the fundamental requirement of putting our management team back in control of the business. ERP was a solution to bad IT, with it we transitioned from a "messy tangle of in-house solutions" with business rules embedded to a "well-ordered closed system" still with business rules embedded. While it solved some of the issues of standardization it came with a terrific cost. We lost our ability to differentiate ourselves around our core value propositions.

BPM 3.0: What's the difference between business process management and the business process reengineering initiatives you launched in the early 1990s?

Rosen: Business process management is the means for reengineering, but it's radically more effective than past techniques. We are able to implement changes to our processes incrementally and in real time. Our consultants work with us within the business, supplementing our own business leaders and supplying specialized process design skills. We've not found it necessary to implement large change programs. The business process management system propagates change throughout the enterprise, naturally and unobtrusively. Our process portal (part of our intranet) gives everyone an insight into our business from their perspective, that of other functions and in the context of our overall objectives. Past reengineering projects at ACME Express were really one-time events. No one thereafter paid much attention to those changes. The rigid computer systems of the time prevented us from making changes without great pain or implementing a new business model.

My CIO tells me our processes were too embedded within the applications themselves so we could not manage or change the processes. To make matters worse, our legacy applications only implemented segments of our overall end-to-end processes. There was no connection between applications at the business process level. Even if we could break down these stovepipes in our company we could not ext approach to our partners. Only when we finally realized that we to focus on processes not applications did we make real progress. It provides a single logical view of our entire company.

BPM 3.0: How has your BPM approach helped you tackle the problem of integration with your customers and suppliers?

Rosen: As we see others adopting the BPM approach we're finding that we can much more rapidly agree on how we can work together. In fact we are taking a leading role in our value chain using BPM, driving adoption because of the streamlined approach to designing and delivering processes and collaborating with our partners. Both ACME and our partners are now armed with a clear definition of the processes we wish to share and those private processes we wish to keep to ourselves for reasons of competitive advantage. In fact, I see a time soon when I'll expect our suppliers to be BPM compliant if they want to do business with us. Or we may even extend BPM capabilities to them, acting as their process outsourcer. Initially, however, many of our customers hadn't adopted BPM. Nevertheless we did see an immediate improvement in the integration process through a much better understanding of our own processes and the speed by which we could implement a customized process tailored to our and their needs. We could model our partner's process for them, without any changes to their applications.

BPM 3.0: ACME has continued to expand globally. How has BPM helped in this regard?

Rosen: Now that we have a clear understanding of our most valued processes we have found it easier to strike the balance between global standardization and local freedom to act. This has resulted in an understanding by all parties in our federated organization and has allowed us to implement localized versions of our business processes. Our country level operations have found this extremely liberating and have been able to become much more responsive in their respective markets. In addition, we have recently been expanding through the acquisition of a number of local delivery operators. Again, clearly defined knowledge of both our global and in-country processes has given us the ability to better assess the applicability of these additions to our network and to more rapidly integrate them regardless of their IT legacy. That's not to say that BPM solves all the problems around the integration of an acquired business, it's just that it's become a more manageable process.

BPM 3.0: A recent publication described how you were creating BPM systems for supply chains in your role as a Fourth Party Logistics Provider. Could you expand on that?

Rosen: Having proved the BPM ecosystem concept within our organization, focused on our core express delivery business, we decided to use the concept as our launch pad into the Fourth Party Logistics (4PL) business, also known as a Lead Logistics Provider. Being a 4PL is all about negotiation based on trust and accurate information. The objective is to provide added value to all participants in the supply chain. Needless to say, overseeing and tracking an entire supply chain requires business processes that work together seamlessly. We could see that each supply chain we looked at had its own set of values that were slightly different from those of any one participant and therefore could be seen as a BPM system in their own right. We took the decision to leverage our experience and BPM platform for this business model. We act as an intermediary, managing, orchestrating and analyzing supply chain processes. We outsourced the execution piece to a third party BPM hosting provider to demonstrate neutrality to partners and to keep our IT folks focused on managing and maintaining ACME's global process infrastructure.

BPM 3.0: Barry, as ACME's CIO, how do you describe the key technical features of your new process management systems?

Jay: Technically our business process ecosystem is composed of a number of artifacts. We use the Business Process Modeling Language to define the behavior of all of ACME's activities and systems. It is an XML schema designed to represent business processes. You won't be surprised to hear that we manage these knowledge assets on the system called a Business Process Management System (or BPMS for short). It is the execution and management environment for our processes and consists of part model repository and part transaction monitor. It is coupled with process design, simulation and analysis tools. For automated access we use a language designed for the purpose. It allows us to manipulate and interrogate processes and their design, much like we use SQL in our database environment. It's called Business Process Query Language (BPQL). Like BPML, it's also based on XML.

BPM 3.0: How would you differentiate BPM from workflow solutions and, to some extent, collaboration tools?

Jay: In the past, both task management and collaboration tools tended to be centered around human activity and to a large extent have been seen as poorly integrated additions to our core, mission-critical applications. They are unable to provide the necessary continuity of the real-world processes that span our entire business. We sometimes use the term "ecosystem" to describe our BPM environment because it is exactly that—a value management system that encompasses all aspects of business activity. The BPM environment covers human activity, application processes, infrastructure services, business-opportunity discovery, business simulation and the implementation of our new business concepts.

BPM 3.0: Models, repositories and executable code; that sounds a lot like Integrated CASE. What's the difference?

Jay: Yes it does sound like I-CASE, but there are significant differences. BPML and BPMS work together to provide both a language for defining all aspects of the business and a means by which business level transactions can be executed. The execution engine is more akin to a transaction monitor than to a traditional executable application program. This engine maintains the state of business process transactions as they are executed by a wide variety of underlying applications code and human activities. Remember that the primary role of the process management system for ACME Express is not to supplant applications but to support a higher-level business purpose by orchestration. BPML, on the other hand, is the means by which the business can be modeled, simulated and then once proven, implemented via the BPMS engine. A tangible difference is the direct way in which we can execute changes to the processes. There is no concept of the traditional lifecycle of requirements definition, application design, implementation, test and deployment. Changes are made "live" on the system. Instead of testing, we simulate the impact of change before deployment. We have also found that BPM provides the platform for developing new applications since they then get visibility of end-to-end processes and so can play a much greater role in adding value to the business.

BPML is not a CASE language. It's a meta-language that because of its mathematical roots and its cross-model applicability can act as a translator between a wide variety of modeling techniques and the execution of business transactions. For example, we have integrated Unified Modeling Language, SCOR (supply chain operations reference model), Activity-Based Costing and Balanced Scorecard models using BPML as the *lingua franca*. BPML is the means by which we've been able to capture a set of executable rules that are presented to the process-server which then coordinates business transactions within and between IT applications. In other words, it is neutral to both the modeling technique employed and the underlying IT execution environment.

BPM 3.0: How did you manage the transition to Business Process Management?

Jay: One of the best features of our process management systems is their ability to support migration. Applications can be participants in other processes. It's possible to model application behavior by what's called Process Projection. An application can be a participant in another process, exchanging messages as required to orchestrate end-to-end. We found the BPMS slotted right into the enterprise mix and we were able to deploy processes literally from the very first week. We just started in one area of the business and implemented processes among existing applications. Over time we started to perceive the new system as the means to extend our processes to all parts of the business. BPM has become the central aspect of the way we approach the use of IT within business development.

BPM 3.0: It seems that tool and package support of a process modeling language is critical. Aren't you at the mercy of the software vendors?

Jay: You make a valid point. We first discovered the BPM approach back in 2000 when it had just started to gather momentum through the Business Process Management Initiative. We were among the first end-user organizations to speak to the BPMI.org. Our objective was to satisfy ourselves that the concept would work and that there was a critical mass of IT tool and package vendors working on the language standard before embarking on a pilot of our own. It's true that in the early days we had problems finding software with native support for BPM. But, because BPM is in fact an application of XML, we were able to work with our BPM vendors to easily develop a range of BPM adapters. We are now, however, seeing a wide variety of vendors, both ISVs and service providers offering native BPM support within their products and services.

BPM 3.0: What's been the impact of BPM on the IT function with ACME?

Jay: The impact to the IT organization has been significant. We are now more focused on providing a broad and deep set of infrastructure services to the business. We find that because the business is now more horizontally focused and that business requirements are expressed within the context of overall business processes, we are able to better identify opportunities for common, application level components that span functional and geographic boundaries. The business analysis activities that used to take place within the IT department are now the primary responsibility of our Chief Knowledge Officer. We've found that works for us, but at first it took me by surprise. This has resulted in a much more holistic approach to the management and development of corporate knowledge. Previously, our Knowledge Program was limited to human communication and as a result was perceived as a mechanism for implementing technologies to improve collaboration independent of our core processes. Now it's seen by the entire enterprise as the vehicle for analyzing all behavioral aspects of our processes and is of direct relevance to all aspects of the business. In the role of CIO, I find I have refocused on technology innovation and service level management.

From a third party service perspective, the clarity around core and contextual processes has allowed us to cherry pick services that we wish to outsource and BPM has given us a far greater control over the negotiation and management of such services. It's not, however, a one-sided win, we've found that service providers have benefited from a more explicit understanding of our needs.

From a technology innovation perspective, I found that, despite the transition of the business analysis activities to the KM function, my staff members are highly motivated because they can see where they can add the most value and aren't constantly being blamed for failure to deliver business solutions. On the contrary, we've been able to deliver a number of innovations that have been widely appreciated for their relevance to core business processes. IT processes and business processes are now one—and the IT function and IT systems are as much a participant as an enabler. My sense is that we've finally found our place in the business. Not everyone will view IT the same way but they will find it necessary to get the business involved in process design. The tools are quite natural to use and the processes run at the end of the modeling session, not the end of the year!

BPM 3.0: Hilary, what do you see going forward? How has BPM impacted your financial performance?

Rosen: Innovation and change are our watchwords. We are starting to experiment with automating the adaptation of processes in real time. There are some situations where the ability to implement so-called "smart" processes, that adjust to the needs of our customers, makes sense. An example is ACME's response when a shipment or package goes missing. Because our processes are now explicit they can be read and written by other software, and integrated with sensing systems out there in the real world. We're working with some new vendors that focus in this area of "Process Smarts." Because BPM is based on XML we can extend it to support the new processes we want to develop with partners—as you know we are doing a lot of outsourcing and alliance activities at the current time. We already put time and cost metrics in the process design and have real-time accumulative information as a result, which helps us to stay in control. But this is just the beginning. The results of these calculations can then be associated with switch points within the process based on thresholds or probabilities. We can't tell you exactly what we are doing for competitive reasons, but we can confirm that we intend to protect these innovations in law as far as we can. There are some processes we wish to patent and some for which copyright protection may be appropriate. We'll be using BPM to provide a clear and unambiguous definition. The combination of our BPMS and the explicit process blueprints, clearly demonstrates our ability to execute these unique processes.

BPM 3.0: Fascinating. Thank you.

EPILOG

Experiments never fail.
—Dale Dauten, The Max Strategy

To business people, it seems that technology is always getting more complex. Technical people feel the same way. Over the last five years, delivering business applications has become much more complex, with layer upon layer of new infrastructure requirements and new features. While this has been good for IT industry players that sell new products for new layers, it is not necessarily so good for companies that use them as business tools. When complexity mounts and eventually becomes unmanageable, it's time for action. As Walt Disney once said, objecting to a proposed sequel to his *Three Little Pigs* cartoon, "You can't top pigs with pigs." In the world of business, stacking a thousand doghouses one atop the other to build a skyscraper is a great proposition for doghouse vendors, but not for future occupants. Skyscrapers need an architecture of their own—their own paradigm, not a sequel to the doghouse paradigm.

The spreadsheet is a simple yet eloquent example of a useful paradigm shift. The convenience and low cost of the breakthrough was so striking that it led to the PC revolution in business. The spreadsheet could not have been successful had it not been for the fact that personal computers—a standards-based commodity—were spreading like wildfire elsewhere in society. To the business, the PC loaded with a spreadsheet meant a radical simplification of routine calculations, transferring to the everyday business person a function that had once required special programming skills.

A similar simplification and transfer of functions is needed by those pursuing business process development and optimization, for as the management prophets foretell, the next phase of corporate development will require systematic control of the value chain, rather than narrow-gauge process fixes. Michael Hammer has admitted that managing such wholesale change is mind-numbingly complex. In fact, it is no longer possible without computer assistance. The technology-planning horizon for Global 5000 companies is now a synthesis of software engineering *and* process engineering. With the widespread adoption of application servers, component-based development and Web services, the field is ripe for the wildfire spread of process management.

Some paradigm shifts created by the IT industry have been truly "radical"—disruptive, costly and unappealing. BPM is different. The architects of the third wave bowed low to the futility of trying to persuade business to switch from one three letter acronym to another. They paid close attention to the urgent needs of businesses to *preserve, extend* and *flex* their existing investments, as well as to enable future opportunity and growth. Building on what already exists in companies everywhere, the third-wave innovators have provided a new level of convenience—the open vista of native process management. Those seeking a sound business and technology architecture for building the process-managed enterprise will think twice before stacking doghouses, and then calling the result "The Company of the Future."

Our message is equally clear for technicians, both in the software industry and the IT shops of major corporations: Build new applications on a process foundation, for the CxO team expects nothing less.

We might well have concluded by paraphrasing the conclusion of Hammer and Champy's original work on reengineering: "Business process management is the only thing that stands between many corporations and disaster." Instead, we prefer to offer this simple, straightforward advice: Embrace process management in the way companies adopted data management decades ago by separating out data for application-independent management, analysis and controlled sharing. At that time, companies knew they had a data problem, and they responded by recognizing the value of relational data management systems. We believe that companies are now recognizing they have an analogous *process problem*. The balance of power in the business-IT relationship *must* shift, away from the need to squeeze business processes into the prepackaged fashions of the IT industry, and toward the ability to design, improve and transform business processes that BPM enables.

BPM does much more than facilitate process design. It provides a direct path from vision to execution. As we stated earlier in this book, it's not so much a matter of "rapid application development" as "*remove* application development" from the business cycle. Show the BPM capability to any executive at any level and they will understand inside five minutes how to break through the IT logjam. Some may still want to prevent managers from defining business processes themselves, saying it is too complex a job and should be left to specialists. That may be true right now, but it won't be by the week after next.

In conclusion, it might be well to recall what Peter Drucker once said about predictions:

> It is not so very difficult to predict the future. It is only pointless. But equally important, one cannot make a decision for the future. Decisions are commitments to action. And actions are always in the present, and in the present only. But actions in the present are also the one and only way to make the future.[1]

Winning companies will invent, not forecast, their own futures. BPM provides the ability to create the future by *innovating with process*, without the costs of reengineering or adding more layers to the already complex technology stack.

A business experiment that fails is a business that failed to experiment. The third wave of BPM is new, and it needs to be done—now.

References

[1] Drucker, Peter F., *Managing in a Time of Great Change,* Truman Talley Books, 1995.

Appendix A

The Language of Process

One of the images I have in mind when I contemplate the universe, is that it is constructed upon a simple pattern of order that may be seen in any and all phenomena, no matter how complex.
—Jonas Salk

Consider carpentry as a field of human activity. "Hammering," "sawing," "screwing," and "measuring," using "hammers," "saws," "nails," "screws," "screwdrivers," "glue guns," "levels," "measuring tapes," and "carpenter's pencils": these words form a vocabulary describing the operations that can be performed in this field, and the means for carrying them out. Now consider business processes as a field of human activity. Processes, process data, activities, messages, rules, computation, process branching, compensating activities, exceptions, sequences, joins, splits, operations, assignments, transformations, schedules, rules and time constraints: These likewise form part of a vocabulary describing the operations that can be performed in the field. The tools for realizing these operations are process modeling languages. These languages provide semantics for business processes and unify the different vocabularies of process development, system integration, workflow, human interaction and transaction management, much as blueprints help the architect and the carpenter find a common language that enables them to work together.

An Open Process-Modeling Language Standard is the Enabler

Today's global telephone system simply couldn't exist without standards. The Internet, the network of networks, couldn't exist without standard protocols. It's easy to imagine that if each computer company offered its exclusive version of network protocols or Hypertext Markup Language, the Internet would utterly lack its "inter," its role as a network that connects machines and processes all over the computing and geographical world, each of which may use different vocabularies to describe what they do. Plenty of proprietary network protocols and private networks were to be found on the market in the past, but the availability of an open, universal standard changed everything. The Internet is ubiquitous, radically inexpensive to access and use, but still allows companies to build all manner of commercial offerings on top of it. Netscape was the first stratospheric commercial offering built atop the new network of networks; many other such commercial projects have come along, and many have passed on, since. Their success or failure was determined by the marketplace, not by the technology of the Internet itself.

It's easy to imagine that if each computer company offered its exclusive version of a modeling language for business processes, chaos would reign and the market for process solutions would remain small.

An open, universal language for describing business processes would, and, we hope, will, provide a ubiquitous business process management platform atop which computer companies can build new value.

A complex mix of marketplace dynamics, set against the compelling mathematical foundation inherent in process calculus, will govern the success of any modeling language vying for attention in the marketplace. Some computer companies will naturally seek to enforce their will on the process battleground by carving out their own proprietary language of process, believing they can use their market power to secure competitive advantage and lock in their customers. In the long run, however, the marketplace always wins. The Internet itself bears witness to this truth, since no one company or group controls the standards that make the Internet the Internet. Those standards are open to all. But more importantly, the correct routing of Internet packets depends upon algorithms that no one can argue with. We believe that for the emerging business process automation industry to flourish and fulfill its potential, similar principles should apply to the definition of process standards. You can't buck math!

Although several process modeling languages have been developed or are on the drawing board, along with a raft of associated Web services standards proposals, we focus in this book on a business process language that was conceived and developed from the ground up to enable the third wave of business process management, and based on a nonproprietary, royalty-free specification open to all.

Other process-oriented language specifications have been devised based on individual paradigms such as the needs of manufacturing, task management, application integration and Web services orchestration. In addition, there is a considerable body of work within academia referred to as the ontology of process representation. It aims to meet the needs for solving problems in particular application domains, for example planning and scheduling. These roots are significant, for as we explained in Chapter 5, "... the business process itself needs its own technology, its own organizing principles and its own paradigm. Hacking at the holistic BPM paradigm by throwing a grab-bag of individual paradigms at it is just that—hacking." Likewise, pushing task management, integration or nascent Web services technologies beyond their natural limits by adding more features and layers to the products already in use in business won't provide the BPM *management* capability envisaged of the third wave—an environment built from the ground up with a rich process entity at its core. A unifying and simplifying step is required, on which the members of the industry of "BPM technology suppliers" can build new products and new services.

If such systems are to succeed in the marketplace, they will be built on a strong mathematical foundation, as were relational database management systems (DBMS) before. To date, the RDBMS is perhaps the most successful of all enterprise computing infrastructure products. The mission-critical BPMS that end-user companies now demand will likewise stand on the shoulders of giants in the field of process calculus, workflow management, the ontology of process representation, concurrent programming, finite state automata, and other technical disciplines. Its success will, however, depend not so much upon whether it implements one standard or another, for standards-acronyms are only fully understood by members of esoteric committees, but upon the capability it provides to business—the BPMS' features, performance and robustness. This in turn depends not on the detail of individual standards, but upon adherence to the mathematics required for process management to work in practice.

Therefore, because we want to convey the comprehensive requirements for a universal language of process, and not because we choose to ignore other work, we focus our discussion on the Business Process Modeling Language (BPML)[1] published by the non-profit Business Process Management Initiative (BPMI.org). Based on process calculus, BPML pays close attention to the needs of companies wishing to build process-managed enterprises. We do not claim that other approaches are defunct or invalid. Nor do we claim with certainty that other new languages oriented to process management will not emerge in due course. It is possible that a number of process modeling languages will co-exist and that there will be a need for interoperability among them.

Fortunately the process paradigm provides an answer to interoperability: A process expressed in one language can become a participant in another process expressed in a different language. This is called a process interface. It, too, is a process. Therefore, BPMI.org can be expected to continue to develop BPML as a superset of the semantics required for modeling both end-to-end processes and process interfaces. The industry will benefit from interoperability and choice. Although some software vendors may have to provide support for multiple languages for some time to come, those end users and vendors that understand the significance of the process calculus foundation and insist on it will withstand any changes in process standards that one or more vendors may impose on their customers.

The Business Process Modeling Language

BPML is a specification both for building process management systems and for modeling business processes. BPML provides the required abstract model for all processes, along with a standards-based XML schema and syntax for expressing and managing business processes. BPML is the language for process management, just as XML is the language for business data and HTML is the language for hyperlinked Web pages.

Although it is possible for business analysts and technicians to model and execute processes using BPML directly, process management tools built on top of BPML hide the details from non-technical users. The scenario is similar to the way HTML is used: Technically oriented people use it directly while business people use high-level tools built on top of it. Although most users of process management systems will never know that its foundations are steeped in process calculus, this mathematical foundation provides consistency and ensures that everything "works." The same assurance was achieved in the management of data through strict adherence to the relational data model and within data query languages built from relational algebra.

A key characteristic of BPML is that it is directly executable on an IT infrastructure. It relies therefore on the existence of an execution environment. This is not the same as rapid application development, where executable code is generated from a model—BPML *is* the executable code. BPML is executed by a "process virtual machine" within the process management system. This is comparable to the way a Java program is executed by a "Java virtual machine" provided by a computer operating system.

BPML defines only what is required for expressing business processes, not any details relating to the systems developed to run it. Therefore, software companies are free to innovate in terms of the performance, scalability, robustness or other aspects of their products that businesses may look for when comparing different process products and solutions.

BPML defines just what is required to establish a standard for processes, just as the relational model defined just what was required to establish a standard for data. This means that BPML covers aspects such as business activities of varying complexity, business transactions and their compensation, process data management, concurrency, exception handling and operational semantics. BPMI.org does not aim to standardize the approach vendors take to the internal construction of a BPMS. Rather, it provides standards for the formal process model a BPMS should support and should expose to the business via process query languages and process design tools.

BPML processes are clear. The meaning of a BPML expression and what it will do when it executes are never ambiguous—a declarative specification. A BPML process transferred from one vendor's implementation to another both means, and does, precisely the same thing, just as transferring data between databases has no effect on the meaning of the data to the business that originated it.

BPML provides a vocabulary for enabling the persistence and interchange of process definitions across heterogeneous systems and modeling tools. This is crucial to businesses and the process industry alike. Companies want to build their process management infrastructure using best-of-breed components. Much as companies now procure a database from one vendor and applications from another, they will want to do the same for processes. They will also want to incorporate process models they have developed in the past.

BPML defines an abstract model and grammar for expressing any business process, Web service choreography or multiparty business collaboration. It does not define any domain-specific semantics, such as the details of supply chain logistics, enterprise resource planning or customer relationship management. Nor does it contain anything specific to any particular vertical industry.

BPML is the language of choice for formalizing the expression, and execution, of collaborative business interfaces. This includes both the data exchange requirements and the process interface by which data is exchanged. BPML defines process data using XML schemata, allowing industry data standards to be used in conjunction with process definitions. BPML can express the inclusion of the data definitions from an industry standard. An example would be, the content of a purchase order exchanged by two process activities, together with the industry's standard procedure for doing this.

The industry has developed visual high-level BPML modeling tools that can be used to describe both collaborative and transactional processes, in a way that business people will understand. BPML is open to the whole community of process engineers, business analysts and system architects, helping companies coordinate and streamline the development of processes inside and outside the enterprise.

Users of BPML can share process descriptions without divulging the technical implementation details of their companies. The approach breaks the proprietary programming cycle that spawned internal e-business solutions that outside developers could not manipulate and business users could not read or understand. BPML provides the business confidence needed in collaborative commerce.

Business people need to be able to communicate in a way that is comfortable for them. The full potential of any standard language remains unrealized until business people can communicate using it. Like complex XML and HTML syntax, BPML is not designed to be easily readable by most business people. Therefore, BPML also has an equivalent graphical visual notation, the Business Process Modeling Notation (BPMN). BPMN uses a simple set of drawing symbols that represent BPML elements. Users manipulate the symbols—various geometric shapes, arrows, and the like—and link process flows graphically. Underneath its "graphic skin," the model is expressed in the form of BPML that more technical staff can use. To those old-enough to remember, BPMN resembles high-school flow-charting.

BPML and BPMN are unique in their ease of use yet powerful enough to develop sophisticated end-to-end processes. These processes can be as complex as traditional software-based applications. Much as spreadsheet programs provide powerful macro capabilities that allow advanced users to develop complex numerical models, though not all spreadsheet users use, understand, or care about these features, BPML can be used by all users, regardless of their level of "technical" expertise.

As shown in Figure A.1, there is a one-to-one correspondence between BPML and BPMN. The diagram represents the code and the code represents the diagram. There is no loss of information when moving between the two. The clear advantage is the ability to depict processes in a way that business users can both understand and execute.

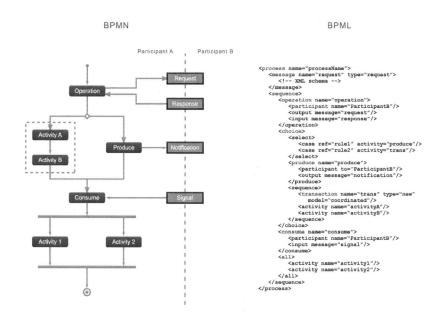

Figure A.1. The Business Process Modeling Notation (BPMN) and
Business Process Modeling Language (BPML version .4, March 2001)

Although BPMN meets the urgent need for process communication on one level, many new and innovative notations for BPML are likely to be developed, built on the foundation that BPMN has established. For example, a project plan is a type of business process, and whereas plans *can* be represented in BPML using timing, resource and constraint attributes, viewing such a plan model in BPMN may not be the best choice; Gantt charts were invented for that purpose. Businesses can expect more and more commonly used business tools such as project planning software to be based—underneath—on process modeling languages. This will allow the planning process, in fact all business information, to be put directly into operation. If the plans a company develops using its preferred desktop tools are based on BPML, they can be directly executed across the entire business, and the company's business partners as well. The "live" plans will link to live systems, inform employees of work to be done, close the loop with managers and supervisors and provide everyone with a live view of project status.

The formal foundation of BPML provides the reliability, coherence and simplicity needed for users to be able to manipulate processes with great confidence. In the past, deploying a new process (application) was fraught with danger and therefore subject to all manner of checks, balances, tests and validation. The risks of rolling out a new application that proved to be unreliable were so huge that weeks or months could pass before it was deemed ready for production. Business processes, on the other hand, are always valid and ready for use. Deploying them is no more complex than saving the design file. Removing a bad process is just as simple. This does not, however, mean that every process design will have the desired impact on the business. Simulation in advance of use is required for complex, high-impact processes. Much as aerospace firms subject their jumbo jets to intensive testing, businesses will put their high-impact processes through a workout before final deployment.

Because the focus of process management is often collaboration between departments or between companies, BPML offers complete support for distributed, concurrent, executable processes. BPML supports multiple process participants, allows for the production and consumption of messages, and supports dynamic process branching, transparent persistence, embedded business rules, nested processes, distributed transactions and exception handling.

In BPML, collaborative process models can contain as many, or as few, execution details as the process designer considers necessary to share between partners or business units. BPML also supports a high level of abstraction, in which execution details can be hidden. This approach promotes collaboration among business partners. A model of the process can be shared even as certain details of implementation can be left to each partner. This is a vital breakthrough for true interoperability, taking integration one step further, to true process collaboration.

BPML copes with the complexity of collaboration among business partners by permitting arbitrarily large numbers of participants to play a role in end-to-end business process designs, at any level of nesting and concurrency. Participants communicate freely with one other, right across the value chain. BPML achieves this by separating and interleaving control flow, data flow and event flow, while adding complementary and orthogonal design capabilities for business rules, security roles and transactions. Messages exchanged between participants contain the process data that is needed for process collaboration.

Tools that create BPML processes from users' actions create new possibilities for innovative IT systems. For example, the concept of "assigning a task" can be defined in BPML. The business manager sends team members a message containing a description of a task, also expressed in BPML. Team members respond with a message indicating whether they can perform the task. The final message goes from the manager to the team member chosen to perform the task. Managers may then make their decision based on process data exchanged between the participants in these interactions. For example, the team members' acceptance messages could include their estimated time for completing the task. The manager could pick the team member with the lowest time estimate, or could examine records of past performance and select someone else. The entire logic of this process can be defined in BPML and shared across the business.

Similarly, in a telecommunications call center, customer service representatives do not think in terms of processes, but this does not prevent process management from forming the basis of minute-to-minute activities. When a customer service representative gets a request from a customer to configure a new circuit, he or she will not say, "What process do I need for that?" Instead, the service representative will interact with the network management system and instigate a process that will do everything necessary for the customer—with no thought given to the term "process," a new process nevertheless comes into being. This may itself be a complex and unique variant of a generic "customer pattern" designed especially for the individual customer, including everything required to ensure that the configuration of the network service meets that customer's requirements.

In a world of business process management systems, more and more operations on IT systems will be instructions to start, stop or interact within processes. Because the process management system has complete knowledge of the state and structure of all its processes, queries and updates can be constructed to modify processes in flight. Just as databases facilitate data transactions, process management systems will enable powerful manipulation of, and updates to, long-lived persistent processes. Extending this further, actions by users of BPM systems could generate dynamic processes "on the fly" that get put directly into operation. It's not an overstatement to claim that such capabilities are rendered technically trivial with the advent of BPML. The creativity and inventiveness of systems developers to read, write, generate, process and manipulate BPML should never be underestimated. BPML is built upon the same set of powerful XML-based technologies that are already in use for a wide range of other purposes in every company and every software development shop on the planet. Those familiar with handling XML will be able to handle BPML.

The Impetus and Design Goals for BPM

In the middle to late 1990s there was an explosion of experimentation with new business models and business-to-business (B2B) integration over the Internet. Various standards proposals were put forward to address the problem of messaging and document exchange between business partners. The CommerceNet eCo Framework Project was the first and most profound examination of the use of XML for e-business. None of these initiatives, however, provided a way to manage a complete e-business scenario. What global corporation would open its back-office systems without a complete overview and a clear description of the processes governing their use? Everyone knew that something was missing. Some even named the missing elements, using words such as "orchestration," but it was not until after much practical experimentation had taken place that it became clear that process management was part of the answer.

Lack of a common language for expressing complex end-to-end business processes—not only the interoperation of services—was hindering the development and adoption of e-business. BPML was therefore developed by the BPMI in the spring of 2000 to provide a foundation for the new class of mission-critical enterprise infrastructure, the then abstract concept of the "BPMS." Such an infrastructure would no longer differentiate between internal and external integration: It would manage complete business processes, not just the public interfaces shared by business partners. In place of having to use separate tools inside and outside the enterprise—enterprise application integration (EAI) internally and B2Bi externally—companies could use one formalism to express all processes in the value chain, paving the way for the development of systems that could execute such processes directly.

BPML was indeed a radical innovation: a language that could model business processes in a way that would translate real-world ideas—the objectives of CEOs, supply chain managers, and strategists—directly to operations, empowering the business user of the system. The language was based on a concept called "design-driven architecture" (DDA). In such an architecture, the "executable" elements are rendered, not as software, but as "data" that is interpreted by an external "engine." The "data" schema (the design) is chosen to perfectly match the intended purpose of the "engine," in this case, the representation, execution and management of business processes. A spreadsheet uses this technique, with rows and columns representing formulae "executed" by the spreadsheet program. The user simply models what is required and the model runs.

Processes such as order management, customer care, demand planning, build to order, product development and strategic sourcing were among the types of end-to-end processes the BPML development group wanted to be able to represent. They recognized that to achieve this would require extending the design-driven principle even to distributed concurrent computation. Their vision was not only to enable "e-business," but also to establish a permanent new foundation for all business systems. This approach, they felt, would make IT infrastructure much more adaptable to the actual, real-world, messy business processes inherent in any enterprise. It could lead to tools that would facilitate the management of constant change. It would be a step-up for the IT industry itself, complementary to the progress that had been made in distributed object based systems.

The developers of BPML realized that to succeed, such a language would need a rigorous mathematical foundation for the new "process data" so that systems built upon it could be as resilient as any existing mission-critical system, such as databases and ERP. They chose to employ a declarative semantics based on process calculus and a concurrent-processing model, so that process management systems could provide end-to-end process analysis, prediction, simulation, metrics and visibility across all participants. Although the mathematical theory may be difficult to understand, as is the relational algebra of the database, the benefits are easy to appreciate.

The Business Process Management Initiative developed rigorous design goals and a charter for the proposed representation and system. These included:

Bridge and unify internal and external integration. In order to unify internal and external integration, the Business Process Management Initiative sought to sharply distinguish the concept of an end-to-end process design from the concept of an interface process design. This functional separation allows each design process to be managed independently, and supports the fluid movement of process work among partners, systems and their security firewalls. The creators of BPML found that this distinction added to, rather than detracted from, the security of e-business, since the rules for permissible, coordinated interactions between partners—the logic governing the flow of business information and the enforcement of business collaboration agreements—would be encoded in the processes themselves, not in technical systems interfaces.

Consolidate human-oriented workflow and machine processes. Previous process-oriented approaches assumed a sharp distinction between the work done by humans and the work done by computer systems. The developers of BPML recognized that this distinction had to be eradicated if such technologies were to "cross the chasm" and become mainstream elements in IT architecture. The workflow community, experts in this area, eagerly joined in to ensure this was the case.

Exploit the growth of hosted services. Web services technologies render "software as a service," a concept that has generated significant interest in the possibility for remote delivery of applications and business services over computer networks, and given rise to the application or business services provider (ASP, BSP) . In recognition of the potential of networked service delivery, BPML was designed to allow the inclusion of hosted services within process definitions and to describe the behavior, discovery and advertising of such services. The developers expected loosely coupled, hosted and network-resident services to play an increasingly important role in how businesses build, source and interact with outsourced third-party business services.

Include key back office systems. Recognizing that legacy systems contain millions of lines of potentially reusable code, BPML was designed so that it could accurately represent existing software and procedures. In this way, past investment in software development could be protected and leveraged by allowing existing procedures to be reused in the design of new processes. The largest, most complex, legacy systems can be tapped for their functionality, and even the tiniest, fine-grained application components can be exposed to participate in business processes. A future refinement of this capability is to automatically allow the representation of standardized packaged applications as business processes, a technique known as *introspection* and *process projection*. This technique is already available for some standard packages.

Build on, rather than replace, middleware. Over the years companies have acquired a variety of infrastructure systems, including messaging, transaction processing, integration brokers, database management systems, object request brokers, directories, rules management systems and a variety of system management tools. More recently they have acquired application servers, enterprise application integration hubs and rules engines. Recognizing the value of prior investments in middleware infrastructure already in place, the BPMI group designed BPML so that new process management systems could sit atop standard middleware components, such as application servers, directories and messaging. The idea was that such existing investments would be integrated once, and only once, to the process management system. Thereafter, numerous processes could be developed and deployed in a stable IT environment with no need to "integrate" individual processes "technically."

Support business change. Based on an analysis of existing process modeling approaches, tools and methods, the design of BPML permits it to represent processes that can react and adapt to changing business requirements in real time. The designers recognized that real-life "business processes" were very different from the "applications" with which companies were most familiar. A real-life business process might evolve, amoeba-like, in quite unexpected ways during its lifecycle, acquiring new participants and new capabilities. BPML makes such "live" structural evolutions independent of the initial process design. The evolving structure is open to analysis by other computer programs.

Distributed execution. Because BPML was designed to be mission-critical, it had to be highly distributed: spanning systems, departments, businesses and even industrial value chains. Distributed "agent-based" architecture was key to the design: Each participant in the end-to-end process is a fully autonomous process. The processes had to operate correctly even if different participants in the process were running on different computers and using different process management software. The design challenge was not merely to enable distributed execution, but also to allow a distributed process to be managed from a single management console. Two different types of distribution had to be supported: distributed execution of the process, on multiple process management systems, and a distributed process management system (for example a cluster or federation), with flexible control of process deployment and partitioning.

Exchange and reuse processes offline. The founders of the BPMI believed they were building the foundation for a new "process industry," and they looked forward to the time when there would be many suppliers of both new processes and new process management systems. Naturally, the full implications of this could not be foreseen, but the essential requirements for the exchange of adaptable packaged processes, both offline as well as online (peer-to-peer), were taken into account. Conventions for this were borrowed from the emerging XML standards. This approach allows complex process data to be freely exchanged and manipulated by commercial and open-source developers alike. For example, a process marketplace might emerge in which processes are sold on CD-ROM or downloaded from a file-swapping Web or FTP site. The BPML developers felt that corporations needed a similar mechanism in-house for sharing "best practices" internally and with partners, and that this would be one of the first applications of a process sharing service.

Reuse processes. BPML was designed so that processes could leverage existing process patterns, enabling a high degree of reuse. Drawing on lessons learned from previous approaches to software reuse, BPML emphasizes composition and adaptation, rather than specialization and generalization. One key goal of process-level reuse is to lay a foundation for the "process factory" and the process manufacturing industry. They sought to enable the rapid assembly, adaptation and packaging of new processes from pre-existing process patterns, much as industrial engineers reuse elementary shapes and objects to build complex three-dimensional product models.

Enable the combination of best-of-breed solutions. No single software company can provide a complete solution or be best of breed in all areas. BPML was designed to allow straightforward integration of commercial off-the-shelf (COTS) products. BPML was also designed to help software companies develop complete best-of-breed BPMS solutions, combining visual modeling tools, process engines and simulators, a trend similar to the emergence of the so-called fourth-generation languages (4GLs) in the field of data management. In this sense, BPML is as adept at integrating processes and applications at run time as it is at integrating software products at build time.

Build on, not replace, existing standards. The BPMI charter recognized the importance of using existing standards and technologies, including standards for the exchange of information and events, business transactions, service advertising and discovery, real-time collaboration and Web services. BPMI adopted the philosophy of "federating" useful standards, and its design methods adhered religiously to this principle. BPML binds to existing and emerging standards, eliminating the fear people naturally have that the standards they have invested in may become obsolete. There are limits to this strategy however. Since much is at stake in the "standards-making" process, the future of process standardization cannot be accurately predicted. Fortunately, this is not an overriding concern for many end user companies who are simply looking for better tools with which to manage their business. Nevertheless, instability in standards can hinder the uptake of new ideas. BPMI insisted on an open process, balanced with the need to get work done and achieve results.

Orchestrate Web services. During 2001 and the early part of 2002, Web services became the marketing banner under which the IT industry rallied a number of important new standards for service interoperability. Considerable efforts were made by BPMI to ensure that process standards and Web services standards were compatible. Web services technology is not a new concept however; it's the convergence of service-oriented architecture—a software trend that began with object orientation in the 1960s—and Internet technologies that began in the 1970s. Web service technology is the latest manifestation of a long line of distributed computing architectures such as Microsoft's DCOM/COM+ and the Object Management Group's Common Object Request Broker Architecture (CORBA and CCM).

Web services technology is important because it removes proprietary barriers to application integration and provides a low cost, universal method for building composite applications. It is to business-to-business interaction what the World Wide Web itself was to business-to-consumer interaction: a radical and low-cost simplification. However, it is not a panacea solution, by any means.

Users of BPM do not require applications to participate using Web services. An over-emphasis upon Web services standardization misses the point that developers of BPM products may wish to develop their solutions in different ways internally, yet still expose a standards-based capability to the business buyer. Pushing Web services standardization too far limits the potential of the industry to innovate, creates overly complex "standards stacks" and leads to "standards battles," since so much is at stake for vendors who choose "the wrong standard." BPMI therefore envisaged the use of Web services as primarily assisting the development of a standard process interface at the business process level, rather than imposing a standard approach to the development of a BPMS.

Apart from the radical reduction in costs they offer, however, Web services suffer the same problems as the EAI solutions they replace. Both EAI and Web services are focused on applications, not business processes. They share an IT, not a business, heritage and bias. They share the Application Programming Interface (API), not the business process, as their conceptual "first-citizen" foundation. The commonly held bottom-up view of Web services is that existing, discrete, components can be combined to form larger composite services and that these can eventually attain the status of a complete business process. This is not BPM. BPM is a new method and new technology for manipulating processes as a whole, not just composing services to create composite applications.

The top-down "whole system" view of BPM says that although Web services are useful as components of a process, the process design and its management must be oriented by conscious, business-led decisions, themselves often processes. BPM includes metrics, computational logic and business rules that can be embedded in process definitions and can constrain processes in accordance with business goals, such as limiting time, cost and resources. Web services are not inherently suitable for handling these process-oriented tasks, and how this family of technologies will evolve is anybody's guess. Do not confuse a software development paradigm, Web services, with BPM.

In reality, however, software developers have choices. Web services are an essential tool for application integration because they provide an intermediate step in the transition from traditional business applications to third-wave business processes as an organizing principle for software. BPML and Web services go hand-in-hand, as do bottom-up and top-down process design. From the point of view of Web services, the system designer's aim is to achieve more flexibility about how services and assemblies of services can be used. From the point of view of process management, the systems designer's aim is to let the process management system establish a common environment in which all services are visible and available for reuse in processes. These subtle distinctions are hard to understand initially, but over time and as process engineers and software engineers work together and gain more experience, they will gain a full understanding of the roles process engineering and software engineering will fulfill.

A Universal Process Language

Business processes are perceived and described in different ways by people with different roles within the business. Software engineers, for example, understand business processes at the level of software implementation. They use a variety of notations and methods such as the unified modeling language (UML) for representing processes as software objects. Business people, however, understand processes at the level of material flows, information flows and business commitments. Often they don't think about technology at all unless it has become a routine element in their business.

Business people imagine ready support for integration and automation and often do not understand why technicians cannot make these happen easily, right away! They don't understand why integration at all levels—people, systems, processes and businesses—is so hard to achieve. Enter the business analyst, someone who bridges the gap between the non-technical business person and the software technician. He or she uses a variety of business architecture and modeling methods and tools to represent business processes, such as the Zackman Framework, IDS-Scheer ARIS and Computer Sciences Corporation's Catalyst. Analysts understand processes in terms of organizational coherence and business outcomes. They use a variety of methods to manage and improve process, including Six Sigma, TQM Activity Based Costing and reengineering. They have a very different perspective to technicians. They deal with "the process" more directly, whereas the software engineer deals with it indirectly, through the distorting lens of software artifacts. BPMI sought to change this. Their answer was a single process model, BPML, shared by all disciplines.

Business analysts are also experts in the processes of specific industries and participate in industry standards initiatives, such as the standards developed by the Telemanagement Forum for Service

Provisioning in the telecommunications sector, or the architecture for Straight Through Processing (STP) developed for the financial sector. Sometimes these models are developed out of a need to facilitate collaboration in the industry. Examples include the SCOR reference model developed by the Supply Chain Council; the Collaborative Planning, Forecasting and Replenishment (CPFR) protocols of the VICS committee, made up of retailers, manufacturers, and solution providers; the high-tech industry's RosettaNet Partner Interface Processes (PIP); the manufacturing industry's STEP framework for product lifecycle management; and FpML (Financial Products Markup Language) for securities trading. These standards are essential to business process collaboration, and BPML is able to model and describe all of them. The implications are far reaching. Industry experts can now turn paper-based specifications into executable processes, no matter what role or skill set they have.

Government regulations and the guidelines set out by professional standards bodies also drive demand for formalized process frameworks. Companies are required to implement and manage such business processes without adding to the cost of their products and services. These industry frameworks create many different perspectives on the nature and management of business processes in those industries. Process management systems and languages can now play a major role in helping companies reduce the cost and complexity of implementing mandated processes. Executable process languages such as BPML help align legislation and best practices with process models.

Companies in every industry probably feel that their own processes are unique. Yet each shares a single underlying model of behavior, but expressed in the standards of its industry. For example, in the retail sector, processes span many business partners, and are oriented to the sharing of information up and down the supply chain. In the financial sector, processes are more centralized: Often one internal process is used to receive and send messages. In the telecommunications sector, processes govern the day-to-day operation and configuration of service and network elements, responding to requests from customers for new services and providing an end-to-end view of all of the network infrastructure elements and their operational support systems (OSS).

Rather than trying to create different solutions for each industry, the BPMI group designed BPML to adapt to and amplify a variety of standards. CPFR, STP, SCOR, HIPAA, RosettaNet, STEP, FpML, GAMP and CIDX can now all be expressed using BPML and be adapted for use by businesses within those sectors. BPML unifies the semantics of a number of different approaches to process definition, making possible the implementation of a universal virtual machine that can execute, literally, any business process.

A Rich Language for Process Engineering

BPML is the meta-language of process, a language for developing process languages that capitalize on BPML patterns. BPML can be adapted for use in different industries by assimilating the required vocabularies. Much as lawyers use specialized legalese and refer *by name* to individual statutes of bodies of case law, BPML can accommodate specialized languages to refer to *patterns* of process design. This will be vital to industry standards groups establishing best practice processes, but using their own vocabulary to do so. Every element and every design pattern in BPML can be named and referred to explicitly using their native vocabularies. An industry can therefore develop its *vocabulary of processes.*

BPML is rich enough to represent and express material flows, information flows and business commitments:

- *Material processes* transform raw materials or components into subassemblies and finished products, using resources such as people, machines and computer systems. These are based on the traditions of industrial engineering, whose key concepts are assembly, transformation, transport, storage and inspection.
- *Information processes* describe the storage, retrieval, manipulation, display and communication of structured and unstructured data and knowledge. These are based on the traditions of computer science and software engineering, whose key concepts are sending, calculating, transacting, invoking, deciding, saving, forwarding and querying.
- *Business commitments* and relationships articulate and satisfy conditions in interactions between customers and partners. These are based on structures of human communication and cooperation found in all languages and cultures. Key concepts are requesting, promising, offering, declining, proposing, canceling and measuring.

BPML excels at representing discrete, distributed, transactional, computational and collaborative processes in any field, whether material, information or commitment based. The language is used to express the manner in which participants (people, systems, data, applications, trading partners and marketplaces) work together to achieve common business goals. This means that employees and business partners can achieve a common understanding of terms in the domain, such as *activity*, *exception*, *message* and *choice* as they work together. In fact, any set of terms can be defined and associated with BPML design patterns.

BPML has rich abilities for expressing business logic, control flow and information flow. Participants in the process can be back-office systems (such as a database or ERP system), software components (such as a Java component or Web service), users (such as a purchasing manager) or partners (such as a supplier or customer). Business transactions (for example the fulfillment of a purchase order) and system transactions (for example a transaction on a database table) can all be defined as part of a process. *Business* transactions usually involve two or more partners (e-business), while *system* transactions can involve multiple back-office packages (distributed transaction).

Processes can be defined to bind participants closely together, as in straight-through processing, or to be loosely coupled, as in supply chain management. Loose coupling is especially important in collaborative commerce, because partners will almost never share the same applications and systems, and they will certainly not allow others to gain direct control over their mission-critical back-office systems. Such processes involve rules, roles and renewal procedures and place fewer restrictions on participants with respect to the order in which activities must be performed. Few existing technologies support this kind of loosely coupled, reliable, behavior, and fewer still support it across different technology platforms and network protocols. BPML does. Each of these characteristics is essential, however, if collaborative commerce is to become widespread. BPML frees companies from such constraints and allows them to deploy the innovative new business models that they need to compete—as tightly or as loosely coupled as necessary, but with the required level of coordination and control.

These collaboration features are part of the process design model itself, not an attribute of a hard-wired application. For example, a product manufacturer can, using BPML, define the way in which customers obtain all required product support services: consulting, configuration, fulfillment, installation and training. Each of the partners providing these services can operate quite freely but in the context of coordinated processes defined by the product supplier. The product manufacturer's end-to-end process model would describe just the coordination required between partners to provide the integrated service to the customer. As experience with the process deepens, it can be tuned to improve the customer experience, and to reduce cycle times.

BPML enables an unlimited degree of nesting, parallelism and concurrency in process design, and can accommodate both process-level transactions and compensating transactions. Think of a process transaction as the equivalent of a database transaction, but right across some subset of an end-to-end process. It has business meaning, quite independent of any "technical" transaction requirements. Furthermore, processes can be designed to be both reliable and self-healing. If constraints or restrictions are required by a business relationship, limits can be placed on the data exchanged by participants, the time spans of activities and the availability of services and participants.

Recognizing that the value chain is always going to be heterogeneous, the developers of BPML designed it to encompass the process semantics inherent in any other process language. BPML can be used to build bridges and process interfaces to other systems using other process modeling formalisms. For example, a company can use BPML to define its order-to-pay process even if another system, based on another process language, was used to define the order requisition part and yet another was used to describe invoicing. BPML can serve as a *lingua franca* for process languages. It should be possible to express any process in BPML that can be expressed in any other process language. Test this assertion in practice.

BPML simplifies interactions between processes running on disparate systems and across business domains. It has to exist in the heterogeneous, distributed, computing environment because that's real life. BPML processes can model anything that occurs in a typical Fortune 500 network infrastructure, including the different processing paradigms inherent in complex IT systems such as teleprocessing monitors, remote procedure calls, object request brokers, and publish/subscribe messaging systems and queues. The unification of the dual notions of "business" and "technical" process played a major role in its design.

A Foundation for Collaborative Commerce

A business process involves two or more business partners. Each partner brings many "process participants" to the table, usually comprising the partner's back-office systems, e-business applications, employee interactions and other third-party elements. The process systems deployed within, or extended toward, each partner are responsible for the management of that partner's process participants. Thus the process management system can be seen as a gateway—a process-level firewall—connecting business partners that each have their own process management system or systems.

For collaborative commerce, the expression of a logically distributed process alone would not be sufficient. Even a single process with a centralized business design may need to be executed across a set of physically distributed systems, including systems owned by different companies. Because business partners normally interact with a large number of suppliers, customers and trading partners—hundreds, or even thousands—companies often need to establish a common "interface process" in order to simplify the required *technical* integration at the network level. To this end, BPML supports the concept of "public interfaces" and "private implementations."

A process deployed by a company on its BPMS usually instantiates the private implementation of a larger e-business process involving business partners. Partners participate by interacting through a public interface, usually defined jointly by both sides. For example, the Partner Interface Processes (PIPs) defined by RosettaNet and the Uniform Code Council (UCCNet), comprise a combination of standard data and standard interface process. This enables the reliable exchange of data in the context of commercially binding business commitments. BPML systems generate the required interfaces for collaboration to occur. In a collaborative purchase order management process, for example, the enterprise's private implementation can be described as a procurement process while the supplier's private implementation of the same e-business process can be described as a fulfillment process. The enterprise's procurement process and the supplier's fulfillment process are two private implementations of the same end-to-end business process. These implementations interact with one another through a common public interface.

The private implementations and public interfaces of an e-business process give rise to corresponding notions of "private processes" and "public processes." But do public processes really exist? The BPMI advocates the concept of a private process, but only as a restricted case of a business process that does not involve a participant other than the enterprise itself—in other words, a strictly internal business process. Moreover, the notion of a public process makes sense only if a single entity is responsible for its execution—for example, an EDI network, an electronic marketplace or a process service provider (e-hub). Even in such cases, however, the hub or marketplace is not really the entity responsible for the execution of some imaginary public process, but rather a business participant in the overall end-to-end process, with real internal processes of its own.

The private implementations of an e-business process are the only parts of a business process that must be executed. Its public interface is nothing more than a vector for the collaborative execution of the e-business process by its participants. Such a public interface is not executed independently but rather consists of the various private implementations of the e-business process—one per participant. It's like looking at the behavior of internal processes from the outside, in terms of their interactions with others.

Business interfaces change infrequently—to align with industry standards for example—and yet companies must be free to continuously innovate along the entire length of the end-to-end process. Although participants in a collaborative process may be internal or external, a BPML process model does not distinguish between the two types. Process systems can be developed that will allow flexible and secure process outsourcing or the division of responsibility among partners, while maintaining a consistent business interface. In fact, the business interface can itself be described as a process and used as a pattern in the design of the end-to-end process, allowing each to evolve at its own pace.

In some cases the interface may itself be a complex process. For this reason, the BPMI has developed BPML-based languages to allow interfaces to be defined independently of end-to-end process designs, using what is known as a *process interface definition language* (PIDL). The messages exchanged between any two process participants constitute a process and can be explicitly modeled as such. BPML itself can be used for such a purpose, although other languages for doing this have been and will continue to be developed; their requirements being not as complex as for an end-to-end modeling language.

One way of visualizing this to imagine a virtual participant sitting between two (or more) real participants; the virtual participant being responsible for mediating between the internal processes of the others. Or think of a Coke machine. On the one hand there exists the end-to-end process of obtaining a can of drink and consuming it. On the other hand there exists the coin slot and drinks dispenser—the interface between the machine, with its internal processes and the human, with his or her internal processes that enables the transaction known as *satisfying one's thirst*. BPML can describe the whole process, including the behavior of the interface. For example, BPML would define the fact that it is possible to put a coin into the slot, but not take one out, and that the converse is true for the drink dispenser. BPML could also define the fact that the human could obtain a drink if and only if he or she deposited the proper number and type of coins. On the other hand, BPML could also describe the private internal processes of the user and the machine: the raising of the arm to put money in the slot and the mechanism inside the machine that drops a can of soda into the bin. Similarly, the enterprise's procurement process and the supplier's fulfillment process are two private implementations of the same end-to-end business process—which we could call "order to pay"—that interact with one another through a common public interface. The interface could adhere to an industry standard such as a RosettaNet PIP. The BPML approach allows separation between different parts of the order-to-pay process —requisition and invoicing. The company can also describe the flow of messages required to process an incoming purchase order, the exchange between buyer and supplier, independently of larger processes in which such a reusable pattern is required.

Both illustrations—the Coke machine transaction and the order-to-pay—are business processes. Each can be modeled, described and executed in BPML. The distinctions between end-to-end processes, internal and external processes, interfaces, real participants and virtual participants are subtle. The point is that any fit-for-purpose process modeling language should be able to model everything required for end-to-end management and execution. For e-business integrators the advantage is the ability to implement an interface once, covering all participants, without limiting in any way the ability of those participants to collaborate across the boundary. Even if an industry requires a particular interface process—for regulatory, security or other reasons—or has developed an effective one in the past, companies can go ahead and use it. If it is already working and in use, BPML can adapt to it.

To make process design practical for collaborative commerce, users will either establish a common process repository and management system, or will support the import of processes to local tools allowing modifications by partners. Sophisticated repositories are not always needed and could be regarded as overkill. Processes can be freely shared using a variety of mechanisms including File Transfer Protocol (FTP), the Web and e-mail. Distributed authoring and versioning of business processes is already supported in process management products using the widely adopted WebDav (World Wide Web Distributed Authoring and Versioning) protocol published by the Internet Engineering Task Force (IETF), a standard for collaborative authoring on the Web.

WebDAV is a set of extensions to the Hypertext Transfer Protocol (HTTP) that facilitates collaborative editing and file management between users at separate locations. WebDAV is expected to have an impact on the development of virtual enterprises by enabling remote groups to work together in new ways. For example, WebDAV-compliant tools can be used by a virtual organization to develop business plans, create software or develop libraries of information. Together, WebDAV and BPML provide the basic foundation for collaborative process development.

BPML does not create processes, nor does BPML limit the ability to define processes in other languages. BPML simply allows a definition of these processes to be exchanged between software tools and provides a basis for the development of open process systems. BPML is an implementation-neutral interchange format for expressing processes, much as EDI is an implementation-neutral format for expressing business transactions and as HTML is an implementation-neutral format for expressing the presentation of Web pages. And just like HTML, business users are highly unlikely to work with BPML directly, but instead will use a variety of tools that rely on BPML as a common language, much as Web authoring tools such as Adobe's Dreamweaver, Microsoft's FrontPage and countless others allow people to develop and maintain Web sites without needing an in-depth knowledge of HTML.

BPML makes all processes explicit by representing them separately from the software infrastructure in which they reside. Similar developments have occurred before in the history of computing. Operating systems dramatically simplified software application development by removing machine-language-level considerations from application development. Likewise, many corporations manage their business rules in a separate business rules management system (BRMS) rather than embedding rules in each and every application. Much as the database removed responsibility from the application for the precise arrangement of data, the BPMS and its BPML foundation remove responsibility for the management of processes from process components. Extending this "separation of concern" to business processes means freeing information system developers from largely clerical, machine-oriented tasks, so that they can take on the more interesting and rewarding challenges of enterprise process design.

Tomorrow's Process Landscape

Every CEO, CIO, CFO, supply chain director and management consultant on the planet has imagined business models and the associated business processes that they would like to implement, right away. They are not short on new ways of imagining how to improve their businesses. Until the third wave every new business process has been hard to achieve in practice due to the cost, time and technical effort needed to implement the required software. BPML has eradicated that difficulty.

Before the BPM innovation, putting new business models into operation depended on the use of complex distributed computing, messaging and integration solutions. With the advent of BPML, these complex and expensive solutions will become simpler, less expensive and ultimately disappear from the mind's eye of the information systems developer. How many young database developers know the details of logical and physical input/output control systems (LIOCS and PIOCS)? They are still there, but the DBMS and high-level languages such as SQL push them down into the plumbing—out of sight, out of mind. Likewise, the complex plumbing of distributed systems can now be managed by the new process technologies that offer simpler, more cost effective and manageable alternatives.

Further radical simplifying steps will no doubt be taken as the process era unfolds. Some companies evaluating BPML have already noted that it is possible to model and execute value chain-wide business processes on a single centralized computer system. The *design* of the end-to-end business is fully "distributed," but its *execution* takes place on a single system. All the participants in the supply chain are present —suppliers, manufacturers, distributors, customers—but the technical implementation and *its management* can be centralized. The process-center, like the data-center, will soon be commonplace. Even in such a centralized environment, the business-level participants still exchange "messages" with each other—they still maintain their own "state," their own process data available to query. Transactions, business ones that is, can still be unwound.

The centralized execution of massively distributed business level process designs is going to be something many organizations will want to explore, especially if they want to incorporate the "little big men" in the value chain. In the U.S. these are the millions of small and medium size enterprises (SMEs) that can be the weak links in any value chain. They are the suppliers' suppliers and typically employ 50 or fewer employees and perhaps have nothing more that an Internet connection and spreadsheets for business technology. Yet they are the backbone of the American economy. A single, multi-company, business process management system, can be responsible for coordinating the activities defined by the end-to-end process (sequencing, synchronization and scheduling); managing process instances (lifecycle, persistence); and processing distributed transactions (two-phase commit protocol, open nested transactions and compensating transactions)—things the SME never imagined, but the very things an industry's 800 pound gorilla can extend to its suppliers' suppliers' suppliers to the benefit of all.

Like data management systems, the business process management system will, over time, move into the background becoming part of the technology infrastructure taken for granted in every company. The innovations built on data management have been truly mind boggling— an infinite variety of data-aware applications. The applications built on BPM will be equally surprising—an infinite variety of process-aware applications. But here and now, one immediate advantage of BPM is the ability to align process design with organizational objectives, a first step in understanding the wider implications.

BPML cannot be used to model the high level values and goals of the business—these activities will remain forever in the domain of human insight, creativity and intelligence. BPML can, however, play a key role in helping identify whether goals are being met. For example, queries against a set of process instances can build a view (past and present) of whether goals are likely to be met. It is also entirely possible to query BPML to determine which participants (systems, users or processes) are responsible for achieving goals or what might cause a goal to be unreachable. BPML is the foundation for a process level of business intelligence.

Putting It All Together

As the medium for the convergence toward process-oriented enterprise computing, BPML provides interoperability between applications, process management systems and a host of new process tools. BPML was designed for complete business process management —discovery, design, operation, optimization and analysis. It is the foundation upon which both software companies and businesses can develop the next generation of process-aware systems, tools and applications.

Business processes have heretofore been second-class citizens in IT because of the challenges in developing a representation, and execution environment, able to cope with the dynamic, expanding, contracting, changing activities of the business. Founded on process calculus and the computer science of mobile processes, however, BPML is designed to manage this complexity and dynamism so that business processes can become first-class citizens again.

The theoretical basis for BPML, like all formalisms, is complex. The same is true for the deceptively simple data model where the underlying relational algebra provides confidence in the safe storage and utilization of the business assets managed by the database system. Ditto process management systems build on the foundation of process calculus. Fortunately software developers and business users do not work directly with the formalisms. They use high-level tools and many are unaware of the formal foundations on which those tools were built. Languages being developed such as the Business Process Query Language (BPQL) enable the gathering of metrics and decision support information for all of the industrial and enterprise processes.

Using the first principles of architecture, the design of BPML is a balance of goals and constraints meant to fit its purpose. It couldn't be so complex that software vendors couldn't implement it, nor could it be trivial. The first principles underlying process management systems had to be applicable to a wide range of purposes. BPML was designed using this bottom up approach—from theory to implementation—so that all higher-level languages and systems built on it would inherit the benefits of its strong foundation. Historically, progress in the development of computer systems has been accomplished in this way, beginning with the foundation of the binary numbering system chosen by Dr. John Vincent Atanasoff when he built the first electronic digital computer during 1937 – 1942 with Clifford Berry at Iowa State University. The binary numbering system continues to serve as the formal underpinning of today's computers, yet computer users couldn't care less. Today, Pi-calculus has been chosen as the foundation for the new "business computer." In the future, business people won't care less.

Few worthwhile endeavors are easy, and BPML is no exception. Moving the workflow document and the application interface out of the center of the computing universe to focus on processes is a paradigm shift for software companies, and for any business, but a necessary shift. Some have said that BPML and all that goes with it exceeds current needs. But for those who have implemented significant integration projects using previous technologies, the old proprietary and point-to-point solutions are an even more daunting prospect. Since companies can almost never be exactly on the curve, their choice is to be behind it or ahead of it. Being ahead of the curve is so much easier in this case.

References

---

[1] Arkin, Assaf, *Business Process Modeling Language (BPML) Specification*, BPMI.org (www.bpmi.org)

Appendix B

Business Process Management Systems

Firms will need process integration servers that model and carry out broad business processes.
—Forrester Research, 1999.

The Business Process Management System (BPMS) enables companies to model, deploy and manage mission-critical business processes, that span multiple enterprise applications, corporate departments, and business partners—behind the firewall and over the Internet. The BPMS is a new category of software and opens a new era of IT infrastructure.

The BPMS can be viewed in one of two ways: either as a new platform upon which the next generation of business applications will be constructed, or as a new capability deeply embedded within existing categories of business systems. In each case the analogy is between the existing RDBMS and the new BPMS, between relational data and processes, between the lifecycle management of data and the lifecycle management of process. In either case, by acquiring BPMS now companies gain unprecedented control over the management of their business processes, supplementing their existing systems and accelerating the achievement of business objectives.

Companies will either procure process management systems from a vendor specialized in BPMS or they will wait for BPMS capabilities to arrive in a subsequent version of a business infrastructure that they have already procured. In either case they will use process management systems along side existing IT investments.

Process management borrows and combines features from a number of familiar tools and technologies, but differs in its central focus on processes. Practitioners from many disciplines are going to feel at home with third-wave BPM, and vendors of existing products in related areas are already moving to a process-centered future.

BPM feels similar to Computer-Aided Software Engineering (CASE) because of the emphasis on graphical notation, collaborative discovery and design. It shares with workflow management a focus on scripted events and task management. The rigor, control and exception recovery that systems administrators apply to data and systems management can be extended to processes. From the viewpoint of systems architects, comparisons can be drawn with transaction processing (TP) monitors and application servers. For ERP practitioners, BPM's focus on process definition and optimization will have strong associations. Developers who have struggled with legacy system integration and who have employed EAI solutions that use processes to define and implement integration paths will recognize similar ideas in BPM. New process analysis tools used in conjunction with the BPMS will be familiar to users of online analytical processing (OLAP). Finally, those implementing business-to-business integration (B2Bi) will find in BPM such familiar concepts as process participants, location independence and non-invasive integration. BPMS is going to astound and delight, but companies existing IT skills can be readily transferred. Our experience is that the learning curve is entirely manageable.

Business process management products are available from many vendors, in versions ranging from departmental workgroup solutions to enterprise-scale infrastructure—a range of solutions to meet all needs. It is possible that personal BPM tools, akin to the commodity databases that form part of commonly used office productivity suites, will emerge. Imagine a "Process Office" suite, providing an integrated, process-centric approach to collaboration, computation, work management, process modeling and simulation. Such a vision is entirely realistic if based on a third-wave approach.

Processes management is going to be a rich source of innovative new approaches for all suppliers of enterprise software, in both horizontal and vertical industry solutions. Why do we make this claim? Simply because the mark of the third wave is far more than a new software package, it is a far reaching shift in business-IT thinking toward "all things process" becoming the central focus of attention—for all packages. The next fifty years of IT will be dominated not by separate data, application, document and business object paradigms, but by living, breathing *holistic* processes.

How will this trend be absorbed by end-user organizations? There is no doubt that users heavily dependent upon ERP systems will continue to look to their preferred supplier for BPM innovations. But there will also be huge demand for independent Business Process Management Systems (BPMS). Companies need BPMS capability today. We are equally convinced that all enterprise applications will eventually be rebuilt upon a BPMS foundation.

For all of the reasons above it is not possible to describe a "typical" BPMS. Some vendors may not even use that term. Terms such as the *fourth tier, business services orchestration* (BSO) and *composite application* are all indicators of the BPM movement. Marketing terms such as *next-generation workflow, smart middleware, hyper-tier* and *real-time enterprise* are also part of the unfolding story, each shifting "processes" to the center of IT.

In this book, therefore, our only option is to sketch the features of a BPMS based on our current understanding of the potential of BPM. Real products may differ from the descriptions that follow, but if they are "third-wave" they will have more than mere "process-inside": they will treat processes as their *first-class entity*. We have, therefore, chosen to describe an enterprise-class, "plain vanilla" BPMS. Analysts report that this thing called "BPM" is rapidly becoming the business platform of choice for Global 5000 organizations. We believe that this is the basic capability companies are seeking in their search for control of enterprise processes.

In look and feel, the BPMS is to the process designer what a design workstation is to the automobile designer. The computer-aided-design and computer-aided manufacturing (CAD/CAM) system of the automobile designer becomes the computer-aided-modeling/computer-aided deployment (CAM/CAD) system of the business process designer.

Unlike shrink-wrapped packages, BPM adapts to a company's processes, not the other way around. The BPMS is targeted at a new hybrid business role—that combines the skills of the enterprise data architect and enterprise business architect. The *process architect* will be the true architect of 21st century business.

Underlying the BPMS, as in the case of CAD/CAM systems, is a digital *simulation* of the real "thing" with which the designer is working. While the automobile designer works with digital models of such artifacts as tires, engines, body frames, aerodynamics and so on, the process designer works with digital models of such artifacts as orders, the fulfillment services of suppliers, third party billing services, bills of materials, the shipping schedules of trading partners and so on.

When the automobile engineer pushes the "make it so button," the computer-aided manufacturing part of the system actually implements the building of the new car. When the business process engineer pushes the "make it so button," the computer-aided deployment part of the system actually implements the *mission-critical* end-to-end business process.

What about all the C++, Java, scripting, EAI, and other computer technologies that are involved? Where did they go in all this? They are still there, only now it is the BPMS that deals with them, not the designers and other business people who use the business process workstations and their underlying BPMS.

With the BPMS, business information systems are developed and evolved by manipulating the business process directly, using the language and concepts of business, not the language and concepts of machines. The BPMS sits right in the middle of the two worlds of humans and machines, letting people speak in their native tongue and enabling machines to understand them—a paradigm shift in the world of business automation that has a significant impact on the way businesses structure and perform work. Business change now proceeds unhampered by the rigid machine-oriented business technology of the past.

The Process-Managed Enterprise

Throughout the last decade companies have been using increasingly complex processes to maintain their operations, but have yet to see an IT infrastructure capable of fully supporting these processes. The great benefit of the last decade's enterprise resource planning (ERP) packages was supposed to be their ability to promote integration—everything the business needs, all in one place—but realizing this goal was not really possible until now, with the advent of BPMS.

Competition and the escalating influence of the business Internet, have put pressure on companies to create new processes and extend existing ones to customers, trading partners and suppliers. Processes used to be embedded in ERP and other monolithic systems. It didn't take long to realize that embedding processes in software was a bad idea, but no better ideas were available. The reason for this is threefold. First, packaged enterprise applications such as ERP systems manage only those parts of the business process that have to be automated at any cost—typically such processes as materials resource planning and financial reporting. Second, the deployment of new end-to-end processes on some IT infrastructures requires prior organization of enterprise data, a formidable process that has already taken several decades to complete. Third, the processes ingrained in most application packages cannot be changed easily nor combined with others, let alone integrated or freed up for collaboration.

For these reasons, ERP and similar systems require massive process reengineering efforts even for internal processes; it is therefore unlikely that any *packaged* enterprise software will be able to automate the countless possible interactions between the processes of multiple business partners. There are both theoretical and practical reasons for this.

From a theoretical standpoint, the complexity of integrating multiple processes increases exponentially with the number of processes and the internal complexity of each process. Take just one example: a standard application for automating the build-to-order process. How could such an application be suitable for all companies in all industries? To claim that it could is comparable to claiming that a universal application had been found for implementing the "dollars-to-more-dollars" process! Application developers who stick to a paradigm based on data and procedures face an uncertain future. Their business model is based on perfecting processes that appeal to all companies and all situations in all industries. That model is absurd, and developers will soon abandon it: When you find yourself in a hole, stop digging.

From a practical standpoint, business partners have heterogeneous IT infrastructures provided by various vendors, and as a result, cannot rely on a single solution to cover every possible case. Even if one company does manage to standardize on one application, this standard can rarely be imposed on others. Industry gorillas that believe they can impose a standard across a value chain are deluding themselves. The long lead times for deployment and customization of any standard package is debilitating. Companies seeking value-chain integration should instead separate process innovation from process integration. Integrate applications once, to the BPMS, and be free ever after to manage end-to-end processes.

The problem of integrating the IT infrastructures of multiple business partners in a vendor-agnostic fashion will be solved in part by the standardization of collaborative business-to-business interfaces. Examples include, RosettaNet in the high-tech industry, ACORD in the insurance industry and CIDX in the chemical industry. Nevertheless, there remains the question of how to integrate these interface processes with existing IT infrastructures, which consist of multiple packaged enterprise applications that are increasingly complemented by new e-business applications such as procurement, fulfillment and service-chain management. But that's not all. Partners want to innovate rapidly and deploy innovations from end to end, not just establish a standard interface at the boundary between companies. Standards organizations must not repeat the mistake of packaged software suppliers: They must focus on a *standard process representation*, not *standard processes*.

Companies should abandon piece-meal individual integration projects and instead use a process foundation for building a coherent IT infrastructure—an enterprise architecture—that encompasses all packaged, departmental and enterprise systems. In this way, unique processes can be extended to business partners and customers—a method we call multi-channel, multi-system and multi-company integration. It's an "integrate-once and customize-many" approach. It contrasts sharply with the approach of distributing packaged software across the industry, which puts a company's proprietary process at risk of being replicated, destroying its competitive edge.

The BPMS enables implementation of business processes directly on the IT infrastructure without the prohibitive cost of software reengineering. The key element of a BPMS is what we call the *process virtual machine*, although different vendors may use different names. This is a scaleable concurrent-processing execution environment for business processes that execute the language of business process much as the Java virtual machine executes the computer programming language Java.

The BPMS does not replace existing applications, although its ability to easily define and execute new processes will be used to replace some application development as experience gives companies the confidence to take that step. Existing heritage systems, however, remain valuable for both internal and external process-based development, because their functionality, currently ingrained and embedded, can be tapped and encapsulated by the BPMS as software components that contribute to new or improved business process designs. Nor do we dismiss any newly invented "best-of-breed" applications that companies may wish to integrate into end-to-end process designs. The flexibility is desirable not only from the point of view of end users but also from that of software suppliers that want to build a repository of application components from other vendors, which they can use to manufacture processes that meet the needs of particular industries or individual customers. This convergence of application and process will deepen over time. Process management systems already exist that "project," or view, standard software in the form of explicit, manageable, process data. This flexibility is what end-user organizations need, and vendors that do not listen will ultimately pay the price.

Benefits of a BPMS

The BPMS, whether purchased as a separate system or included with next-generation application packages, will enable the enterprise to live by the adage "Say what you do, and do what you say."

Since a packaged application cannot adequately address the challenges raised by the integration of business processes, the only alternative, in the absence of a BPMS, is extensive custom development involving traditional programming. Even if the software development approach is versatile, a major drawback remains: Software code does not directly reflect business processes, and thus becomes incredibly difficult to maintain over time, as processes require modification. Although internal processes can be successfully maintained if current development methodologies are carefully adhered to, the same is not true for processes that extend to partners. Traditional approaches can no longer handle the complexity of the task: All the programmers in the world, even if a company could afford them, could not keep up with the growing demand for end-to-end business processes.

The intermediary step between the definition of business processes and their implementation on the IT infrastructure can be avoided with a process-centric infrastructure (Figure B.1). This, in turn, confers upon the IT infrastructure the advantages of adaptability and control.

Adaptability: The BPMS is the primary business velocity engine. Companies are under great pressure to embrace the unprecedented changes fostered by the economy, manage dynamic relationships with business partners and retain an edge over the competition. Business analysts customize business processes through user-friendly design tools and through business rules expressed in natural language. This dramatically reduces the time required for the deployment of new business processes.

Manageability: The BPMS enables business process intelligence. For the same competitive reasons, the enterprise needs to measure its performance directly. Analysts, never shy about introducing new three letter acronyms, refer to this as enterprise performance management (EPM). The "P" in EPM ought to stand for "process." EPM is not an amalgam of existing ERP, CRM and SCM applications, as some analysts have defined it, but should be defined as the third wave of business process management and heralds a shift to BPMS as the foundation for enterprise architecture.

Traditionally, business measurement—what analysts call "business intelligence"—has been based on the analysis of *data* extracted *after the fact* from past operations of implicit business processes. The BPMS, on the other hand, enables business analysts to do real-time process analysis—to *directly measure the business value of explicitly defined business processes.* These processes can now be optimized on the fly without the need for additional software development, tremendously simplifying the management of their design over their lifetime.

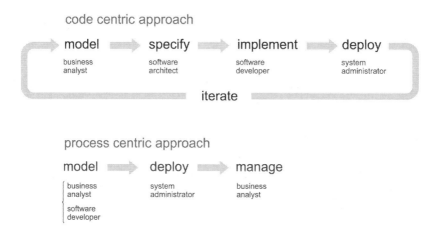

Figure B.1. Software versus Process Development Lifecycle

Requirements for the BPMS

The BPMS must meet three mandatory requirements: extreme flexibility, reliability and security. It must be able to model, deploy, and manage any business process, in any vertical industry, across any enterprise application, corporate department or business partner. This requires a high degree of flexibility, which is provided by the process representation used by the BPMS. The system must possess scalability, fault-tolerance and quality of service if it is to be viewed as a mission-critical infrastructure component. And since the BPMS serves as the frontier between internal IT infrastructure and that of business partners, it must also offer advanced process-level security. No other enterprise software infrastructure has ever provided all of these features.

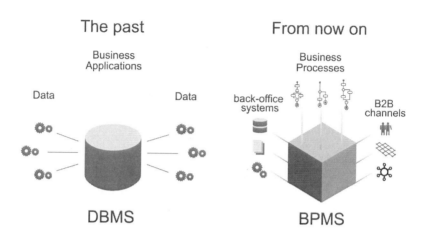

Figure B.2. Mission-Critical Enterprise Software Infrastructure[1]

Flexibility. Just as flexible relational database management systems were based on the powerful relational model for the modeling, indexing, and retrieving of data, the business process management system must be built around a powerful business process model for the modeling, deployment, and management of enterprise-wide business processes.

Therefore, as Gartner's David McCoy advised,

> Enterprises should begin to take advantage of explicitly defined processes. By 2005, at least 90 percent of large enterprises will have BPM in their enterprise nervous system (0.9 probability). Enterprises that continue to hard-code all flow control, or insist on manual process steps and do not incorporate BPM's benefits, will lose out to competitors that adopt BPM.[1] Business process management's potential for business improvements through advanced process automation is the most compelling business reason to implement an 'enterprise nervous system' (ENS). Where ENS implementations risk being seen as infrastructure in search of a

---

[1] The cube is the symbol adopted by the Business Process Management Initiative to represent the BPMS, as opposed to the cylinder that has traditionally denoted the database management system. The cube and is not a trademark of the BPMI nor of any member of the BPMI. The top face of the cube always represents processes. The left and right faces can be used to represent either internal applications and external business channels, or information sources and process participants.

problem, BPM allows enterprises to raise the level of discussion and make specific business process support the primary reason for application integration efforts.[2]

The BPMS must knit process components together and allow the accurate measurement of the performance of business processes using advanced business-process intelligence technologies. It must enable business analysts to customize existing business processes for specific market segments, trading partners and customers. The system must enable the enterprise to leverage its existing IT investments by providing an open architecture based on industry standards, simplifying its integration with any back-office system, enterprise middleware, or packaged application, on any platform or operating system. Most importantly, the system must support standard business-to-business collaboration protocols, without requiring business partners all along the value chain to be running the same business process management system. This flexibility will be augmented by means of building interfaces between process systems, mediated by interface processes that partners agree to use for collaborative, distributed process management.

Reliability. A process-oriented business infrastructure must provide a foundation for existing mission-critical applications that rely on it to gain access to core process services. This has been the case for ERP packages, which typically rely on an external database management system provided by a third party. In addition, BPM is based on parallel (concurrent) computing, which means that the business process management system must offer an extreme degree of scalability and reliability—including support for clustering, load balancing and failover—so that the continuous execution of processes is never interrupted.

Reliability is usually the result of multiple factors, mainly of a technical nature. Scalability must be offered in terms of both scope and complexity so that the business process management system will be able to support a broader range of business processes that span an increasing number of enterprise applications, corporate departments, and business partners. Fault-tolerance should be provided through a proper architecture that minimizes the number of single-points-of-failure and supports the redundancy of critical components. Quality of service must be guaranteed based on process-level agreements negotiated between business partners, and embodied in explicit digital process interface designs.

The same criteria that companies have applied to existing products can be used to evaluate the BPMS. However, it will also be necessary to evaluate the capabilities of process management systems in terms similar to those used to evaluate early database management systems. For example, it is possible to determine the degree to which a relational database product adheres to the relational data model as set out by E. F. Codd:[3]

- Large data banks must be protected from having to know how the data is organized in the machine (the internal representation)
- Activities of users and most application programs should remain unaffected when the internal representation of data is changed
- Changes in data representation will often be needed as a result of changes in query, update, and report traffic and natural growth in the types of stored information
- A model based on *n-ary* relations, a normal form for data base relations, and the concept of a universal data sub-language are introduced
- Three of the principal kinds of data dependencies need to be removed from existing systems: ordering dependence, indexing dependence, and access path dependence

Replacing the word "data" with "process," similar criteria can be extended to BPMS—and we encourage vendors to take this step. Reliability will be paramount. Will BPMS work in the correct manner under all conditions, and can the outcomes of executing processes be predicted?

Security. The BPMS must serve as a "business firewall," offering security and auditability. In any open environment, across companies or across internal-divisions, security is, not an optional feature that can be added over time through point solutions, but a *mandatory feature* that should be addressed in the early stages of development. Whether it sits on a private community network or the open Internet, the business process management system is the boundary between a relatively unsecured IT infrastructure and a community of partners that, unfortunately, are not always trustworthy or well intentioned.

For example, business partners commonly require the ability to validate the employment of a person claiming to work for the other partner. In the past, this problem was typically solved by providing one partner access, over a virtual private network (VPN), to the human resources systems of the other partner. The VPN grants physical access to desktop computers, servers and mainframes, however, leaving potential security holes. It provides access to far too much information, even within the HR system alone, when all that is really needed is a confirmation of employment. Because trading partners need to reach deep into one another's systems, companies are not able to change any of their existing systems without coordinating explicitly with partners.

BPMS eradicates this constraint by mediating the connection between partners. The BPMS can receive a partner's request, access the correct information, provide a response in an agreed-upon way and modify the rules for doing so as needed—all expressed explicitly in a process design. The boundary between the partners is the process interface. The private implementation component of the process resides inside a particular partner's security boundary. The boundaries between private and publicly shared process-design information and process data content can be adjusted dynamically according to the needs and wishes of the partners and the different security roles granted to specific users. The BPMS is, a *business process firewall,* as illustrated in Figure B.3.

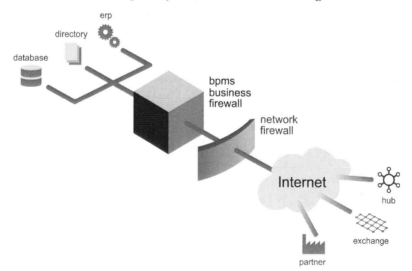

Figure B.3. The BPMS as Business Firewall

In contrast to the rigidity of most hardware firewalls, the configuration is flexible and can change according to the needs of the business—without compromising security. Processes can be used to define and execute a security policy. Process participants can act as mediators in an end-to-end security process.

As a business firewall, the BPMS enables the enterprise to audit the security of its IT infrastructure. In a distributed environment, users must be identified with certitude, and therefore the business process management system must support user authentication through digital certificates. Furthermore, security policies must be deployed at the enterprise level, which requires integration with existing directory services. Finally, communications with business partners must be encrypted to guarantee the proper level of confidentiality. Consequently the BPMS must support existing public key infrastructures (PKI). In this way, business partners establish the process-level of identity required to authenticate members of trade communities.

The Business Process Management System

Beyond compliance with complex technical requirements, the business process management system must provide the foundation for a *straight-through process integration* methodology. As shown in Figure B.4, the BPMS *integrates once* with existing IT systems so that the enterprise can leverage its previous investments while retaining the ability to innovate rapidly in the area of process design. In addition, it must provide an evolutionary path to support future business-to-business *collaboration protocols* that will grow dramatically in scope and complexity over the coming decade. Companies are now looking for products that implement process management in general, not the specifics of particular protocols. Such hard-coded solutions will be left in the dust by the BPMS.

AMR Research[4] enumerates the ten typical capabilities that will be embodied in a business process management system:

1. Process Modeling	6. Process Automation
2. Collaborative Development	7. B2B Collaboration
3. Process Documentation	8. End-User Deployment
4. Process Simulation	9. Process Analysis
5. Application Integration	10. Knowledge Management

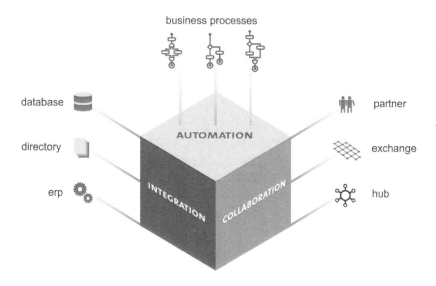

Figure B.4. The Business Process Management System

Model, Deploy, Manage. The business process management system enables a three-step, straight-through process integration methodology for the integration of business processes. When a BPMS is first employed, these steps should involve different categories of users—business analysts, software developers and systems administrators—with the constant participation of business analysts over the entire lifecycle.

First, business processes are modeled with a graphical user interface (GUI) and the underlying process design patterns are stored in a process repository. The process repository is responsible for the distributed authoring of business processes by multiple users over Internet-based networks.

Second, business processes are deployed from the process repository to the business process management system with process management tools accessible from any browser. Processes can be deployed and updated in real-time, without any interruption to the process server. Tools for users can dynamically query the state of any process instance, as well as the status of the business process server itself.

Third, business analysts and system administrators can begin to manage business processes with system management tools using standard business process query languages. For example, operators are able to manage the division of work between partners in the execution of processes. BPMS must provide for the fluid movement of process activities and responsibilities across organizational boundaries, which is so important in value chain integration and business process outsourcing.

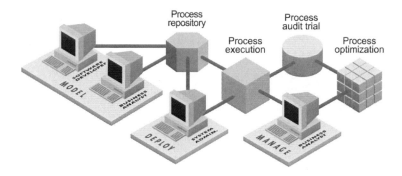

Figure B.5. The Model, Deploy and Manage Methodology

Process management offers a clean approach to the division of responsibilities between business and IT in the management of the process-centric enterprise infrastructure. The "process-neutral" BPMS infrastructure is owned by the corporation and entrusted to IT to manage—either in-house or through outsourcing to a third party. The processes running on the BPMS are owned by the corporation, by lines of business or by functional workgroups, depending on how the processes are segmented and designed. High-level end-to-end processes are probably owned by the corporate office. Controlled adaptations of these processes will be owned by local entities, particularly in federated organizations, where it is necessary to "think globally, but act locally." The BPMS will be the repository of organizational learning and best practices.

The extent to which IT is involved in the design of processes will vary from company to company and from process to process. It will depend partly on culture, partly on skills and partly on the type of processes being deployed. Although we have consistently used the phrase *business process* in this book, we do not exclude IT processes, such as data center operations or IT service management, from the scope of our definition, for these are business processes in their own right. IT will naturally be more involved in the managing of its own processes than it is in processes owned by HR or logistics.

Most importantly, BPMS will empower the business side as never before. The business side will focus mainly on process discovery, design, optimization and analysis, and will share responsibility for process deployment, execution and operations with IT, although as processes bed in, even those responsibilities will fall to the business, not IT, whose focus will be to assure the business continuity of the BPMS service itself. In addition, software engineers may still be required to implement some "last-mile" aspects in all process design. Vendors will seek to minimize these out-of-process-bounds activities.

Business analysts will design high-level process patterns (process skeletons). Business people will use these reusable processes to create their own actual processes and put them into operations on the BPMS. There will be no set pattern either for how the BPMS should be used or how the organizational structures should grow up around it. Companies will find that BPM adapts to the way they work.

The BPMS will inevitably be used with a wide variety of existing tools in the company, including those shown in Table B.1.

Process discovery tools	Rules management systems	Integrated development environments
Simulation	Modeling tools	Integration brokers
Transaction servers	Source code control	Publishing systems
Application servers	Directories	Groupware
Databases	Systems management tools	Public key infrastructure (PKI)

Table B.1. Existing IT Tools To Be Integrated With BPMS

IT will be responsible for integrating these with the BPMS where they already exist in the enterprise, or will decide which BPMS products contain the richest and most complete set of tools. Standards will play a major role.

Integration, Automation, Collaboration. In order to support such a methodology, the business process management system must provide a high-level abstraction of the peripheral entities with which it must interact. Modeling, deployment, and management of business processes must be totally independent of the mundane details related to any specific back-office system or business-to-business collaboration protocol. This "model once, deploy many times" philosophy is enabled by a three-tier architecture comprising, at its most basic, an integration tier, an automation tier, and a collaboration tier, as shown in Figure B.6. This diagram is deliberately abstract and simplified; because we encourage end user companies to examine real products and services from vendors and consulting firms.

The integration tier is responsible for the integration with back-office systems, enterprise middleware, and packaged applications. It offers a schema-driven mapping framework and off-the-shelf connectors to leading databases, directory servers, message-oriented middleware, transaction-processing monitors, application servers, and packaged enterprise applications.

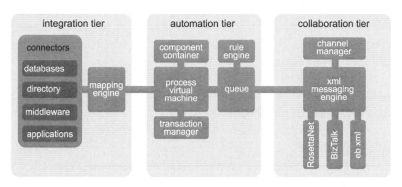

Figure B.6. The Abstract, 3-Tier, BPMS Architecture (Simplified)

The automation tier is responsible for the reliable execution of business processes and the processing of business rules. It relies on advanced distributed and concurrent computing technologies including a message queue, a transaction manager, a component container, a rule engine, and a process virtual machine.

The collaboration tier is responsible for the support of standard business-to-business collaboration protocols, as well as any future standards or any custom protocols such as those already in use by industry. It is built on top of a versatile XML messaging engine and offers customizable implementations of leading business-to-business (B2B) collaboration protocols as well as a hierarchical channel manager.

Process Integration Environment. The business process management system is not simply an execution engine for business processes. Rather, it's a complete platform for the modeling, deployment and management of all process-related information. While this environment is specifically targeted at business analysts and supports distributed collaborative development, it is also designed to inter-operate with existing integrated development environments (IDE) used by software developers. Existing repositories of enterprise "software" assets must be accessible to the BPMS. Completing the platform are system management tools designed for system administrators.

A Process Server

Just as today's data management systems can be accessed from different programming languages using structured query language (SQL) or other connectivity tools, the same will be true for process management systems. The DBMS is a general purpose "data server"; the BPMS will be a general purpose "process server." Although it will be possible to work entirely using BPML, we can expect a variety of software engineering techniques to grow up around the BPMS. One of the most significant will be the process equivalent of SQL, the Business Process Query Language (BPQL). This will enable the development of "process-aware" applications, regardless of platform or programming language.

The reason that software developers will readily adopt BPQL and process servers is that they simplify the development of applications in the context of *entire processes.* In traditional development, pieces of a business process are scattered; a piece in one application; a piece in another; a piece in my system, a piece in the system of a partner. Implementing "e-business" using such an approach is extremely time consuming. Process-aware applications, on the other hand, see all processes and all process data, limited only by the rules of process-level security (itself defined as a process). With BPQL, it will be trivial to write software programs that monitor, interrupt, interact with and intercede in end-to-end processes. The "e" in "e-business" stands for integration, collaboration and coordination. When processes are first-class citizens, the "e" is pre-built into every process and doesn't have to be "e"-programmed for each, just like Lego bricks are designed to snap together.

BPQL will also make it possible to write the equivalent of database "stored procedures and triggers" whereby the process server can invoke, interrupt and interact with business processes on the fly. We expect developers to be very inventive—perhaps too inventive—finding ways to write all kinds of code to manipulate processes offline, online or even during process execution. This process-centric application development environment will not be different in kind from traditional programming, but it will be incredibly more powerful. Process-aware code will have a 360-degree view of the processes—past and present—spanning systems, departments and businesses.

Remarkably enough, process-aware applications can be written in such conventional programming languages as COBOL, Java and RPG, as well as in such database query tools as SQL, ODBC and XPath. If *process* is the new "data," then a raft of new techniques will emerge, offering a rich palette of opportunities for new technology start-ups that choose to build on, not re-build, the new process foundation the BPMS provides.

Although the advocates of process management systems envision a world in which the business process design alone supersedes the application as the organizing principle for software, old habits die hard. Application development using established programming languages will continue for the foreseeable future. But the trend is clear: BPMS will greatly simplify application development in the way that DBMS did in days past. In a world of processes, don't expect software to go away. Companies should develop guidelines for determining when the different paradigms—process aware (BPQL), data-aware (SQL)—should, and should not, be used.

The Integration of Applications and Processes

Companies that set out to define and execute processes using a BPMS will be surprised to find how easy it is to integrate existing applications into process design. Although the system will be most commonly used to integrate existing back-office systems, it has far greater potential. For example, many companies already use simulation and other business-intelligence tools. These can now be extended into the realm of executable processes. When the simulator has been integrated, once, to the BPMS, it can freely participate in any process design, requiring nothing more from the user than drag-and-drop operations on the process design desktop user interface. The user specifies using BPML how the simulator's process exchanges information with the processes of other participants. The simulator becomes a new agent in the system. It can add intelligence to the process and oversee and predict the behavior of entire processes. For example, it could provide a running simulation of market response to new products.

Integrating a simulator in this way provides *simulation as a service* to every process participant. But BPMS vendors and some companies may take simulation a step further, providing access from the simulator to the process server using BPQL. In this way, all persistent process data will be available to the simulator, opening up vast possibilities for new business insight. Companies should count on this being possible today and start to plan the applications it enables.

Any existing IT system can be integrated to the BPMS or included within a process design as a participant. For example, supply-chain planning tools and value-analysis tools can now have access to the end-to-end process data they need from across the whole chain. It's no more difficult to achieve than designing the required process.

Process Management and the IT Industry

The emergence of process management systems does not mean that packaged "software" is going to go away—far from it. It is possible to package a digital process in the same way that it is possible to package software objects. Packaged processes are a form of packaged software.

Software companies that develop and sell enterprise packages want new ways to customize their products. Process management systems offer an answer. Many software companies are considering strategies for componentizing their current monolithic products, and several have already made significant progress in this effort. Their goal is to allow customers to pick and choose only the components they need, as they are needed. Others are exploring the possibility of packaging software components as "business services" and selling them using an ASP (application service provider) or BSP (business service provider) approach.

If we extrapolate such activities into the future, we can envision the era of building application packages giving way to an era of "process manufacturing." Package suppliers, including those who strive to offer a "complete" solution, can embrace the principles of mass-customization in their offerings. Initially these suppliers will use process management to adapt their existing packages to the needs of vertical industries—a process that has already begun—then to niche markets, and eventually to individual customers. Providing process solutions to small and mid-size enterprises (SMEs) , which cannot afford the huge ERP packages of the past, is a considerable market opportunity.

Packaged software is poised to change in two significant ways. Firstly, packages will look more like processes and suppliers will provide process management tools for adapting them to the enterprise. In days of old, package suppliers urged their customers to avoid customization, for they well knew the consequences. When a company did modify a package and things went astray, the suppliers often threw up their hands and said, "It's not our fault." Tomorrow, packaged software suppliers with process management systems embedded in their offerings will encourage customization. They know that this is how competitive advantage is achieved and they want prosperous customers. In the era of BPM, when a customer modifies a package, the suppliers will throw up their hands and say, "Let's celebrate!"

Secondly, a wave of new "process software," built on the foundation of the BPMS, will emerge. Although the notion of "process software" may sound inconsistent with the principles of the third wave of BPM—the eradication of software development and IT involvement in process design—it is really no different than the emergence of support tools for data management. These tools will fall into one of two general categories:

- Advanced tools provided, not by the BPMS supplier, but by companies specializing in various aspects of the process lifecycle, such as discovery, design, operations, optimization and simulation.
- Applications built on the BPMS and taking advantage of its capability to persist and manage the state of end-to-end processes. For example, future ERP, SCM, CRM and workflow—indeed all applications—will be built on, or evolve toward, the BPMS.

Such developments are inevitable: The BPMS is not a silver bullet or panacea, any more than any other packaged system is. However, because the step from data to process is so profound and so powerful, many companies may find less need for specialized applications, relying instead upon the general-purpose process management system. This is the experience of companies that have already deployed the first generation of third-wave BPM solutions. They are finding they have a very powerful "application" (process) development environment. Not only this, but the "applications" (processes) they develop work together with no further integration work required from IT.

Crossing the Process Chasm

As end-user organizations, software providers and consultants move to process-centered information systems, the pattern of adoption will be similar to that of the migration to the database platform: There will be early adopters, mainstream adopters and the laggards. In tables B.2 and B.3, we compare key factors in the migration to the standards-based database platform with those involved in the migration to the BPMS.

	Preexisting Applications	First Generation Innovators	Mature Data Applications
Data	Embedded	Partially explicit	Fully explicit
Data representation	Proprietary	Proprietary	Standard (relational)
Data query language	None	Proprietary	Standard (SQL)
Data management tools	Ad hoc	Proprietary	Platform (RDBMS)
Business impact	Unable to easily manage data within and between applications	Easier to manage stovepipe data but no enterprise data query	Enterprise wide (shared) data management (and data-aware applications)

Table B.2. Evolution of Data Management

First-generation BPM innovators represent where we are today, and the industry is poised to take the next step. Most businesses and the software companies that supply them are in a headlong race to obtain process-management capabilities, although much of the effort thus far has been spent on finding ways to extend the existing "data-application" paradigm by embedding "application-interface" integration brokers with packaged applications. As companies experience increasing pressure to find new competitive advantage, and as they recognize business process management as the means to that end, the race to BPM maturity will set a new speed record for the mainstream acceptance of a radical breakthrough.

	Preexisting Applications	First Generation Innovators	Mature Process-Applications
Process	Ingrained	Partially explicit	Fully explicit
Process representation	None or implicit	Proprietary, and, possibly not first-class citizen	Standard (BPML)
Process query language	None	Proprietary	Standard (BPQL)
Process management tools	None	Proprietary	Platform (BPMS)
Business impact	No ability to change processes without software engineering	Some discrete processes manageable (point solution)	Enterprise wide (shared) process management (and process-aware applications)

Table B.3. Evolution of Process Management

A New Era of Business Infrastructure

The introduction of the business process management system will lead to pervasive yet evolutionary changes in the corporate IT infrastructure. First, new packaged enterprise applications will leverage the BPMS as a mission-critical process execution facility. Second, the BPMS will act as a business firewall, federating multiple directory services across the enterprise—the foundation for future enterprise-process repositories. Third, the BPMS will be tied to future process-analysis servers—the cornerstone of the next generation of business process-intelligence technologies. As a result, the BPMS will become the center of gravity of the modern enterprise architecture.

Over the last two decades, companies have undertaken many

business-reengineering initiatives, with mixed success. As a result, they are much more experienced in discovering, understanding and modeling their business using processes. We believe that companies are ready to take the next step, adopting business process management as the primary mission-critical enterprise software infrastructure governing process innovation. In fact, many are going to be surprised by how liberating that step will be, thanks primarily to the design-driven architecture (DDA) of BPM, further explained in Appendix C. Those that choose to participate will deploy and manage their own innovative business processes making changes when required, the way they always wanted to. The BPMS is the cornerstone of the company of the future.

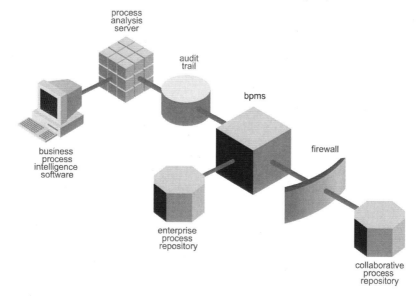

Figure B.7. The BPMS-Centric Enterprise Software Infrastructure

References

[1] Research note, Gartner, April 2001, COM-13-3057.

[2] "BPM – Are you experienced?" Gartner, November 2001, LE-14-8698.

[3] Codd, E.F., "A Relational Model of Data for Large Shared Data Banks," *Communications of the ACM*, Vol. 13, No. 6, June 1970, pp. 377-38.

[4] Source: AMR Research, 2000.

Appendix C

The Theoretical Foundations of the Third Wave

An intrinsic relation between two things A and B is such that the relation belongs to the definitions of basic constitutions of A and B, so that without the relation, A and B are no longer the same things.
—Arne Naess, *The Shallow and Deep Ecology Movements*

While a self-organizing system's openness to new forms and new environments might seem to make it too fluid, spineless, and hard to define, this is not the case. Though flexible, a self-organizing structure is no mere passive reactor to external fluctuations. As it matures and stabilizes, it becomes more efficient in the use of its resources and better able to exist within its environment. It establishes a basic structure that supports the development of the system. This structure then facilitates an insulation from the environment that protects the system from constant, reactive changes.
—Margaret Wheatley, *Leadership and the New Science*

Changing The Process of Change

For those managing change, it often seems there is a sharp distinction between the process of change and the change being introduced, but this is an illusion. David P. Norton, ex-CEO of the consulting firm The Nolan Norton Institute and now a Director with the Balanced Scorecard Collaborative states: "To execute strategy is to execute change at all levels of an organization. Seems self-evident, but overlooking this truth is one of the greatest causes of a failed transformation effort."[1] Whatever we choose to call the "change process"—reengineering, Six Sigma, Change Management, innovation—*it* changes over time and those changes need to be managed, just as *it* exerts control over the processes it seeks to improve or introduce. Any theory of process management must recognize this and break down distinctions between the *process of change*, the *process under change* and *change in both*.

As we have discussed in this book, change occurs for many reasons. Examples include changes in business regulations, audit requirements or improvements in our understanding of how to mobilize and catalyze resources. Distinctions between different types of change only arise as a result of today's inadequate, disparate and disjoint process management methods and technology systems. In the third wave, there is no need for a distinction between the change process (e.g. Six Sigma, project plan) and the process under change (e.g. customer service, product manufacturing)—they can be one and the same. But, of course, some companies applying process management, may still choose to make such distinctions.

Third-wave processes are inherently open to change; theorists call this "mobile" behavior. Mobile systems are systems whose participants freely communicate and change their structure. They do this in two ways. First, links between participants, which represent the relationships between them, may themselves change. New links may be formed, old links being broken. To an observer this looks as though the participants, or the links, are moving. A second type of mobility is the relationship of the linked participants to the environment in which they exist. This in turn looks as though the whole process, or subset of linked participants, is moving. Such "mobile" processes now pervade the *informational* world of computer systems and networks as well as the wider *real* world of which they are a part. Examples include industrial supply chains, the Internet, cellular mobile telephony networks, air traffic control and distributed computing.

In a supply chain, a message may indicate the physical movement of goods or the level of inventory in a warehouse. On the Internet, protocols between routers establish preferred routes for packet switching. In a mobile telephony network, a base station announces the availability of circuits to receivers in the same area. In air traffic control, aircraft move into and out of controlled airspace. In a corporate IT infrastructure, messages create relationships and share data between different business applications. Communication and interaction within such systems is rich and varied. Modeling such behavior is hard, but crucial if effective process management tools are to be developed.

At every level there is change. What we commonly refer to as a "business process" is no different. We now understand that trying to capture these descriptions at a specific instant in time, in a software application, is futile. We need a more mutable digital form: prone to change, capable of change and of being changed.

Participants in a business process include employees, information sources, business units, computer systems, business partners, machines, trucks, goods, even business processes themselves (for example as occurs in outsourcing). Change occurs through the acquisition or loss of these participants, through the growth or contraction of relationships among them and their interactions with the environment. A business process "moves"—as it changes—in the multi-dimensional space of time and structural evolution. Like a living entity under the influence of Darwinian evolution, it exists in the past, the present and has possible futures.

In understanding a business process we therefore distinguish different characteristics such as *state, capability* and *design.*

- *State* can be understood through the *execution* of the process, the values of calculations performed and the information collected and generated along the way.
- *Capability* can be understood as the specific *participants present* within the process at any time: what they are, the *activities* they are capable of performing and the *relationships* established among them and through which they *communicate.*
- *Design* can be equated to the *intentional* characteristics of the process, those put in place during the design process, before the process was set free to execute, to evolve and to change. Thus, we speak of the difference between intentional design and observed behavior.

How can we start to link the world of business *management* with the world of business *technology* using these process characteristics? Perhaps we can think of operations, the everyday running of the business, as being mostly concerned with process state. Perhaps business strategy is largely a matter of intentional process design. Somewhere between the two lies the management of process capability, the actions taken to grow the business, its customers and its market share. If we accept these rough analogies, then:

- Business *intelligence* is an *analysis* of the past and present state, capability and design of business process.
- Business *insight* is a *simulation* of future state, capability or design.

Today, while the analysis and simulation of process state is perfectly well understood, what does it mean to analyze and simulate growth in a processes capability, or changes in its design? The third wave points to possible answers.

A New First-Class Citizen in Computing

In the esoteric world of technology, there are plenty of ways of developing IT applications that automate business processes. The IT marketplace has a nasty habit of regularly generating new technologies that tease developers into trying out new ways to develop computer software. Not only do new computer languages constantly appear, but new methodologies, each with their own "first-class citizen," the center of their computing universe. Recent examples include peer-to-peer, grid and utility computing, self-organizing data networks, the semantic Web and distributed agents. This constant evolution in computing infrastructure, information types, applications and process approaches is confusing to business people. They wish to find technology that reflects the way they understand their business.

When technologists examine the applicability of each of these new techniques, and compare them with more established practices such as component and object-based software development, they are, in effect, examining their *relevance* to modeling and support for the classical six domains of change within a company: process, organization, location, data, application and technology. Yet *process* is not a category. Process encompasses *change* in the representation of the other five. Therefore, in developing a process representation language, the third-wave innovators looked not for a single new theory, but a theory that provided a synthesis of other theories. In process calculi they found approaches that could describe the previously separate descriptions of a company's organization structure, locations of operation, data model, application logic and technology infrastructure requirements. They then asked, "what if this were the basis of a new foundation for computing?"

Just as there are countless ways for technicians to implement an automated business process, there are just as many ways to develop and execute a business strategy. In, *The MacRoscope*, Joel de Rosnay postulates, "The fundamental concepts that recur most often in biological, ecological, and economic models can easily be grouped into major categories: energy and its use; flows, cycles, and stocks; communication networks; catalysts and transforming agents; the readjustment of equilibriums; stability, growth, and evolution. And above all, the concept of the system—living system, economic system, ecosystem—that binds all together all the others." Similar thinking can be applied to existing management theories. Six Sigma, TQM, Balanced Scorecard, Activity-Based Costing, Economic Value-Added (EVA) , Value Analysis, each can be represented using a small set of core concepts—an ontology of commerce—a vocabulary of well-defined primitive forms that can be combined in a recursive procedure to represent any business process, no matter how complex and how expansive.

Examples of such primitives include ideas such as identity, relationship, exchange of value and knowledge about a system. We now we understand that the outcome of a process is nothing more than the result of the flow of interactions among participants at every level, from the digits involved in a calculation to the most complex exchange of assets between two economic legal entities. Formalizing this *business* vocabulary and providing precise *definitions* of these elements will emerge as the counterpoint to the exploitation of process management systems over the coming decade.

Unification of Data, Computation and Interaction

In process calculus, relationships represent anything from a physical link (a lorry arriving at a warehouse) to a business relationship (two parties entering into a contract) to a mathematical property (such as calculating tax). Using just a tiny set of primitives, these theories can unify both the large-scale (macro) structure of mobile process systems and the small-scale (micro) structure representing intricate behaviors, themselves processes.

Previous theories in computer science, notably the Lambda-calculus, focused on the behavior of much simpler computer systems, where there is either a single thread of execution or a set of parallel but non-interacting tasks. Such algorithms are procedural, sequential, goal-oriented, hierarchical and deterministic. All of today's well-known programming languages can be studied using Lambda-calculus, including Fortran, COBOL, Pascal, Lisp, C and Java. By contrast, in process theories such as the Pi-calculus[2], the main focus is on systems that interact and interrupt one another, where there are many deeply nested, independent, but coordinated, interacting threads of execution. Business processes are an example. The differences between these theories are striking, for even our notion of what constitutes a common-sense interpretation of *data* and *value* has changed utterly.

In conventional computer languages there exists the concept of a "type." For example, the type of the number "five" is called an *integer*, the type of the text "hello" is called a *string*. Such types represent *values* —such as 24, "customer name," "purchase order number." These values are then aggregated to form *records* and these are stored in databases. All conventional languages focus upon *computation* using values and records, for example, *counting* customers that match certain criteria or *evaluating* their credit worthiness.

By contrast, in languages derived from Pi-calculus, types represent *behavioral patterns.* In business terms this would mean things like "signing a new customer," "exchanging contracts" or "performing work." In this brave new world, computation is harder to envisage. To do so, think of analogies such as "measuring the acquisition cost of new customers," "understanding the value exchanged through a negotiation" or "analyzing work habits." If brown is the new black in fashion, then behavior is the new data in the third wave.

Process engineers and designers of process management systems respect Pi-calculus because it identifies the concepts that underpin a wide variety of concurrent systems. This is no different from other fields of study. Electrical engineers respect differential calculus. For them, it ties together various frameworks, concepts and thinking without distortion and defines what is common to all *electrical systems.* Likewise, database engineers respect the relational data model originally proposed and defined by E. F. Codd[3].

Process calculus would, however, be of no use if it were wonderful at describing *business* processes but omitted to describe traditional *computational* processes. Fortunately it can do both. For example, the operation to *combine two lists* into one—a common operation in most computer programs—can be regarded as a change in the relationship between the lists, from disconnected to connected. In process calculus the movement of a piece of data inside a computer program is treated exactly the same as the transfer of a message, or indeed an entire computer program, across the Internet. Taking decisions and computing results—in fact all common programming tasks—can be represented and understood as "processes."

This process approach, where process is the new first-class entity, can be applied even to the lowly task of adding two numbers—one plus two equals three. The sum itself is a process. It can be understood as a process in two ways. The first is: The "one" participant joins "two" in the "plus" relationship, which then grows to include the participant "three" in the "equals" relationship. The second is: A participant receives a message containing "one" from another participant, and a similar message containing "two" from a second participant. It then performs the "plus" activity and sends the result "three" in a message to a third participant. These rough analogies hardly give credit to the richness of Pi-calculus, but they help us understand how any calculation can be represented as a process. This perspective gives the third wave of process management its inherent ability to *capture, describe and manage whole processes*—not just integration between existing algorithmic procedures written in conventional software languages and embodied in today's packaged software. This approach to process representation can be applied to a wide range of problems. Other examples include:

- Hypertext links that are passed around, created, or which disappear
- Connections between mobile telephones and base stations
- A job scheduler, allocating work on a production line
- References passed as arguments to methods in "business objects"
- Business partners changing roles in a business process
- Work passing between participants in a business process
- Code sent over a computer network to execute on another system
- A vending machine, serving up a can of Coke
- A mobile device acquiring a new capability over a telephony network
- Procedures passed as arguments to methods in computer systems
- A business process passed to a business partner for execution

Relationships, specifically their namesappear to be something fundamental. They are ubiquitous in computing, in the form of addresses, identifiers, links, pointers and references. They are ubiquitous in business, in the form of purchase order numbers, product codes, organizational roles, the identity of partners, the types of business relationships and the infinite ways of organizing, performing and referring to items and patterns of work. In process calculus the names of relationships can be used for many purposes, such as channels over which processes communicate, the names of processes themselves, the names of objects (as in traditional programming), proxies for physical locations or references to encryption keys. Names received in one interaction can be used to participate in another. By receiving a name, a process acquires a capability to interact with processes that were previously unknown to it. A name can even refer to the specific pattern of a process design. The connections among participants—the structure of the system—can thus change over time and in ways not envisaged by the process designer.

Process-aware Applications

In business, a supply chain director is required to understand complex processes, such as a logistics network, but his or her ability to manage and optimize that network is still very much an art, rather than a science, and presents huge challenges. By contrast, to a software engineer, even the most simple business process, such as the exchange of a purchase order, can be difficult to program and hard to represent. This is because today, most software engineers use constructs such as records, objects and interfaces, first-class entities of a past era, not attuned to the representation of business processes. This mismatch, between the reality of business and the artifacts of traditional software, limits the ability of the software engineer to provide tools to the supply chain manager to help manage real business.

In many industries, business and systems architects strive to create software applications that accurately reflect their business. Sometimes they do not realize that a perfect simulation is their ultimate aim. Architects in other industries know precisely that this is their task. In the logistics industry, companies often model their IT architecture closely around the behavior of the physical logistics networks they monitor and control. The tools they have to achieve this are improving all the time. Gradually architects are finding ways to represent the behavior of complex systems—interconnected and inter-related mobile processes—within the business applications they develop. Soon they will realize that mapping business concepts into artificial IT artifacts such as objects, interfaces and procedure calls, should be replaced, or at least complemented, by the process calculus models of the third wave. These artificial constructs arose to support the composition of software, not the representation of business. Architects are now looking for methods, tools and systems that are purpose built for business. Increasingly they are looking to business process modeling languages for solutions.

Drawing on themes from concurrent programming and agent-based systems, process-modeling languages treat process participants as autonomous "agents." An agent is free to act, having both an internal process that it follows, and an external interface through which it communicates. As it interacts with other agents, it collects information from them that it can refer to in making decisions, calculating results and constructing messages to send to others. It can then pass on this derived information to other participants. Partly autonomous, and partly constrained through process design, agents act in parallel and in consort. The action of any particular agent depends upon both the anticipated actions of the agents with which it interacts or the agent's analysis of the state and structure of the system process in which it exists. Such systems are called "adaptive complex networks" and they occur widely in nature, not just in computing. Examples include the economic networks and value chains studied by economists and business people alike.

Imagine a typical business application today and ask: "Why does it stay the same? It's digital stuff right? So why can't it change? Why does a new version of the application have to be developed for each and every situation? Why can't it adapt to me?" It is now legitimate to ask such questions—IT industry experts are already anticipating software programs that will write themselves to agreed process patterns. IT infrastructures will take on—auto-magically—the form of the organizations that use them. From now on, the business process is the "app," and the "app" is nothing more than mutable data. For this is the "third wave" form of business asset described in this book. Let's move on and build the new "process-aware" applications of the third wave and not try to preserve paradigms that fail to fully represent the complexity of business. Those companies wishing to take this step will need a mission-critical infrastructure designed for the purpose, the business process management system (BPMS), upon which they can manage their "mutable process data."

References

---

[1] Norton, David P., *The Balanced Scorecard Report*, Harvard Business School Publishing and the Balanced Scorecard Collaborative, Volume 4, Number 1, January-February 2002.

[2] Milner, Robin, *Communicating and mobile systems*, Cambridge University Press, and Sangiorgi, Davide & Walker, David, *The Pi-calculus: A theory of mobile processes*, Cambridge University Press.

[3] Codd, E. F., "A Relational Model of Data for Large Shared Data Banks," *Communications of the ACM*, Vol. 13, No. 6, June 1970, pp. 377-38.

Appendix D

Lessons Learned from Early Adopters

There's so much talk about the system. And so little understanding. That's all a motorcycle is, a system of concepts worked out in steel.
—Robert Pirsig, *Zen and the Art of Motorcycle Maintenance*

I'm from Missouri. You've got to show me.
—Willard Vandiver, Congressman from the Show-Me State, 1899.

A number of early adopters are at work establishing BPM platforms and deploying process-based systems, tools and methods. They represent a diversity of industries and illustrate a variety of initial uses of BPM in those industries. These companies have begun to apply BPM to their mission-critical business activities in increments. The following is a summary of lessons we have learned:

A global bank implementing more flexibility in customer-facing systems

Lessons learned: Replace complex layers of BPM middleware machinery with a BPMS capability. Build flexibility into new applications using a business process management system (BPMS). Enable sales teams to manage their own sales processes. Use a BPMS to avoid having to provide complex guidance to application developers so that they can develop inherently flexible applications. Implement a BPMS so that process design and infrastructure development can occur in parallel.

A global pharmaceuticals and health products company responding to competition and an uncertain market

Lessons learned: Renewing the application portfolio is insufficient; cross-functional processes are key. Map and discover processes to understand where best practices lie. Adapt and deploy best practices for local ownership using BPM. Establish a BPM center of excellence. Develop standards for corporate process management. Implement processes to govern the lifecycle of improvement in other processes. Integrate metrics into process designs so that progress can be measured. Avoid seeing BPM as another stovepipe IT project.

An established telecommunications provider moving into broadband

Lessons learned: BPM can facilitate the aggressive acquisition of large numbers of new customers, accelerating beyond the competition. BPM can collect, store and queue orders to ensure that customers do not experience outages from failures in dependent systems operated by third parties. BPM provides control of complex, many-to-many processes typical of telecommunications environments. BPM allows operators to become customer-centric. BPM insulates operators from changes in third-party service providers and the changes arising from the unbundling of service elements as a result of deregulation.

A national department store failing to serve customers

Lessons learned: When core processes are broken and need to be fixed, there is no time for package customization. Integrate new packages with the BPMS rather than performing systems integration to fix individual processes. Process design can start before IT renewal.

The chemical industry learning to collaborate

Lessons learned: Link applications in the value chain using BPM. Map the collaboration processes you wish to use with partners. Offer process management capability to your partners. Deliver process management as a service.

A global consumer electronic and media company moving into new markets with existing digital assets

Lessons learned: Replace a channel strategy based on coarse market-segmentation with process customization. Let customers define the way they wish to interact with your processes and implement processes to meet individual customer requirements. Use process execution and metrics to create valuable billing or other business intelligence. Use processes to implement flexible billing strategies. Equate processes with the design of relationships. Let the BPMS take on part of the burden of customized service response.

Straight-through processing (STP) in the finance sector

Lessons learned: BPM can implement straight-through processing (STP) , removing latency in trading systems that tie up huge sums of money as non-cleared transactions. BPM can also tackle complex exception handling automatically, reducing the need for human intervention significantly. Workflow coupled with rules management and BPMS is more flexible than workflow alone in dealing with exceptions that fall outside automated, and therefore predefined and predetermined, controls. BPM enables a higher degree of automation, even where workflow task lists still generate many exceptions. New regulations, such as the upcoming Basel Accord, generate additional pressures to change or renew IT systems. BPM can encode these new business rules into IT systems and maintain processes in line with such changes thereafter.

A multinational retail bank, trying to harmonize disparate IT systems

Lessons learned: BPM can reduce the cost of IT in a highly federated and syndicated business. For example, in an environment in which individual systems, dedicated to separate functions, reside in different local regions of operation, BPM can provide both flexibility and coherence based on a unified image of IT comprising multiple best-of-breed applications. BPM can adjust to local trading conditions such as national trade regulations by providing best-practice process templates that can be adapted for reuse. BPM can maintain a national process image even as discrete applications are being harmonized. BPM can assist the process of migration to a rationalized IT architecture.

A global logistics and mail company wishing to reduce the cost of providing individual customer IT solutions

Lessons learned: BPM can customize service for different customer segments and individual corporate customers. BPM allows service to be tuned to customer needs. Customizing logistics services for corporate customers is the norm in the logistics industry. BPM can replace the development of an individual customer IT-enabled logistics solution with a single solution (BPMS) configured for each customer using business process design and management. BPM can reduce the cost and complexity of maintaining customer solutions in the logistics industry, and it replaces application partitioning and multitasking.

Agricultural payments agency trying to interpret regulations and make correct awards

Lessons learned: BPM can simplify the development and maintenance of IT systems in situations involving complex relationships among rules, processes and participants. BPM can open up processes for audit by third parties.

A mobile telephone services operator changing from a reactive to proactive market strategy

Lessons learned: Use process agility to respond to unexpected market developments, turning a reactive strategy into a proactive strategy. Use process agility not only to improve existing processes but also to create brand new ones. Use BPM to reduce the cost of performing trials on new processes associated with new products and services. Replace stovepipe applications for individual products and services with a common BPMS layer that allows flexible integration. Implement common reusable processes and rules in the BPMS. Take advantage of BPM's ability to adapt and reuse processes for different product and service lines. Eradicate complexity in IT through process management. Empower marketing, sales and new product development groups to manage their own processes.

A global engineering company exploring common systems for future programs

Lessons learned: In complex engineering projects, use process management to link the hordes of component suppliers, subassembly manufacturers, prime contractors, subcontractors, joint-venture partners, third-party design firms, outside consultants, regulators and specialists. Implement processes that distribute program and product data to everyone concerned, in a manner that's timely and consistent with their specific needs Let the BPMS implement the processes that define the regulations and audit requirements of projects that are closely monitored by prime contractors and third parties. Establish a minimum level of common IT support, in the form of BPM, so that new programs can build on lessons learned from previous programs. Use processes to coordinate the multitude of activities involved in the design, testing and engineering of baselines, throughout the program.

An ASP hosted BPO services provider

Lessons learned: Business process outsourcing is different than other forms of outsourcing. Use BPM to discover the processes of new customers before integrating them into a shared service. Maintain individual service levels by using process automation. Use a process portal for customer access in order to eradicate hand offs and keep everyone focused on the process. Decouple user interface design from process design, so that process change does not impact users. Foreseeing that processes for individual customers will change and deviate from one another over time, build in a process customization capability. Instead of relying on standard processes, use a standard representation of all conceivable processes. Integrate any needed applications once, for all customers, then use processes alone to differentiate services.

A leading manufacturer of audio and video products integrating its disparate IT systems

Lessons learned: Use BPM to integrate processes once thought impossible to integrate using conventional techniques. Integrate back-office systems once, to the BPMS. Integrate B2B systems once, to the BPMS. Separate logical and physical design using BPM. Standardize processes across the globe without having to micromanage the development of each local process variant.

A global fast moving consumer goods company trying to locate and disseminate best practices

Lessons learned: Combine best-of-breed packages with ERP using BPM. Implement BPM to provide end-to-end business visibility. Implement B2B using BPM. Monitor individual department's use of BPM to advance a company-wide platform. Use BPM to converge systems, data and procedures. Align technology strategy with business strategy using BPM. Treat the introduction of BPM like any other project: Develop a blueprint and allow divisions to innovate. Use BPM to create a "joined-up-business." Leverage BPM's capability to uncover best practices. Test and deploy BPM incrementally alongside other initiatives to reduce risk.

A worldwide logistics company looking to extend services to specialized customers and enter the 4PL (fourth party logistics) marketplace

Lessons learned: Consider replacing bespoke approaches to BPM, developed in-house, with commercial products. Extend discrete services to others using BPM to create new revenue. Use BPM to gather the information needed to improve processes company wide. Link shared services to customer-facing processes. Use BPM to standardize the processes facing your partners, and then customize the end-to-end processes with each customer. Implement open BPM standards. Map processes to aid strategic analysis of the business. Link process design to key performance indicators so as to provide incentives for process improvement.

Develop processes based on a common business vocabulary. Delegate responsibility for subprocesses to local divisions. Strike a balance between overly detailed corporate process designs and micromanagement enforced by corporate head-office. Balance necessary support for local process adaptation with a common portfolio of core processes. Recognize that IT alone cannot change stovepipe behavior by departments, even using BPM. Separate process logic from software engineering practices. Integrate process design, deployment and management using BPM to implement a feedback loop of refinement and improvement. Carefully evaluate BPM scalability.

A phone company needing more automation

Lessons learned: Use BPM to eliminate labor-intensive tasks that add little value. Integrate automated processes with human processes so that employees can focus on problem-solving and troubleshooting. Eliminate "swivel-chair integration" using BPM. Assist workgroups in eliminating chronic sources of work backlogs using BPM. Use BPM to make the systems development process more transparent and more reflective of business imperatives. Use BPM to integrate processes inherited from mergers and acquisitions.

A petroleum and energy company extending ERP to remote teams

Lessons learned: Complement centralized systems like ERP with BPM so that processes can be applied everywhere they're needed. Simplify interaction with ERP, reducing screen count dramatically. Integrate intelligence into legacy systems by adding a BPM component. If BPM is successful in one area of the business, find out why and replicate that success elsewhere. Build BPM teams around key skills in process design, business design and project management. Use collaborative process design sessions to help diagnose deeply rooted business problems and achieve buy-in to change. Use BPM to assist the understanding of how departments affect one another—and their effect on customers.

A telecommunications and Internet services start-up

Lessons learned: Use BPM to shave months from new systems development by simultaneously introducing a BPM capability, the integration of package applications and the design of processes—each of which are now performed independently. Use BPM to implement customer self-service. Use BPM to defer process design decisions and to allow rapid process evolution once the market is understood. Avoid package customization: Customize at the process level. Use BPM to enable a larger number of proof-of-concept projects at a lower cost. Make user interface design part of process design so that changing user interfaces is as easy as changing the processes themselves. BPM reduces screen count, by an order of magnitude or more. Don't rely on packaged user interfaces: Integrate a purpose built interface that automatically aligns to the end-to-end process design. Use portals to enable users to interact with processes. Standardize interfaces to applications so that they can be swapped in and out as required. Understand that your intellectual property lies in your business processes, not in the standard applications you buy from vendors.

A global consumer goods company integrating its value chain

Lessons learned: Use BPM to implement data validation among partners in complex supply chains. Use BPM as the backbone of a simpler global supply chain. Recognizing that the barriers to supply chain integration are largely technical, compounded by years of acquisition of disparate systems by everyone in the chain, use BPM to solve the resulting n-dimensional technical integration challenges. Use BPM to glean business intelligence on data passed among participants in the chain, resulting in, for example, improved order and forecasting accuracy that benefits customers because data can now be understood in the context of its use. A technical integration solution cannot do the work of a process integration solution. BPM can include manual steps in cross-system, cross-partner processes to help resolve exceptions. Integrating at the process level enables change at the process level across the chain. BPM is equally applicable to real-time, batched or mixed processes.

A commercial bank trying to streamline deal flow

Lessons learned: Stovepipe systems designed for managers are no substitute for BPM extended to everyone in a "deal flow." BPM can enhance collaboration within the bank and with customers. Include both technicians and business analysts in BPM projects. Let the IT organization own the BPMS. Let business units own the processes. Use visual tools for process notation to assist teamwork and common understanding. BPM is more flexible than older workflow solutions, avoiding the "droneware" syndrome. Use BPM to create personal relationships between bankers and their clients. Offer customers very personalized information using custom processes. Manage the BPM project, not as an IT project, but as a process improvement project. Place process designs under change control and in a central repository. BPM can reduce the deployment time for new processes. Explore the use of BPM to extend banking services to other institutions.

A legal publishing giant entering new markets

Lessons learned: No amount of messaging solutions, EAI or packaged applications can substitute for BPM. Without a process view, different capabilities are used as point solutions based on countless lines of proprietary code, resulting in unnecessary maintenance costs. The publishing industry is changing rapidly—a process-based view is mandatory—for example, to enable publishers to move into new markets and customize services for small-to-medium sized clients.

A large Japanese general trading keiretsu renewing legacy IT architecture

Lessons learned: BPM can serve as a global standard for developing new systems and re-architecting the old. BPM offers a superior return on investment than that offered by a combination of packaged applications. The combination of BPM with such standard application architectures as J2EE or .NET can be highly effective. BPM can relieve the frustration of being locked into processes defined by the lowest common denominator, as embodied in packaged applications.

A large independent publisher implementing open standards

Lessons learned: BPM allows a company to fully automate the business, linking all information sources with all resources across all processes. BPM is the antithesis of the experience of heading down a blind alley due to a lack of attention to open standards.

A Fortune 50 financial services firm renewing its approach to IT development

Lessons learned: BPM can bring business people into an application design process previously dominated by technical Java and XML development. BPM reduces the cost of application design and shortens the application development lifecycle. BPM includes comprehensive debugging capabilities across the end-to-end process.

A division of a Fortune 10 industrial conglomerate, implementing Six Sigma

Lessons learned: BPM allows business analysts to effectively manage the lifecycle of the business processes for which they are responsible, with only minor technical assistance. BPM can enforce Six Sigma CTQs (Critical To Quality). BPM and high-end workflow solutions can govern application behavior at a sufficiently fine degree of control to meet the extreme quality requirements of Six Sigma.

A leading worldwide electronics and industrial firm wanting to use the process maps it developed through BPR projects

Lessons learned: A combination of BPM and existing process assets, as captured by a previous generation process mapping tool, can make existing process maps into process models, that are then executable on an IT infrastructure. BPM can eradicate the process of manually translating process diagrams into requirements for IT systems development. BPM can go straight from design to execution without the traditional waterfall model of software development. BPM can be applied as a global corporate development standard.

A large international express delivery firm streamlining its development process

Lessons learned: Proprietary code, aimed at providing integrated processes, can be inflexible, costly to maintain and sometimes inconsistent in its handling of events such as unexpected exceptions in transactional environments. Getting code from design to production using software engineering is time consuming and resource intensive compared to BPM. BPM provides drastically higher code coverage than traditional process mapping. Even where process maps can be supplemented by accelerated development techniques based on the maintenance of a model, BPM provides for continuous process change after development, without the need for application regeneration and redeployment.

A discount securities brokerage and financial services giant implementing customer-facing systems

Lessons learned: BPM can replace multiple application development projects, particularly where each connects to a mainframe and requires its own modern, Web-based front end. Processes deployed using BPM can unite human participants, applications and back-end systems and can be modeled to respond to customer requirements. While integration solutions can solve integration problems, they, unlike BPM, cannot support the process development cycle itself.

Appendix E

The New MBA Curriculum

Originally appeared in *Internet World Magazine*, August 2002

In January 2002, Ronald Alsop reported in the *Wall Street Journal,* "In 1999, the M.B.A. course 'E-business' was as hot as a high-tech IPO. It was so popular, in fact, that University of Chicago M.B.A. students were required to show their I.D.s to get through the classroom door. School monitors were on the lookout for gate-crashers because only 60 of the 220 students who tried to register for the class had been admitted." Alsop's article was titled, *"Change of Course,"* and that's exactly what has been happening—two years later the course was dropped. With the crash of the dot-coms, e-enrollments took a nosedive—and the "e" has been dropped from courses and curriculums in business schools across the land. But now the pendulum has swung back too far. Although many professors were relieved that they did not create e-anything or hire high-priced professors with e-credentials, these "I told you so" profs continue to teach outdated information systems courses aimed at yesterday's business problems. There is, however, new work to be done, and the business world needs properly trained graduates that can put the Internet to real business use in finding desperately needed new sources of productivity—*a la* GE's company-wide Digitization Initiative.

IBM's Ambuj Goyal summarizes the requirements in a Line56 article, *Achieving Automation,* "Savvy IT companies are beginning to take a fresh approach to managing their systems environment. No longer are they looking at their IT systems as discrete functions, but rather as parts of broader *business processes.* They are shifting their focus to a higher level and asking questions, such as 'How do we reduce the time and effort it takes to step through an order transaction?' and 'How can we more cost-effectively handle customer inquiries?' Doing so requires interactions between multiple business systems, and a top-down and bottom-up view of business processes, as well as the right software tools to integrate, analyze and transform them. The payoff is increased business efficiency. But exchanging data within a company and with business partners and customers is not easy. A survey conducted by IBM of 33,000 companies around the globe found that only five percent of businesses were at this stage of e-business integration. The key stumbling block was integrating work processes—such as supply chain, procurement and customer relations—across disparate computing plat- forms, applications and operating systems." This is the challenge M.B.A. graduates will face as they enter today's workforce—the business process management (BPM) challenge.

While e-commerce and e-business monikers may have been M.B.A. marketing ploys, the real "e" is *e-process*. BPM, along with hands-on automated tools and live case studies, should be integrated into the core curriculum, including courses on operations management, managerial accounting, marketing and production management. In much the same way that SAP provided case studies and software to business schools that wanted to teach their students hands-on skills using ERP systems, it's now time to do the same with BPM software.

Business process management and Web services composition courses, using integrated development environments, should replace yesterday's systems analysis, design, programming and database courses in the more specialized M.I.S. and C.I.S. programs. Enough already —companies no longer build in-house systems. They buy and configure functional application packages like ERP, SCM and CRM. But with the *business process* superseding the *application* as the object of automation, students need to learn about the BPMS as well as the traditional DBMS. They need hands-on experience with BPQL as much as they ever needed SQL skills. The future is not about systems development; it's about business process manufacturing and manipulation, where the object of an information system is end-to-end business processes.

Companies need business process analysts and engineers, not systems analysts and programmers. Now is the time for business schools to provide their graduates with the business process management knowledge and hands-on skills needed in the process-managed enter- prise, the company of the future. The future will be owned by those who don't just improve processes, but who create methodologies and systems that automate their creation to achieve competitive advantage.

Professors, please teach your students to speak BPML, the language of process. Vendors, please give them the tools they need.

Index

About the Authors

HOWARD SMITH is Chief Technology Officer (Europe) of Computer Sciences Corporation (CSC) and co-chair of the Business Process Management Initiative (BPMI.org). With more than 24 years in the IT industry, he is a sought after speaker and advisor. His work in predicting and shaping technology at the intersection with business led him to take an active role in the development and application of the third wave. He is currently researching the application of *business process management* to corporate sustainability, innovation and growth, for which he has global research and development responsibility at CSC.

PETER FINGAR is an Executive Partner with the digital strategy firm, the Greystone Group. He delivers keynotes world wide and is author of the best-selling books, *The Death of "e" and the Birth of the Real New Economy* and *Enterprise E-Commerce*. Over his 30-year career he has taught graduate and undergraduate computing studies and held management, technical and consulting positions with GTE Data Services, Saudi Aramco, the Technical Resource Connection division of Perot Systems and IBM Global Services, as well as serving as CIO for the University of Tampa.

Your Complete BPM Library

Innovation at the Intersection of Business and Technology

www.mkpress.com

—New—

Extreme Competition, **Peter Fingar**
The World is Flat?, **Aronica and Ramdoo**
The Power of Process, **Kiran Garimella**
Thrive!, **Towers and McGregor**
More For Less, **Andrew Spanyi**

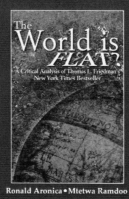

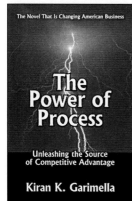

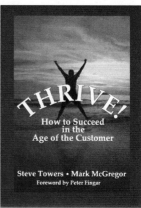

— **www.mpress.com** —